Python Adventures for Young Coders

Alaa Tharwat

Python Adventures for Young Coders

Explore the World of Programming

Apress®

Alaa Tharwat
Bielefeld, Nordrhein-Westfalen, Germany

ISBN-13 (pbk): 979-8-8688-1066-4   ISBN-13 (electronic): 979-8-8688-1067-1
https://doi.org/10.1007/979-8-8688-1067-1

Managing Director, Apress Media LLC: Welmoed Spahr
Acquisitions Editor: Celestin Suresh John
Development Editor: Jim Markham
Coordinating Editor: Gryffin Winkler

Cover designed by David Clode on unsplash (unsplash.com)

Distributed to the book trade worldwide by Springer Science+Business Media New York, 233 Spring Street, 6th Floor, New York, NY 10013. Phone 1-800-SPRINGER, fax (201) 348-4505, e-mail orders-ny@springer-sbm.com, or visit www.springeronline.com. Apress Media, LLC is a California LLC and the sole member (owner) is Springer Science + Business Media Finance Inc (SSBM Finance Inc). SSBM Finance Inc is a **Delaware** corporation.

For information on translations, please e-mail booktranslations@springernature.com; for reprint, paperback, or audio rights, please e-mail bookpermissions@springernature.com.

Apress titles may be purchased in bulk for academic, corporate, or promotional use. eBook versions and licenses are also available for most titles. For more information, reference our Print and eBook Bulk Sales web page at http://www.apress.com/bulk-sales.

Any source code or other supplementary material referenced by the author in this book can be found here: https://www.apress.com/gp/services/source-code.

If disposing of this product, please recycle the paper

Contents

About the Author

Alaa Tharwat is a distinguished PostDoc and Research Group Leader at Bielefeld University of Applied Sciences and Arts, Bielefeld, Germany. He earned his PhD in Electrical Engineering from Ain Shams University in Egypt. His research focuses on machine learning with small data, active learning, and explainable AI for Industry 4.0 applications. Actively engaged in academia, Alaa has contributed to conferences like AISI and organized workshops and tutorials at prestigious events such as ECML PKDD and IEEE WCCI. His numerous publications and tutorials, easily accessible for students, underscore his commitment to knowledge dissemination. Recognized for his exceptional presentations, Alaa has received awards, including Best Presenter, Best Paper, and Best Teaching Assistant. Motivated by a passion for simplifying complex concepts, he extends his expertise to authoring a book aimed at imparting fundamental programming knowledge to readers, reflecting his dedication to spreading knowledge and facilitating learning.

About the Technical Reviewer

Vinícius Gubiani Ferreira is an experienced IT professional with over 15 years of experience in IT areas such as software development, cloud computing, and DevOps. He's been working, learning, and sharing knowledge about Python for about ten years. Currently working as QA team lead, he also worked as a software engineer across several industries in different companies. Graduated in electrical engineering at UFRGS, software engineering at PUCRS, and with an MBA in project management at FGV, he also loves to code, to read other people's code, and to help others achieve what they want with code, be it directly or by guiding them to find out for themselves.

Acknowledgements

I would like to express my heartfelt gratitude to everyone who has supported me on this journey.

Thank you to my family and friends for your unwavering encouragement and love.

A special thanks to **Ahmed Ramadan**, software engineer, for his invaluable help in revising the second chapter. I am also deeply grateful to my son, **Yassin Othman**, a tenth-grade student at Gesamtschule Quelle in Bielefeld, Germany, who carefully reviewed four chapters and provided numerous helpful suggestions. Yassin is not only an enthusiastic reviewer but also part of the target audience for this book, making his insights especially valuable. As a non-native English speaker, he guided me in simplifying complex words and phrases to ensure that the content is accessible to readers. I also want to thank my son, **Adam Othman**, a ninth-grade student at Gesamtschule Quelle in Bielefeld, Germany, for helping to create a great design for the book cover. I would also like to express my sincere gratitude to **Dr. Sara El-Sayed El-Metwally**, Associate Professor, Computer Science Department, Faculty of Computers and Information, Mansoura University, Egypt, for her assistance in revising the first chapter and for her thoughtful suggestions.

Your support has made a significant difference, and I am truly grateful to each and every one of you.

Introduction

This book tells the journey of Kai, a child who wakes up trapped inside a giant robot. One morning, a young child named Kai wakes up to find himself trapped inside a giant robot. Kai quickly realizes that he cannot interact with the outside world. The only way to communicate with the external environment is to interact with the robot, and the robot will communicate with the outside world because the robot has a screen or monitor to show some messages to the external world and can also receive some inputs from people in the outside world. The robot has a window, and from this window Kai can see the world, but no one can see him. He also noticed that the robot speaks in a strange, mechanical language that Kai does not understand.

In a panic, Kai searches the robot's control room and discovers a series of strange documents and manuals – all written in the robot's secret language. Kai realizes that the only way to escape this situation and interact with the robot is to decipher or decode these programmed "magic books" and learn the robot's language. This will help him to communicate with the outside world. So he decided to read and learn from the books around him to learn the language of this robot. In this book, we will tell you what Kai found and learned in his adventure. As this book progresses, each chapter will present a new challenge or adventure that Kai must overcome using his growing knowledge of the robot's programming language – which is, by chance, Python.

Reader's Road Map

Importance of This Book

In today's world, being able to understand and work with computers is very important. This book will teach you and your children or your students about programming, which is the skill of telling computers what to do. Programming is a valuable tool that can be used in many different areas, like science, technology, engineering, and math. Programming also helps you think in a special way called "computational thinking." This means you will learn how to break down problems into smaller steps, think logically, and find creative solutions. These skills are not just for coding; they can be helpful in all kinds of situations, like solving puzzles or coming up with new ideas.

As you read this book, you will go on exciting coding adventures that will spark your curiosity and teach you how to be a problem-solver. Through fun stories, colorful illustrations, and hands-on activities, you will become a programmer and learn how to make computers do amazing tasks. This will prepare you for a future where technology plays an important role in our life.

In this book, we will use the Python programming language. This language is suitable for beginners because it is easy to learn, can do many different things, and is free.

Who Can Read This Book

This book is for anyone who wants to learn how to code and create programs with computers. Whether you are a kid, a parent, or a teacher, this book is for you.

The main readers or audience we have in mind is kids between the ages of 10 and 18 who are interested in learning programming. You do not need to have any previous programming experience – this book is perfect for beginners. All you need is some basic computer skills, like knowing how to use a computer, laptop, or even a tablet.

Parents who want to teach their kids how to code will also find this book very helpful. Even if you do not know much about programming yourself, this book will guide you and your child through the process of learning to code. It is a great way to spend time together and help your child develop important skills.

Teachers and homeschooling parents who want to incorporate coding into their lessons will find this book to be a fun and engaging resource. The stories, activities, and hands-on projects make learning programming enjoyable for young students.

Older kids or teenagers who already know some coding might also enjoy this book, especially if they want to focus on learning the Python programming language or strengthen their understanding of programming basics.

No matter who you are, if you are curious about coding and want to have an adventure with computers, this book is for you. Get ready to become a programmer and learn how to make computers do amazing things.

Why This Book Is Different Than the Others

This book has some exciting features that make it different from other books that teach kids programming. These features are

- **Storytelling and adventure**: This book does not just teach you about programming – it takes you on exciting adventures. As you read, you will find that new coding concepts are introduced naturally as part of the story, rather than just listing out programming statements and concepts. This makes learning fun and engaging, because you get to see how coding can be used to solve problems and create amazing things. By combining education with storytelling, the book sparks your curiosity and encourages you to think critically, solve problems, and use your imagination.
- **Hands-on learning**: This book does not just tell you about coding – it lets you do it. You get to do interactive activities, solve practice problems, and work on fun coding projects. This allows you to apply what you learn and really understand how programming works. And do not worry if some of the exercises seem too hard – we have included easy, medium, and hard levels so that everyone can find something they can do, and we have also included solutions for all the exercises and some explanation of them if there is a new idea in the solution.
- **Creativity and problem-solving**: This book emphasizes creative thinking and problem-solving through interactive coding projects. By exploring programming concepts in a creative context, young coders are inspired to think outside the box and develop innovative solutions to real-world challenges.
- **Easy language**: This book aims to make Python programming accessible to non-native English speakers by removing language barriers. It presents the language in a clear and simple way that makes it easy for young learners to understand the concepts and start programming.
- **Accessible introduction to Python**: With a focus on young programmers, this book provides a beginner-friendly introduction to Python programming. It presents Python concepts in a clear and concise manner, allowing young readers to grasp the basics of programming without feeling overwhelmed.
- **Available code**: The codes for many parts of this book are available on this GitHub link: https://github.com/Eng-Alaa/Programming_4_Kids.

The Book's Main Contents

This book is all about going on an exciting adventure where you will learn how to code using the Python programming language. It is not just a boring reference book – it has illustrative and attractive figures, and the content is introduced in a progressive manner. Throughout the book, you will follow along with some programming adventurers as they explore programming in an ordered manner. As they go on their journey, you will learn the programming skills you need to help them along the way.

The book will have four main parts:

1. **Introduction to Python**: In the first few chapters, you will learn all about Python and how it works. You will set up your own programming environment and write your first lines of code. Python is a really friendly and easy-to-learn programming language, perfect for beginners.
2. **Basic programming concepts**: After getting to know Python, you will start learning about the building blocks of programming, like loops and conditional statements. These are the basic skills you need to start writing your own programs.
3. **Advanced code programming**: Once you have got the basics down, you will dive into some more advanced Python topics like lists and functions. You will learn how to use these new tools to make your programs even more powerful and exciting.
4. **Create coding projects**: The best part is when you get to use your programming skills to bring your own ideas to life. In this final section, you will work on fun, interactive projects that let you be creative and show off what you have learned.

The Story of This Programming Adventure

The book consists of 13 chapters; the knowledge of each chapter is based on the previous ones. Therefore, it is better to start the book from the beginning when you have no pre-knowledge about programming. There are two special checkpoint chapters. These are like rest stops on your coding journey, where you can take a break and look back at what you have learned so far. The checkpoint chapters remind you of important programming concepts that you have covered in previous chapters and show you how these concepts relate to each other. In addition, the checkpoint chapters fill in any gaps or missing information you may have while giving you cool new ideas for using your programming skills. Checkpoint chapters also include helpful sample programs for you to study and fun exercises to test and grow your programming skills. Hence, even if you get a little stuck or confused at any point, those checkpoint chapters will be there to get you back on track and keep your adventure moving forward.

At the end of each of the first nine regular chapters, you will find even more practice exercises. Figure 1 shows an example of how the exercises will appear in this book. The exercises come in different difficulty levels, so you can really put your new programming skills to the test. And do not worry – the answers and explanations for all the exercises are simply found in the appendix of the book. Therefore, you can check your work and keep improving.

At the start of each chapter, we will let you know briefly what you are going to learn – that way, you will always understand how it relates to what came before. This will help keep the flow of the book clear and easy to follow, even as your coding skills grow from chapter to chapter. In addition, you will find a handy glossary at the end of each chapter that explains any new programming commands and statements you encounter. This will be a great reference to help you reinforce what you have learned. It also gives you a few hints about the new adventure in the next chapter.

In some chapters, we have used unique visual elements to call out important information:

- Definitions are contained within a box with a blue background (see Figure 2).
- Cautions, warnings, or important notes are highlighted in a box with a red background as shown in Figure 3.
- Easy, medium, and hard levels of exercises are indicated by green, blue, and red filled circles, respectively. Figure 4 shows an example of the three different levels of difficulty of the exercises in this book.
- The background of the programs in this book will have a unique color, which is black, as shown in Figure 5.
- After running a program, this book displays the output of that program as shown in Figure 6.

●Exercise 1: Print output

What is the expected output of this program?

```
for i in range(1, 4):
    for j in range(1, 4):
        print(i, j)
```

Figure 1. An illustration of how the exercise will appear in this book. It has a somewhat representative title, some given data or hints, and a question

➡**Design Time**
    The Design time is the time when we create and plan our program.

Figure 2. Illustration of how the definition appears in this book

✗ **Case sensitive**: Python is case-sensitive, so using the correct uppercase and lowercase letters in variable and function names is critical to proper program execution.

Figure 3. Illustration of how the warning or caution appears in this book

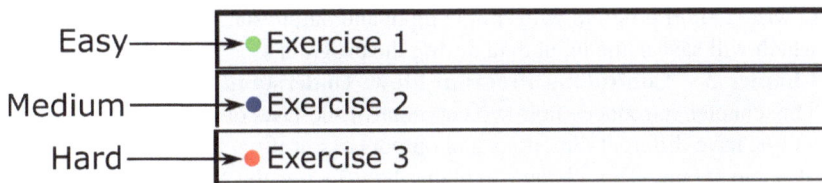

Figure 4. Illustration of the different levels of difficulty of the exercises in this book

```
1  # Generate and print the multiplication time table
2  for i in range(1, 5):
3      print()  # Print an empty line between each row for better readability
4      for j in range(1, 11):
5          result = i * j
6          print(i, "x", j, "=", result)
```

Figure 5. Illustration of how the program appears in this book

```
Enter the number of apples you ate: 2
Enter the number of bananas you ate: 1
Enter the number of oranges you ate: 3
You consumed a total of 304 calories.
```

Figure 6. Illustration of how the output of the code or program will appear in this book. Red text means that this text is user-entered

These visual cues will help you quickly identify key concepts, warnings, and practice opportunities as you work through the material.

It is worth mentioning that some of the illustrations in this book were created using the Artificial Images (AI) image model, which creates images from text. In this book, we used Copilot: https://copilot.microsoft.com/.

The first four chapters, along with the first checkpoint chapter (chapter 5), cover the basics of programming. These core chapters are essential building blocks, so it is important not to skip them. Everything that comes after them relies heavily on the concepts and skills you learn in these early chapters. These chapters are as follows:

- **Chapter 1 – Welcome to the World of Programming!**: In this chapter, we will start our adventure by trying to explore the world of programming. This chapter starts by defining the program and programming languages. Next, this chapter tries to explain why we need to learn programming and how we can find programming in our life. After that, the chapter presents how to get the output, input, and initial knowledge of variables.
- **Chapter 2 – The Basics of Variables: An Introduction to Storing and Manipulating Data**: This chapter provides more information about variables, such as the definition of variables, types of variables, rules for naming variables, and conversions between different variables. After this chapter, you will be able

to write a short program with simple input and output statements using variables, which will save some input data during the program.

- **Chapter 3 – Controlling Program Flow: Understanding the If Statement**: This chapter introduces how we can control the flow of our program, in other words, have different directions and outputs of our program based on the values of some inputs. This chapter explains how to use the "if," "else," and "elif" statements. This chapter also introduces some new concepts, such as the code block, indentation, and the nesting concept.
- **Chapter 4 – Repeating Actions with For Loops**: This chapter is important to explain how to make repeated tasks in your program like printing timetables for all numbers from 1 to 100. The main statement used in this chapter is the for loop statement. The chapter shows how using the for statement makes the program much shorter. Next, the idea of breaking the loop at a specific point under a specific condition will be explained. Further, this chapter shows how to use two or more nested for loops.
- **Chapter 5 – Checkpoint: Strengthening Your Programming Skills**: This chapter is designed to fill in any gaps from the previous four chapters and further enhance the reader's programming skills. The chapter introduces new concepts, such as Python assignment operators, the while loop, logical operators, the break and continue statements, and Python casting. It also shows how to apply basic programming ideas, such as counters, finding maxima, and using conditional statements (from Chapter 4) with loops (from Chapter 3), building on topics covered earlier in the book. The chapter includes numerous solved examples to help make these new ideas clear.

  In addition to the exercises, this chapter contains three "project" assignments for the reader to complete. The goal of these projects is to give the reader practice breaking down a more complex task into smaller, more manageable steps and then implementing those steps using the programming fundamentals you have learned so far. The sample project solutions you see were created by young students who were just learning to code. These students used the knowledge they learned in the first five chapters to create these projects. As a result, the code may not be the best or most organized. But even though it is not perfect, the solutions still have interesting ideas and can perform the required tasks. The focus of this checkpoint chapter is to solidify the reader's core programming skills before moving on to more advanced topics in the later chapters of the book.

The next four chapters, from Chapter 6 through Chapter 9, focus on two major advanced topics: lists and functions. With lists, the reader will learn how to access elements by their indices, rather than just using individual variables. Functions are also introduced as an important way to organize code and make it simpler and easier to trace by encapsulating repeated parts of a program into reusable functions. These chapters are as follows:

- **Chapter 6 – Exploring Lists: Operations and Manipulations**: This chapter begins by introducing and defining the concept of lists in Python. It explains the advantages of using lists over single variables for certain programming tasks. It also covers the various methods for accessing and modifying the elements within a list. To solidify the reader's understanding of lists, the chapter includes many solved examples and exercises related to list operations and manipulations.

- **Chapter 7 – Using Loop Statements for Searching, Removing, and Updating Lists**: This chapter explains how to use looping statements, such as the for loop and the while loop, to access, find, and modify items in lists. Using these looping constructs makes the process of working with lists much easier, faster, and more efficient. Many solved examples are included in this chapter to make the ideas of using lists with loops easier and clearer for the reader.

- **Chapter 8 – Exploring Functions: Building Blocks of Code**: This chapter introduces the concept of functions in Python programming. It explains that in some programs, certain parts of the code are repeated many times, which increases the length and complexity of the programs. By using functions, programs can be made shorter and simpler. Instead of repeating the same code multiple times, we can encapsulate it in a function and call that function whenever we need it, with no limit on how many times the function is called.

  This chapter also covers different types of functions – those with no inputs, single inputs, or multiple inputs, as well as functions that produce no output, single output, or multiple outputs. To help the reader fully understand the role and implementation of functions, the chapter provides many solved examples and exercises.

- **Chapter 9 – Coding at an Advanced Level with Functions**: This chapter delves deeper into the concepts and uses of functions in Python programming. It recognizes that functions are a fundamental and important programming construct, so the chapter aims to help the reader develop an advanced and professional-level understanding of how to use functions effectively. Some of the advanced function topics covered in this chapter include

  - **Recursion**: Explaining how a function can call itself to solve complex problems iteratively
  - **Function calling a function**: Demonstrating how a function can call other functions, allowing for the creation of modular, reusable code
  - **Variable scope**: Exploring the rules governing the accessibility and lifetime of variables within the context of a function

  Additionally, this chapter introduces the concept of built-in functions. It explains how these predefined functions provided by the Python language can simplify programming tasks by allowing the programmer to leverage powerful functionality without having to implement the functions from scratch.

- **Chapter 10 – Checkpoint: Linking Lists and Functions to Strengthen Programming Skills**: This chapter serves as a checkpoint, bringing together the concepts and skills covered in the previous four chapters (Chapters 6–9) on lists and functions. The primary focus of this chapter is to demonstrate how lists and functions can be used together effectively. The chapter also explains how to pass lists as arguments to functions, allowing the functions to perform operations on the list data. This integration of lists and functions is used to enhance and refine the code of the projects introduced in Chapter 5.

By applying the list and function techniques learned earlier, this chapter shows how the existing project code can be made simpler, more concise, and easier to maintain and debug. It demonstrates the power of combining data structures such as lists with modular, reusable functions. In addition, the chapter introduces a new project, giving readers another opportunity to practice applying their knowledge of lists and functions to solve real-world programming challenges. The code for the updated projects, as well as the new project, is made available in the book's associated GitHub repository (https://github.com/Eng-Alaa/Programming_4_Kids). This allows the reader to reference and study the solutions implemented.

Chapter 11 – Saving and Retrieving Data: File Handling Essentials: This chapter focuses on introducing the concepts and techniques of working with files in Python. The goal is to show how using files can solve many problems and make projects more realistic. This chapter covers the following key aspects of file handling, including

- Storing data in files
- Updating, removing, or deleting data in files
- Retrieving data from files when needed

The knowledge gained in this chapter about working with files is then applied to improve the projects that were introduced in the previous chapters. By incorporating file-based data storage and manipulation, the projects can be made more robust, flexible, and representative of real-world applications. The ability to persist and retrieve data in files enhances the functionality and practical value of the projects.

Chapter 12 – From Projects to Play: Designing and Implementing a Fun Game: This chapter focuses on introducing the reader to game development, whether they are children or adults. The main objectives of this chapter are

- Introduce some of the built-in functions in Python that are related to game development
- Guide the reader through the process of creating their first simple game

By starting with an overview of relevant built-in functions, the chapter aims to provide the reader with a foundation of the tools and capabilities available for building games in Python. The chapter then moves into the hands-on creation of a simple game. This practical application allows the reader to put the concepts and functions they have learned into practice, giving them the opportunity to create their own interactive game.

Chapter 13 – Toward Exploring Future Programming Directions: In all the chapters before this one, we have learned the basic skills and knowledge of programming. We have covered things like variables, loops, functions, and more through the funny adventure. Now that we have these strong basics, this chapter will show you some exciting new areas of programming to explore next. There are many different directions you can go to further develop your skills and create even more interesting programs. This chapter will introduce you to several programming topics and ideas that you might want to explore after you finish this book. This will help you decide what to learn and try next on your programming journey. There are many directions, but this book recommends the following:

- Object-oriented programming (OOP)
- Basic data structures
- Introduction to algorithms
- Problem-solving techniques

By highlighting these areas, the chapter acknowledges that the book has provided a solid foundation in programming, but there are many other directions the reader can take to continue learning. The discussion of OOP, data structures, and algorithms suggests that the book is laying the groundwork for the reader to move on to more advanced programming topics and techniques. Chapter 13 serves as a conclusion to the introductory programming journey covered in the book, while also opening the door for readers to explore further areas of study and skill development based on their interests and goals.

Source Code

Since adding all code, especially project code, can increase the number of pages in the book, we have made long code available on our GitHub link: https://github.com/Eng-Alaa/Programming_4_Kids.

Welcome to the World of Programming! 1

Kai had many questions when he unexpectedly found himself trapped inside a giant robot. Kai was just a young boy, but somehow he had become isolated from the outside world, and the only way to communicate with others is through the robot. Some of these questions are "what is the language of this robot (Python)?", "how can I learn it?", and "how can I use this language to send and receive messages to and from the outside world?" The answers to these questions and more will be found in this chapter.

In this chapter, we will learn with Kai how to speak the language of computers and create simple programs. Now, programming is the secret behind it all. It is like learning a new language that allows us to give instructions to computers or robots and make them do amazing actions like display a message to users of the computer and receive data from the users. Together, in this chapter, we will find out what programming is, what programming languages are, why programming is important, and where we can find it in our everyday lives. Step by step, we will learn how to write our first program. Get ready to enjoy this chapter and learn how to communicate with computers by knowing the input and output.

1.1 Introduction to Programming

1.1.1 Definition of the Program

The starting point of this chapter is the definition of the program. If we want to explain to someone who speaks another language, such as Italian, how to perform a certain task, we must first acquire knowledge of the Italian language in order to communicate the instructions effectively. For example, if we want to tell an Italian how to bake a cake, we must first understand the process itself, describe the individual steps, and then translate those steps into their language so that they can successfully understand how to bake a delicious cake. The same principle applies to

© Alaa Tharwat 2025
A. Tharwat, *Python Adventures for Young Coders*,
https://doi.org/10.1007/979-8-8688-1067-1_1

programming. If we want to tell a computer to do a task, we should first learn the computer's language, and then we can explain the task step by step in a language that the computer can understand. If the computer can only understand a certain code (the language of computers), we need to learn that code. Then we can write the steps of the task in the computer's language so that the computer can understand and follow the desired instructions.

For example, let us explain the task of making a cake. As shown in the figure on the right, you can see how the task of making a cake is divided into some simple steps. As we can see, following these easy-to-understand and simple steps, we and many others can do the task of making a cake. After dividing the task into simple steps of instructions, these steps could be translated into any language to make it available to people who speak different languages.

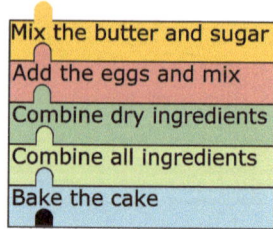

> ➡ **The program**
>
> The program is a set of instructions or codes (computer language) that tells the computer what to do. The person who writes the program is called a programmer.

Oops, does this mean that I cannot tell the computer how to do the task if I do not know how to do it? The answer is yes, but why? The answer is simple, because in order to tell someone or a computer how to bake a cake, for example, we should know how to bake a cake and the steps involved. But if we do not know how to bake a cake, how can we tell it how to do it?

1.1.2   Programming Languages

If we think of programming languages as different ways of talking to the computer, does the computer have only one language or many? And what languages can we use to talk to the computer? We can say that the computer understands many languages (or programming languages). Some scientific reports mentioned that there are more than 250 programming languages. Here are some examples of programming languages:

- **Python**: Simple and friendly, good for beginners
- **Scratch**: Like building with colored blocks, perfect for kids
- **JavaScript**: Helps build websites
- **Swift**: Builds cool applications for cell phones
- **Java and C#**: Develop games and specialized computer programs

Surely, one or two programming languages are enough to do a huge amount of tasks. In this book, we will use Python because (1) it is easy to learn, (2) it is free, and (3) it is used in many fields and scientific directions.

1.1.3 Why Should We Learn Programming?

Before we explain how to create a program, we should first say why programming is important and what the motivations or goals are for learning to program. Imagine that you have a robot, like the giant robot that Kai lives in, or a computer. Programming is telling the robot or computer what to do. So if we are able to write a program, we can easily ask the computer to do very complicated, repetitive, and time-consuming tasks very quickly and very accurately. Therefore, we can say that programming is especially important for tasks that are complicated, require multiple calculations, and/or need to be repeated often. This is because computers follow our instructions exactly and never get bored, making them a great tool for accurate work. Therefore, if you learn to program, you will be like a superhero who can get things done with a computer.

1.1.4 Programming in Our Life

An important question is where we can find programming in our life or what applications in our lives we can use to explain programming. For example, look around and you will see the magic of programming:

- **Games**: Have you ever played a video game? Programmers made them for fun. Every video game is a fun program that takes an action from the user or player and makes fancy reactions like increasing the score, moving objects, and many other actions.
- **Websites and applications**: These allow us to access information, communicate, and enjoy digital content and services. For example, chat programs translate our conversations and send them to other people, making communication fast, easy, and cheap.
- **Smart devices**: When your robot vacuum cleaner cleans the house, it follows programmed steps. This robot does its job repeatedly (perhaps many times a day) and accurately.
- **Simulations**: Engineers use programming to test ideas on a computer before putting them into practice. For example, a simulator is used to test whether people training to be pilots can successfully land an airplane. You can see how these simulators save people's lives and test whether they can fly planes safely and smoothly without losing our lives.

1.2   How to Write a Program

The goal now is to explain how to start writing and running a program. First, we need a special tool called an "editor" to write the program (see the figure on the right). An editor is like a magic notebook or screen where we write our instructions (code) or update our code. Hence, the editor helps us to create stories (programs) that the computer can understand. The program, as we mentioned

```
First line of code
Second line of code
Third line of code
        •
        •
        •
```

before, consists of a set of instructions (code); each instruction consists of some letters, numbers, and symbols. We can define the editor as follows:

> **➡ Editor**
>
> The editor provides a text-based interface for programmers to write and edit code.

After we write a program, we can use the debugger to "debug" or check that code to see if there are any errors. Thus, the debugging tool is like a special software that helps computer programmers find and fix problems, also known as "bugs," in their programs. The process of debugging is all about finding the errors in the program and finding out where these errors are so that these errors can be fixed. This way, the program can work properly without any problems.

> **➡ Debugger**
>
> The debugger is a software tool that helps programmers find and fix problems or "bugs" in their programs. The debugging process is the process of finding the errors and their locations in the program and fixing these errors in the program to ensure its correct functioning.

Once we are done fixing any mistakes or errors in the code during the debugging step, we can move on to "running" the program. Running the program means telling the computer to follow the instructions we wrote, one at a time. As the computer follows these instructions, it will do what we want it to do, and we will see the results or outputs of the program on the screen.

1.2.1   Outputs: How Can We Generate Outputs?

The goal of our first program is to print (or have the computer print) a word or phrase such as "Hello everyone, welcome to the world of programming!" The code to do this is as follows:

```
print("Hello all, welcome to the world of programming!")
```

After writing this program in an editor, we can perform a check or debug it for any errors. If no errors are found, we can proceed to run the program, and the expected output will be as follows:

> Hello all, welcome to the world of programming!

From the above code, as we can see, the first command, instruction, or statement we will learn is "print"; this command prints what is between the two double quotes ("").

In the above example, the code prints exactly this sentence: "Hello everyone, welcome to the world of programming!" If we change the phrase between the double quotes, what will happen when we run the program? For example, if the code is print("123456789"), running the program will print the numbers 123456789. In another example, print("**********") will print the line of ten stars.

An important question here is, can we write different print commands or instructions? Yes, of course; see the code below; it prints different lines:

```
1  print("Hi, my name is Alaa")
2  print("I'm an Engineer")
3  print("I'm a football fan")
4  print("I like programming")
```

The output of the above program will be

> Hi, my name is Alaa
> I'm an Engineer
> I'm a football fan
> I like programming

What happens if we make a mistake in the text between the quotes? Actually, we should be sure that the compiler or debugger does not look at or check what you write between the quotes. Therefore, whatever mistake you make there (such as a spelling or grammar error), the debugger will not catch it. For example, in the following program, the debugger will not check for many spelling errors, and the text between the double quotes will be printed as it is:

```
1  print("Hello all, wilcum tu th wurled of programmeng!")
```

But since the debugger is so flexible about errors in the text between the two quotes, is it always that flexible? Oh, surely not! For example, if you change at least one letter in the main command, the computer will not understand it. For example, if we write "prent" instead of "print," the computer will certainly not understand it because it is a mistake; even if we use PRINT with capital letters, the computer will not understand it. The reason is that "in my opinion" the computer is not intelligent or does not even think. You are the person who thinks and wants to do a task and then tries to translate that task into a set of instructions. These instructions should be written in a language that the computer (or debugger) can understand in order to execute[1] the program. Therefore, if there is an error in the syntax[2] of the instructions, the program cannot be executed, and we will not see the output of the program. This is similar to what will happen if we say a wrong Italian word (the pronunciation or the meaning) to an Italian person; they will not understand what we want or what is the meaning of our speech. However, humans are very smart and can understand things even if there are some small mistakes. But computers are not like that – they are not flexible when it comes to the special language they use.

> ✗ **Attention**: Avoid spelling and syntax errors in your code to prevent unexpected bugs.

1.2.2   Inputs: How to Get Some Inputs to My Program?

Now we know how to print or create output, we need to make our program more interactive. An interactive program means that the user of the program should or can interact with my program. In other words, a conversation could take place between the program and the user who is using the program. For example, let us say we write a program to create a simple game. This game (or program) should have some interaction between the computer running my program and the user or player trying to play this game. A simple example of this interaction is asking the user for (1) their name, (2) their age, and (3) their game mode (easy, medium, or hard), and the user should be able to give an answer. The program will react differently depending on these inputs or responses. For example, if the user has selected the easy game mode, the game missions will be easier than if the user has selected the hard mode.

Why is this interaction important? Suppose you write a program that prints or says your "Hello" and prints the name of the user or person using the program. Anyone using the program may enter a different name; therefore, the output (or printing) of the program will change according to the name that the user enters. For example, if I use the program and enter "Alex," the program will say "Hello, Alex," but if you use the program and enter "Sophie," the program will say "Hello, Sophie."

The question now is what is the instruction that we can use to make an input to the program? The instruction is "input," and to make it clear to the user who is using the program what they should input, we can make the instruction as follows: "input("How old are you?")." This command or instruction asks the user to enter their age, and the program will react differently depending on the answer.

---

[1] To "execute" a program means to run or start the program, so that the computer can follow the instructions and do what the program is supposed to do.

[2] "Syntax" is the special way that a computer program needs to be written so that the computer can understand it. Just like how there are rules for how words and sentences are supposed to be put together in a language like English, there are also important rules for how the different parts of a computer program need to be written. These rules make up the program's syntax.

Figure 1-1. Visualization of
saving a value to a variable

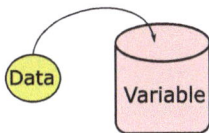

Another question we have is how the answers are stored in our program. In other words, when we ask the user for some information (like their age), we need a place to store this information so that we can use it in our program. This special place is called a *variable*; in this variable, the information could be stored. Now, let us learn how to get an input into our program, for example, to ask for the age of a person, as in the code below:

```
Age = input("How old are you? ")
```

the output will be

How old are you?-

As we can see above, when you run this program, it waits for your answer or response, so try any number. This number is stored directly in the variable called Age (see Figure 1-1). From the above code, we can define the "input()" command as a way for your program to ask a question and get an answer from the person running the program, and whatever the user types will then be stored in the variable called Age. Suppose the user entered the number 30 as the answer. The computer will take that answer and remember it by storing it in the variable called "Age." It is like having a special box where the computer keeps or stores the number you enter.

Later on in the program, if we want to use the age that was entered, we can use the "Age" variable. For example, we can write a program to print a message like this:

```
Age = input("How old are you? ")
print("Your age is:", Age)
```

The output of this simple program will be

How old are you? 20
your age is: 20

Figure 1-2 shows this simple program. When we run this code, the computer will execute the instructions one by one. First, the program will ask the user to enter their age. When the user enters their age, this will be saved in the variable called "Age." Next, the program will print the message "Your age is:" followed by the number you entered as your age; this number was entered by the user of the program and stored in the variable called "Age."

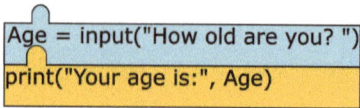

Figure 1-2. Visualization of the steps of our simple program example. The first step is the input instruction, and the second step is the print instruction

1.2.3   Variable: Where Can We Store Our Information in Our Program?

After introducing the "input" command, which gets an input or answer from a user and stores that answer in a variable, we want to explain what the variable is. Imagine you have a magic box that can store a piece of information, like our answer. This magic box is amazing because it can remember this piece of information and even change it whenever you want. In programming, we call this magic box a "variable." For example, let us say we have a variable called "age." We can put an age into this variable, such as 5, 10, or 15. The variable "age" remembers the value we put in it, and we can use it later in our program.

> **➡ Variable**
> In programming, a variable is a named storage location that holds a value. It is used to store data within a program.

Therefore, the variable is like a special container that holds information, and we can give it a name. For example, let us say we have a variable called "age" and we can store the user's age in this variable. Now, whenever you ask the magic box for "age," it will tell you. Thus, a variable in programming is like a magic box with a special name that contains information, and you can use the name of the variable to access or change the contents of the variable. It helps the program to remember and work with different information.

There are many different types of variables. The main difference between these types is the type of data that the variable can store. Each type is like a special box that can hold a specific type of information. The main types of variables are

- **Numeric variables**: Numeric variables are like magic boxes that we can use for mathematics to store numbers. They can be large or small, positive or negative numbers. Examples of the contents of a numeric variable are 5, −3.14, and 1000.
- **String variables**: String variables are like putting words and letters in a box. We can insert any word or group of letters into these string variables. The strings are always enclosed in double quotes. Examples of string variable contents are "Hello," "Python is fun!", "123."

- **Character variables**: Character variables are storing a single letter or character. They are usually part of a string. The characters are always enclosed in quotation marks. Examples of the contents of a character variable are "A," "b," "@."

Now we can make our program a little bigger and ask the user for a lot of information, for example:

```
print("Welcome in our program!")
Name = input("What is your name?")
Age = input("How old are you? ")
Language = input("Which language you speak?")

print("Hello " + Name )
print("you are " + Age + " years")
print("you speak " + Language)
```

This will print the following:

> Welcome in our program!
> What is your name? Alaa
> How old are you? 22
> Which language you speak? English
> Hello Alaa
> you are 22 years
> you speak English

The red parts in the output above represent the information entered by the user. Did you find something strange in our code above? You are right; what is the meaning of this line of code: "print("Hello " + Name)"? As we can see, the print command looks different because it prints "Hello," then there is a "+" sign and the variable called "Name"; this is called "concatenation." In Python, when we want to combine words with information into one sentence to print it, we use this "concatenation." It is like making a sentence by combining words with variables that hold information. For example, in the code above, the line "print("Hello " + Name)" concatenates the word "Hello" with the variable called Name, and this prints the value that is stored in the variable called Name right after the phrase or sentence between two quotation marks. Instead of using "+", we can use the comma, and this will print approximately the same results, as follows:

```
print("Welcome to our program!")
Name = input("What is your name?")
Age = input("How old are you? ")
Language = input("Which language you speak?")

print("Hello " , Name )
print("you have " , Age , " years")
print("you speak " , Language)
```

Now, using the "input" command and with the help of variables, we have a nice interaction between our program and the user of our program.

In another example, suppose we have two users and we want to ask them for their information as follows:

```
 1  print("Welcome to our program: First user")
 2  NameUser1 = input("What is your name?")
 3  AgeUser1 = input("How old are you? ")
 4  LanguageUser1 = input("Which language you speak?")
 5
 6  print("Welcome to our program: Second user")
 7  NameUser2 = input("What is your name?")
 8  AgeUser2 = input("How old are you? ")
 9  LanguageUser2 = input("Which language you speak?")
10
11  print("Hello " + NameUser1 + " you are the first user")
12  print("you have " + AgeUser1 + " years")
13  print("you speak " + LanguageUser1)
14
15  print("Hello " + NameUser2 + " you are the second user")
16  print("you have " + AgeUser2 + " years")
17  print("you speak " + LanguageUser2)
```

The output of the above program is

```
Welcome to our program: First user
What is your name? Alaa
How old are you? 22
Which language you speak? English
Welcome to our program: Second user
What is your name? Ahmed
How old are you? 10
Which language you speak? Arabic
Hello Alaa you are the first user
you have 22 years
you speak English
Hello Ahmed you are the second user
you have 10 years
you speak Arabic
```

Another clearer example is to ask the user to enter two numbers. Getting the two numbers is easy (see the code below). What if we want to add them? This would be easy for you except for one thing; it is how we can perform an operation like adding, subtracting, dividing, multiplying numbers. Why not? Since we have the two numbers, I think we can add them. This is not quite right, because the variables we have are not numbers. In other words, we can say that there are different types

of variables, some of which can be used to do some calculations. We will explain
how to solve this problem in the next chapter.

```
print("Enter two numbers: ")
Num1 = input("The first number ")
Num2 = input("The second number ")
```

The output of this code will be

Enter two numbers:
The first number 5
The second number 7

The figure on the right shows that the two variables defined in this
program are like two boxes, each with a different name. Each variable
stores the value that was entered by the user.

Num1 5
Num2 7

1.3 Exercises

● **Exercise 1: Line of stars (horizontal)**

Write a program that prints a horizontal line of stars using the print
statement.
    The program should print

    ****

● **Exercise 2: Line of stars (vertical)**

Write a program that prints a vertical line of stars using the print statement.
    The program should print

    *
    *
    *
    *
    *

● Exercise 3: Print a pattern

Write a program that uses the print statement to print a pattern. The pattern should consist of multiple lines and can be any shape or design you like. Here is an example of a simple pattern:

```
*
**
***
****
*****
```

● Exercise 4: Square pattern

Write a program that prints a square pattern of asterisks (*) with five rows and five columns. Each row should have five asterisks. Here is an example:

```
*****
*****
*****
*****
*****
```

● Exercise 5: Number pattern

Write a program that uses the print statement to print a pattern of numbers from 1 to 5. Each line should display the numbers in ascending order. Here is the output:

```
1
1 2
1 2 3
1 2 3 4
1 2 3 4 5
```

● Exercise 6: Diamond pattern

Write a program that prints a seven-line diamond pattern using asterisks (*). The middle line should have seven asterisks, and each line above and below should have two less asterisk than the previous line. Here is an example:

```
      *
     ***
    *****
   *******
    *****
     ***
      *
```

● Exercise 7: Find the mistake

What is the mistake(s) in the following program and what is the output of this program?

```
1  Score = input("Enter your Score: )
2  print("Your score is " + score)
```

● Exercise 8: Find the mistake

What is the mistake(s) in the following program and what is the output of this program?

```
1  name = input("Enter your name: ")
2  print("Hello, nice to meet you, " + name
```

● Exercise 9: Find the mistake

What is the mistake(s) in the following program and what is the output of this program?

```
1  favorite_color = INPUT("Enter your favorite color:")
2  PRINT("Your favorite color is" + favorite_color)
```

● Exercise 10: Welcome message

Ask the user to enter their name, age, nationality, and gender, and then print all these details. For example, if the name is Alaa, the age is 43, the nationality is Egyptian, and the gender is male, print Welcome Alaa, you are an Egyptian male and you are 43 years old.

The expected output of this program is

Enter your name: Alaa
Enter your age: 43
Enter your nationality: Egyptian
Enter your gender: male
Welcome Alaa, you are an Egyptian male and you are 43 years old.

● Exercise 11: Favorite things

Ask the user to enter their favorite color, animal, and food. Then, print a message that combines these details. For example, if the favorite color is red, the favorite animal is a lion, and the favorite food is pizza, the program should print

What is your favourite color? red
What is your favourite animal?: lion
What is your favourite food? pizza
Your favourite color is red, your favourite animal is a lion, and your favourite food is pizza.

● Exercise 12: Enter three numbers

Ask the user to enter three numbers and then print the three numbers.
The expected output of this program is

First number: 5
Second number: 8
Third number: 10
The first number is 5 and the second number is 8 and the third number is 10

1.4 Glossary

Term	Definition
print	A command used to display output on the screen.
input	A command used to receive input from a user during program execution.

1.5 Our Next Adventure in Programming

In this chapter, Kai learned the first steps to communicate with the robot. He has learned how to make an output to display it on the screen on the robot, then the other people can read this screen and get some information from the robot or from Kai. Kai also learned how to get some inputs from the outside world or the users. This means that he can ask the people in the outside world and get answers from them. Finally, Kai got some knowledge about variables.

Understanding variables is crucial for Kai's ability to control the robot and create more smart programs. Variables allow Kai to store, manipulate, and retrieve[3] different types of information, which forms the backbone of how he can make the robot respond dynamically to inputs and perform a wide range of tasks. In the next chapter, we will dive deeper into how Kai can use variables to explore the full power of programming the robot.

---

[3] To "retrieve" something means to get or obtain it, especially information that is stored or hidden somewhere. In programming, we often need to retrieve data from variables, lists, or other parts of the code in order to use it, for example, retrieving data from a file to help solve a problem.

The Basics of Variables: An Introduction to Storing and Manipulating Data

2

In the previous chapter, we explored the following with Kai:

- Why should we learn programming?
- Where can we find programming in our life?
- The definition of programming.
- Some examples of programming languages.
- How do we write a program?
- "print" and "input" commands.

In this chapter, we will dive deeper into the world of variables, exploring different types of variables, how to properly define them, and the important rules for naming them. You will learn how variables give Kai the power to store, retrieve, and manipulate all sorts of data – from numbers and text to more complex information. With a solid understanding of variables, Kai will be able to take his programming skills to the next level and create truly dynamic and responsive robot programs.

2.1 New Definitions

2.1.1 Design Time vs. Runtime

In our journey of programming, it is important to know the difference between design time and runtime.

Design time is the phase (or time) when we create and plan our program. It is like making a plan before building a house. Therefore, the design time is when we are busy creating our program in the editor. In the design time, you can add, update, or modify your code (modify the program).

© Alaa Tharwat 2025
A. Tharwat, *Python Adventures for Young Coders*,
https://doi.org/10.1007/979-8-8688-1067-1_2

> **➡ Design time**
> The design time is the time when we create and plan our program.

Runtime is the phase when the program is actually running or being executed. In other words, runtime is the execution phase, when the program runs and performs its tasks. It is like when you press the play button on a video or start a game on your computer. During runtime, the program comes to life and starts doing the things it was designed to do. It interacts with the user, performs calculations, displays information, and responds to various inputs or events. Therefore, we usually cannot change the design of the program at runtime; we can only do so at design time. Then we can say that the runtime always comes after the design of the program is finished at the design time.

> **➡ Runtime**
> The runtime is the time when the program is actively running or being executed.

Figure 2-1 explains the difference between design time and runtime with a simple example. As shown, in the design time the child is trying to build a car from their brick toys or Legos. During this time, the child can experiment and change the design of the car as much as they want. They can try different arrangements of the bricks, add or remove pieces, and figure out the best way to make the car. Hence, this design time is when the child is planning and creating the car, before it is fully built. Now, in the runtime, the child has finished building the car. The car

(a) Design time   (b) Runtime

Figure 2-1. Illustrative example using brick toys to explain the difference between the design time and the runtime. In the design time, the child is trying to build a car, and during this time, they can modify the design as they wish. In runtime, once the car is built or assembled, it is ready to play with

is now assembled and ready to play with. During this runtime, the child cannot really change the design of the car anymore – the car is already built, and the child can play with it. Therefore, the design time is when the child is designing and building the car, while the runtime is when the child is actually playing with the assembled car.

2.1.2   Making Comments

Comments are like little notes in your code or program that you or other program-mers on your team can read. Therefore, we use comments to explain what our code does and to give the reader more information about the program. Comments are not executed by the editor or the debugger. Therefore, the editor (or debugger) does not check or pay attention to comments. This means that the comments may contain errors, spelling mistakes, or be written in another language. The comments start with # and do not affect the execution of the program. For example, the comments could be a line like this:

```
1  # my comment
```

or many lines as follows:

```
1  """ Comment1
2  Comment2
3  Comment3
4  Comment4
5  Comment5
6  Comment6 """
```

We can add a comment to explain the function of a variable in our program as follows:

```
1  # Name is a variable to store the name
2  Name=input("Enter your name")
```

2.2   Defining Variables

As we have learned in the first chapter, variables are like special containers that can hold information. When you create a variable, it is like reserving a small space in the computer's memory and giving it a name; this is the name of the variable. This name helps us identify and access the information stored in that space. When we put a value into a variable, it is like putting that value into a container. The value is stored in the reserved memory space assigned to the variable.

For example, let us say we have a variable called "score." We can reserve a space in memory for it and give it the name "score." Then, we can put a value into the variable, like 10 or 20. The variable "score" remembers the value we put in it, and we can use it later in our program.

Variables are really helpful because they allow us to store and manage information easily. It is like having our own little storage drawers to organize things. We can give them meaningful names, like "score," "name," or "age," so we can remember what kind of information they contain.

2.2.1   Types of Variables

In general, when you write code in programming, you need to tell the computer what kind of information you are working with. This is called a "data type." For example, if you are working with a number, that's a different type than if you are working with words or letters. In some programming languages, such as Python, you do not actually need to tell the computer what type of information you are using. That is because Python is really good at figuring it out for itself. Therefore, when you write code in Python and give a variable a value (like a number or a word), Python looks at that value and automatically assigns it the right type. Python allows you to create variables of different types:

- **int**: This defines a variable that holds integers (positive or negative) without decimals.

```
1 age = 10
2 apples = −5
```

- **float**: This is used to define a variable that holds numbers with decimal places.

```
1 height = 1.75
2 temperature = −3.5
```

- **str**: This is used to define a variable that contains text or strings (sequences of characters (letters, numbers, or symbols)).

```
1 name = "Alice"
2 greeting = "Hello, World!"
```

- **char**: This is used to define a variable that contains a character (or strings of length 1).

```
1 first_letter = 'A'
2 punctuation = '$'
```

- **boolean**: A boolean variable is a variable that can have one of two values: True or False. It is used to represent a logical state or condition.

```
1 is_raining = True
2 is_sunny = False
```

Figure 2-2. Visualization of
defining five variables

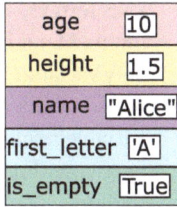

Here is an example of defining many variables (see Figure 2-2):

```
1  # Define variables
2  age = 10        # int
3  height = 1.5    # float
4  name = "Alice"   # str
5  first_letter = 'A' # char
6  is_empty=True # boolean
```

Figure 2-2 shows how the variables in the above example are stored in memory. As shown, different colors represent different types. Further, each variable is like a box that has its own name and it has content. For example, in the top box, the variable is called "age" and its content is 10.

Can a variable have two values? Definitely not, because, as already mentioned, the variable is a container or box that contains information. Therefore, the variable only contains one value. So what about the output of the following program?

```
1  name="Ahmed"
2  name="Tom"
3  print(name)
```

This will surely print "Tom," which is the last value in the variable. This means that we can assign different values to the variable, but the variable will only keep the last value. But what about the other old values? If the variable has one value (e.g., name="Ahmed") and then we assign another value (e.g., name="Tom"), the variable will overwrite (or delete) the old value and keep only the last value. As a result, the above program will print "Tom."

2.2.2   The Rules for Naming Variables

When it comes to naming variables, there are a few rules to keep in mind:

- **Begin with a letter or underscore**: Variable names must begin with a letter (lowercase and uppercase letters, from a to z) or an underscore (_). They cannot start with a number. For example, it is invalid to have a variable name like "5Age" because it starts with a number or "*Name" because it starts with a special character other than "_".

- **Use letters, numbers, and underscores**: Variable names can contain letters, numbers, and underscores after the initial character. They are **case-sensitive**, so "myVariable" and "myvariable" would be considered different variables.
- **Avoid reserved words**: You cannot use reserved words (also called keywords) as variable names. These are words that have special meanings in the programming language. For example, you cannot use "input" or "print" as variable names in Python.
- **Be descriptive**: It is good practice to choose variable names that are meaningful and describe the purpose of the variable. For example, instead of using a generic name like "x" or "a," consider using more descriptive names like "age," "username," or "total_score."
- **Use lowercase or underscores**: There are several naming standards you can follow. One of them is the camel case method. In camel case, the variable name looks a bit like the humps on a camel's back – each new word in the variable name begins with an uppercase letter (e.g., "myVariableName"). Camel case gets its name from the uppercase letters, which create a humped appearance similar to a camel. Alternatively, you can use underscores to separate words (e.g., "my_variable_name"). It is important to be consistent with the naming style you choose.
- **Variable name length**: Variable names can be of any length, but only the first 255 characters are important. If a variable name is longer than 255 characters, the interpreter deletes extra characters.

Based on the above rules, there are two important things to remember when choosing names for variables. Let us call them "cautions," warnings, or "things to be careful about."

> ✗ **Naming conventions**: Variable names in programming must begin with a letter or underscore and can include letters, numbers, and underscores. They should avoid using reserved words and be descriptive to convey their purpose, and variable names can be of any length but are limited to 255 characters.

> ✗ **Case-sensitive**: Python is case-sensitive, so using the correct uppercase and lowercase letters in variable and function names is critical to proper program execution.

Examples of invalid variable names:

```
1  2name = "Alaa"  # starts with a number
2  print = 10  # reserved word (print is a reserved word in Python)
3  my−variable = 5  # contains a hyphen
```

Try the examples above and see what kind of errors the interpreter reports. Examples of valid variable names:

```
1  name = "John"
2  age = 25
3  total_score = 100
4  xprint = 10
```

2.2.3 Variable Type Conversion (Typecasting)

In the previous chapter, we started to use variables. It is important to tell you that all the information we get from the input command is just strings. This means that even if you enter numbers or other types of data, they will be treated or considered as text, and the computer will consider those numbers to be strings. When performing calculations or comparisons with this input, we need to convert the text to the appropriate data type to get accurate results. Keep this in mind to avoid any confusion or unexpected outcomes.

The code below explains how to ask the user to enter two numbers and save each number in a variable:

```
1  # Program1
2  print("Enter two numbers: ")
3  Num1 = input("The first number: ")
4  Num2 = input("The second number: ")
5  print("The first number is " + Num1 + " and the second number is " + Num2)
```

Try the code and check the output of this program. The output of this code will be

---

Enter two numbers:
The first number: 5
The second number: 7
The first number is 5 and the second number is 7

However, we cannot perform any mathematical operations on these numbers directly. For example, we cannot add these two numbers because the computer (or the debugger) considers them as strings. The Python language (and also other programming languages) solves this problem by providing the ability to convert between variable types. This means that we can convert a string variable to a numeric variable. This is clear in the code below where we used "int"; what does this "int" mean? This is an abbreviation or shortcut for integer, and this simple command converts the string to an integer; then we can add the two numbers.

Another hint in the code below is that after adding the two numbers, we used "str" in the "print" statement; what does that mean? The "str" command converts the contents of a variable to string. As you remember, we have converted the two variables ("Num1" and "Num2") to numeric variables (integer), then the addition of them is still numeric, but I forgot to tell you that the "print" command deals with homogeneous strings. Therefore, after adding the two numbers, we should convert the result of this addition to a string, and this is the reason why we used "str" in the code below:

```
# Program2
print("Enter two numbers: ")
Num1 = int(input("The first number: "))
Num2 = int(input("The second number: "))
print("The sum of the two numbers is:" + str(Num1+Num2))
```

Enter two numbers:
The first number: 5
The second number: 7
The sum of the two numbers is: 12

As we mentioned before, the red text in the above output represents the numbers entered by the user, and the computer performs the addition process to add the two numbers (whatever the user entered), and as shown, 12 represents this sum.

The above program is similar to this one (below):

```
# Program3
num1 = "5"
num2 = "7"

result = int(num1) + int(num2)
print("The sum of the two numbers is: " + str(result))
```

The only difference between "Program2" and "Program3" is how we get the numbers used in the program. In "Program2," the user has to choose the numbers, while in "Program3" we have already decided on the values and assigned them to the variables.

Let us consider a scenario to better understand this difference. In "Program2", we could ask a friend, "Hey, what are the two numbers you want to add?" and they would tell us the numbers. We would then use those numbers in our program. In contrast, in "Program3", we are like a teacher who says, "In this exercise, let us add the numbers 5 and 7." Hence, in "Program3," we have already decided on the values and entered them into the program before we run it. Therefore, the main difference is that in "Program2" the user enters the numbers at the time the program is run (runtime), while in "Program3" the values are preset within the program's design of the program (design time) without any user input.

There are many other mathematical operations that we can use in Python, for example, addition (+), subtraction (-), multiplication (*), and division (/). Hence, we can update the above program to print the sum, difference, and multiplication of two numbers (see the code below):

```
# Program4
print("Enter two numbers: ")
Num1 = int(input("The first number: "))
Num2 = int(input("The second number: "))
print("The sum of the two numbers is: " + str(Num1+Num2))
print("The difference between the two numbers is: " + str(Num1−Num2))
print("The multiplication of the two numbers is: " + str(Num1∗Num2))
```

The output of the above program is as follows:

```
Enter two numbers:
The first number: 9
The second number: 4
The sum of the two numbers is: 13
The difference between the two numbers is: 5
The multiplication of the two numbers is: 36
```

Even though we are still in the second chapter, we can certainly think about different solutions (codes) for the same problem. I mean, programming is not like math where you should know a certain method to solve a problem, but could be considered as a tool (like a Lego) that we can use flexibly to achieve a certain task. Therefore, for the same problem, we can have many creative programs or solutions. For example, the above program could be written as follows to do the same task:

```
# Program5
print("Enter two numbers: ")
Num1 = input("The first number: ")
Num1=int(Num1)
Num2 = input("The second number: ")
Num2=int(Num2)
Num_addition=Num1+Num2
Num_subtraction=Num1−Num2
Num_multiplication=Num1∗Num2
print(str(Num1) + "+" + str(Num2) + "=" + str(Num_addition))
print(str(Num1) + "−" + str(Num2) +"= "+ str(Num_subtraction))
print(str(Num1) + "∗" + str(Num2) +"= "+str(Num_multiplication))
```

```
Enter two numbers:
The first number: 9
The second number: 4
9+4= 13
9-4= 5
9*4= 36
```

The output of the above program ("Program5") may look a little different than "Program4," but it still performs the same task as "Program4."

2.3   Solved Examples

In this section, we will try to solve and discuss some examples and write programs with the aim of practicing what we have learned in this chapter and the first one.

2.3.1   Solved Example 1: Square a Number

Ask the user to enter a number and then print the square of that number. Use ** for exponentiation. For example, the square of 5 is $5 \times 5 = 25$. In Python, you can use $5 ** 2$, which is 5×5. The expected output of this program is

> Enter a number: 5
> The square of 5.0 is 25.0.

```python
1  # Solved example 1
2  # Ask the user to enter a number
3  number = float(input("Enter a number: "))
4
5  # Calculate the square of the number
6  square = number ** 2
7
8  # Print the square
9  print("The square of", number, "is", square)
10 #print("The square of" + number + "is" + square)
```

In the above code, we start by asking the user to enter a number, convert it to float, and then store the value in a variable called "number." The "input" function allows us to get an input from the user; let us say it is 5. Next, the program calculates the square of the number. The ** symbol means "to the power of." Therefore, if the user has entered the number 5, "number ** 2" means that we multiply 5 by itself, which gives us 25. Finally, the program prints the result, which is 25.

2.3.2   Solved Example 2: Multiplication Table

Print the multiplication table for a number entered by the user. Assuming the user has entered 7, the program will print $7 \times 1 = 7, 7 \times 2 = 14, 7 \times 3 = 21$, and so on until $7 \times 10 = 70$. Can you print the multiplication table for the numbers from 1 to 10? (This will be covered in Chapter 4.)

The expected output of this program is as follows:

```
Enter a number: 7
7 × 1 = 7
7 × 2 = 14
7 × 3 = 21
7 × 4 = 28
7 × 5 = 35
7 × 6 = 42
7 × 7 = 49
7 × 8 = 56
7 × 9 = 63
7 × 10 = 70
```

```
1  # Solved example 2
2  # Ask the user to enter a number
3  number = int(input("Enter a number: "))
4
5  print(number, "x 1 = " + "=", str(number*1))
6  print(number, "x 2 = " + "=", str(number*2))
7  print(number, "x 3 = " + "=", str(number*3))
8  print(number, "x 4 = " + "=", str(number*4))
9  print(number, "x 5 = " + "=", str(number*5))
10 print(number, "x 6 = " + "=", str(number*6))
11 print(number, "x 7 = " + "=", str(number*7))
12 print(number, "x 8 = " + "=", str(number*8))
13 print(number, "x 9 = " + "=", str(number*9))
14 print(number, "x 10 = " + "=", str(number*10))
```

In the above code, the program starts by asking the user to enter a number. The "input" function allows us to get input from the user and save the value in the variable called "number." The "int" function is used to convert the input into a number (integer). Next, the program prints out the multiplication table for this number. As you can see, these print lines represent the multiplication table. In the above program, we need more than ten lines of code to print the multiplication table for one number; what if we want to print the multiplication table for the numbers 1 to 100, how big is our program? This repetitive code could be easier if we used the for loop, for example, which we will introduce in Chapter 5.

2.3.3   Solved Example 3: Rectangle Area and Perimeter Calculator

Write a program that asks the user to enter the length and the width of a rectangle. The program should calculate and print the area and perimeter of the rectangle.

Given the length (L) and the width (W), the area of the rectangle is $A = L \times W$, and the perimeter is $P = 2 \times (L + W)$. Example output:

> Enter the length of the rectangle: 4
> Enter the width of the rectangle: 3
> The area of the rectangle is 12 square units.
> The perimeter of the rectangle is 14 units.

```
1   # Solved example 3
2   # Ask the user to enter the length and width of the rectangle
3   length = float(input("Enter the length of the rectangle: "))
4   width = float(input("Enter the width of the rectangle: "))
5
6   # Calculate the area and perimeter of the rectangle
7   area = length * width
8   perimeter = 2 * (length + width)
9
10  # Print the calculated values
11  print("The area of the rectangle is", area, "square units.")
12  print("The perimeter of the rectangle is", perimeter, "units.")
```

The code above begins by asking the user to enter the length and width of the rectangle. The input function allows us to get input from the user. We use float to allow decimal values for the length and width. Next, the program calculates the area of the rectangle by multiplying the length by the width and also calculates the perimeter of the rectangle by adding the length and width, multiplying the sum by 2, and storing the result in the perimeter variable. Finally, the program prints the calculated values using the print function.

2.4   Exercises

> ● **Exercise 1: Valid or invalid variable name**
>
> In the following variable names, which ones are valid and which ones are not? Explain why.
>
> ```
> 1  alpha_beta = "gamma"
> 2  23_variable = 5
> 3  student_score = 85
> 4  my variable = 10
> 5  _private_data = 100
> 6  super@hero = "Batman"
> 7  myVariable = "hello"
> 8  color123 = "blue"
> ```

Exercise 2: Age in months

Ask the user to enter their age and print this age in months (the year has 12 months). For example, if the user is 14 years old, print $14 \times 12 = 168$ months.

The expected output of this program is as follows:

Enter your age in years: 20
Your age is 240 months.

Exercise 3: Seconds to minutes

Ask the user for a number of seconds and print out the time value in minutes. You know that 1 minute corresponds to 60 seconds.

The expected output of this program is as follows:

Enter a number of seconds: 180
180 seconds is equal to 3 minutes.

Exercise 4: Circle area

Write a program that asks the user to enter the radius of a circle. The program should calculate and print the area of the circle. The area of the circle with radius r is $A = \pi r^2$, where $\pi = \frac{22}{7} = 3.14$.

The expected output of this program is as follows:

Enter the radius of the circle: 5
The area of the circle is 78.53975 square units.

Exercise 5: Speed converter

Write a program that asks the user to enter a speed in kilometers per hour (km/h). The program should convert the speed to miles per hour (mph) and print the result. Assume that 1 mile is equal to 1.60934 kilometers.

The expected output of this program is as follows:

Enter the speed in kilometres per hour: 60
The speed in miles per hour is 37.28227153424 mph.

● **Exercise 6: Temperature converter**

Write a program that asks the user to enter a temperature in Celsius (C). The program should convert the temperature to Fahrenheit (F) and print the result. Note: $F = (C \times \frac{9}{5}) + 32$.

An example of the output is

> Enter the temperature in Celsius: 25
> The temperature in Fahrenheit is 77.0 degrees.

● **Exercise 7: Calorie calculator**

Our user is on a diet to lose some weight. Tell them that an apple has 49 calories, a banana has 95 calories, and an orange has 37 calories. Ask the user to enter the number of apples, bananas, and oranges they eat and calculate the number of calories consumed.

The expected output of this program is as follows:

> Enter the number of apples you ate: 2
> Enter the number of bananas you ate: 1
> Enter the number of oranges you ate: 3
> You consumed a total of 304 calories.

2.5   Glossary

Term	Definition
int	It is used to convert values from other data types (such as float or str) to the int data type.
str	It is used to convert values from other data types to the string data type.
float	It is used to convert values from other data types to the float data type.
char	It is used to convert values from other data types to the char data type.
Mathematical operations	+, -, *, /
#	Comment (does not affect the execution of the program).

2.6   **Our Next Adventure in Programming**

In this chapter, Kai learned more about variables, their types, how to define them, and the important rules for naming them. This improves Kai's knowledge and gives him the ability and flexibility to deal with different types of data, which allows Kai to store, retrieve, and manipulate different types of data.

In the next chapter, we will take Kai's fresh variable skills to the next level by exploring the "if" statement – a fundamental construct in programming for making decisions. The if statement enables conditional execution of code, allowing developers like Kai to control the flow of a program based on certain conditions. For example, we can ask the user to enter a number, then check whether it is negative or positive, and perform different actions depending on the result. This ability is important for making decisions, implementing logic, and creating more dynamic and interactive programs that respond intelligently to different scenarios.

Controlling Program Flow: Understanding the If Statement

In the last chapter, we have learned with Kai about variables, types of variables, the rules for naming variables, and how to convert from one variable type to another, which is a fundamental chapter in programming.

In this chapter, we will explore the power of the "if statement." Imagine if you could teach your computer to make decisions just like you do. With the "if statement," we, with Kai, can create programs that react intelligently to different situations. For example, if the number in a variable is positive, the program will output something completely different than if the number is negative. Then we could have two or more possible ways/routes for our programs, not just one. Get ready for a fun journey where you will learn how to write code that makes your programs think and act on their own. Discover the magic of the if statement and explore your creativity.

3.1 If Statement

3.1.1 Definition of the If Statement

The if statement allows your program to make decisions. If a condition is true, a line or block of code (many lines of code) is executed. First, we have a condition. This is something we want to test. It can be a question with a yes or no answer. For example, we could ask "Is the number greater than 10?" Next, we use the "if" keyword to start the "if statement." This tells the computer that we are going to check a condition. After the "if" keyword, we write the condition. For example, if we want to check if the number in the variable "x" is greater than 10, we can write

© Alaa Tharwat 2025
A. Tharwat, *Python Adventures for Young Coders*,
https://doi.org/10.1007/979-8-8688-1067-1_3

"if x>10." Here is a clear example of the "if statement" in Python that checks if the number in the variable "x" is greater than 10:

```
1  x = 5
2
3  if x>10:
4      print("Greater than 10")
5
6  print("End of the program")
```

In a step-by-step approach, the above code begins by assuming that there is a variable "x" that holds a value, in this case, "x" is 5. Then, the if statement checks the condition "x > 10" to determine whether it is true or false. If the condition "x > 10" is true, the code inside the if block is executed, which, in this case, prints the string "Greater than 10." However, when the condition "x > 10" is false, the code inside the if block is skipped, and the program continues with the next line after the if statement. The program execution then proceeds with the next line of code, which prints "End of the program" at line 6. The figure on the right shows the if statement, and as shown, if "x" is greater than 10, the program will print "Greater than 10." In this case, we can say that the condition we want to check is "$x > 10$," and if this condition is true, the next line after "if" will be executed, as in the code above.

Hence, in simple terms, the if statement allows us to make decisions in our programs and to control the flow of the execution based on certain conditions. It is a fundamental building block in programming and helps us to create more dynamic and interactive programs.

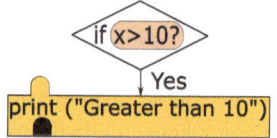

There are many comparison operators or relational operators (see Table 3-1) in the if statement:

- Equal (==)

```
1  if x == 5:
2      print("x is equal to 5")
```

Table 3-1. Python comparison operators that are used to compare two values

Operator	Explanation	Example
==	Equal	x == y
!=	Not equal	x != y
>	Greater than	x >y
<	Less than	x<y
>=	Greater than or equal to	x >= y
<=	Less than or equal to	x <= y

Figure 3-1. Visualization of
the if statement with a block
of code that is executed when
the condition is true

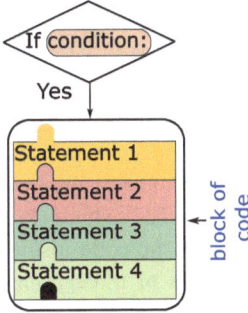

- Less than ($<$)

```
1  if x < 3:
2      print("x is less than than 3")
```

- Greater than ($>$)

```
1  if x > 3:
2      print("x is greater than 3")
```

- Less than or equal ($\leq$)

```
1  if x <= 3:
2      print("x is less than or equal to 3")
```

- Greater than or equal ($\geq$)

```
1  if x >= 3:
2      print("x is greater than or equal to 3")
```

- Not equal ($!=$)

```
1  if x != 10:
2      print("x is not equal to 10")
```

It is also possible to have many lines after the if statement instead of just one, as shown in Figure 3-1. This block of code is executed when the condition in the if statement is true.

The next program shows an example of the if statement with a block of code. In this example, we are checking to see if the value of the variable called "age" is lower than 13, which indicates whether the person is a teenager. The program looks like this:

```
1  #Program 1
2  age = 12
3
4  # Check if the person is a teenager
5  if age <= 13
6      print("You are a child!")
7      print("Enjoy your childhood years.")
```

```
8    print("Have fun!")
9
10   # Code continues executing here
11   print("Program continues...")
```

In the above program, we assume that there is a variable called "age" that holds the age of a person. In this case, we set it to 12. The if statement checks the condition "age ≤ 13," which checks if the age is smaller than or equal to 13. If the condition is true, the code inside the block will be executed. In this case, the block of code consists of three print statements that display messages related to being a child. After executing the code inside the if block, or skipping it if the condition is false, the program continues to execute the code after the if statement. In this case, it prints "Program continues..." on the screen.

The output of the above program is

> You are a child!
> Enjoy your childhood years.
> Have fun!
> Program continues...

3.1.2   If-Else

The else statement is a powerful component of the if statement that allows us to specify what should happen if the condition in the if statement is False. In other words, it gives us an alternative way to execute if the condition is not true. Therefore, when using an if statement, we often want to (or can) specify what happens if the condition is true as well as what happens if it is false. The 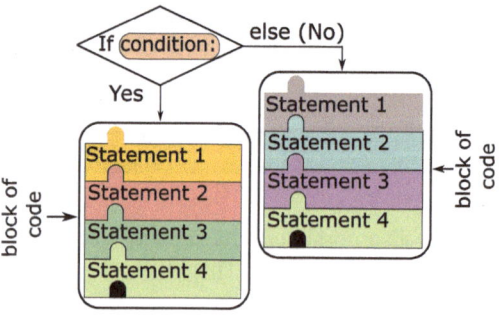 figure on the right shows how there are two blocks of code, one of which is executed if the condition in the if statement is true; otherwise, the other block of code is executed.

Here is an example to illustrate the use of "else," where the if statement prints "Positive" if the number is greater than zero; otherwise, it prints "Negative."

Figure 3-2. Visualization of the if-else statement to print positive if $x > 0$; otherwise, print negative

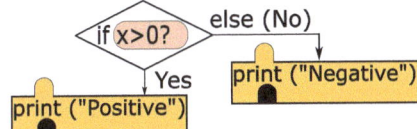

```
1  #Program 2
2  number = 5
3
4  if number > 0:
5      print("Positive!")
6  else:
7      print("Negative")
```

In the above example, as shown in Figure 3-2, we check if the variable number is greater than zero. If it is true, the program prints "Positive." Otherwise, it executes the code in the "else block" and prints "Negative."

After covering "if" and "if-else" statements and learning how to use them for decision-making, there is another interesting tool related to the "if" statement called "elif." It is like a bridge between if and else. Do not worry if it seems confusing at first – we will demonstrate how it works in the second solved example.

3.2   New Definitions

3.2.1   Block of Code

➡ **Block of code**

In programming, a "block of code" refers to a group of statements or instructions that are grouped together and executed as a single unit.

A block of code is typically used within control structures such as for loops (next chapter), conditional statements such as if statements, or function definitions (discussed later). It helps organize and control the flow of a program by specifying a set of actions to be performed (see Figure 3-1).

In the following example, if the condition is true, the block of code consisting of four statements – "statement1," "statement2," "statement3," and "statement4" – will be executed:

```
1  if condition:
2      statement1
3      statement2
4      statement3
5      statement4
```

3.2.2   Nested Concept

Nesting blocks means putting one block of statements inside another block of statements. It is like having a box inside another box, where each box contains a set of instructions. Nesting helps us organize and structure our code. It allows us to group related statements together and make our code easier to read and understand. Generally, the nested concept in programming refers to the practice of having one construct (such as an if statement) contained within another construct of the same type.

> ➡ **Nested concept**
> In programming, this concept refers to the practice of having one construct contained within another construct of the same type.

Let us explore the concept of nested if statements with a simple example:

```
1  #Program 3
2  x = 10
3
4  if x >= 0: # outer if
5    print("x is positive")
6    if x % 2 == 0: # nested if
7      print("x is even")
8    else:
9      print("x is odd")
10 else:
11   print("x is negative")
```

Before explaining the above code, we want to mention that in Python, the "%" operator is known as the **modulo operator** or the **remainder operator**. It is used to calculate the remainder of a division operation. Here is how the modulo operator works:

```
1  result = dividend % divisor
```

In the example above, the "%" operator calculates the remainder when the dividend is divided by the divisor. The result is the remainder of the division operation. Here are some examples to illustrate the use of the modulo operator:

```
1  # Example 1
2  result = 10 % 3
3  print(result) # Output: 1
4
5  # Example 2
6  result = 16 % 7
7  print(result) # Output: 2
8
9  # Example 3
10 result = 21 % 5
11 print(result) # Output: 1
```

Figure 3-3. Visualization of the nested if statement. The first checks if "x" is positive; if it is, the program prints "x is positive." The nested if checks if "x" is even; the program will print "x is even"; otherwise, the program will print "x is odd."

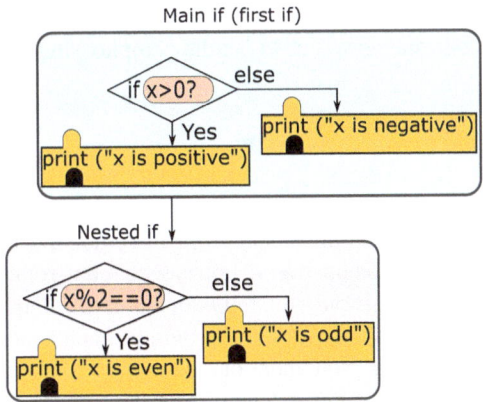

The explanation for the above example is

- In Example 1, the modulo operation 10 % 3 calculates the remainder when 10 is divided by 3, which is 1.
- In Example 2, the modulo operation 16 % 7 calculates the remainder when 16 is divided by 7, which is 2.
- In Example 3, the modulo operation 21 % 5 calculates the remainder when 21 is divided by 5, which is 1.

As a result, and from the example above in "Program3," the modulo operator % can be used to determine whether a number is even or odd (by checking whether the remainder is 0 or 1, when the divisor is 2). In this example, "x %2==0" calculates the remainder of dividing "x" by 2. If this remainder is zero, then "x" is even. For example, if "x" is 8, then 8%2=0, so "x" is even. Further, in "Program3," we have a nested if statement within the outer "if statement." Here is how the code execution flows as shown in Figure 3-3:

- The first if statement (outer if) checks if "x" is greater than or equal to 0. If the condition is true, the code inside the if block is executed.
- Inside this outer if block, after printing that "x is positive," we have a nested if statement. It checks if "x" is even by checking if "x% 2" is equal to 0.
- If the condition of the nested if statement is true, the code inside the nested if block is executed, which prints "x is even."
- If the condition of the nested if statement is false ("x" is odd), the code inside the else block of the nested if statement is executed, which prints "x is odd."
- If the condition of the outer if statement is false ("x" is negative), the code inside the else block of the outer if statement is executed, which prints "x is negative."

By nesting the if statement within another if statement, we can create more specific conditions and control the flow of the program based on multiple levels of conditions. This gives us more control over the execution of different blocks of code and allows us to handle complex situations effectively.

3.2.3 Indentation

Before explaining the indentation, let us explain the scope of statements within our code. Let us think about scope in Python like the lights in different rooms of a house. Imagine you have a big house with many rooms. Each room has its own light switch that controls only the lights in that room. This is like "scope" in Python. The whole house is like your entire program. Each room is like a different part of your code (like an "if" statement or a "for" loop (see next chapter)). The light switch in each room is like the indentation in your code. The area where the light shines is the "scope" of that room. When you turn on a light switch in one room

- The light only shines in that room. This is like the "scope" of that part of your code.
- It does not light up other rooms. Just like how code in one scope does not affect other scopes.
- If you want to light up another room, you need to use its own switch. Similarly, in Python, you need new indentation for a new scope.

Indentation plays a crucial role in Python because it determines the scope and execution of statements within a block. The vertically indented lines that follow a control structure, such as an if statement or a for loop, are considered part of the block of code associated with that control structure. It is like using the correct spacing or alignment when building something with blocks.

Imagine you have a set of blocks, like the one shown at the right, and you want to build a structure. When you build the blocks on top of each other, you need to make sure they are properly aligned. In Python, we do something similar with indentation. Indentation in Python means adding spaces or tabs at the beginning of a line to indicate that it belongs to a particular block. As shown in the figure at the right, there are three levels of indentation, a, b, and c, each

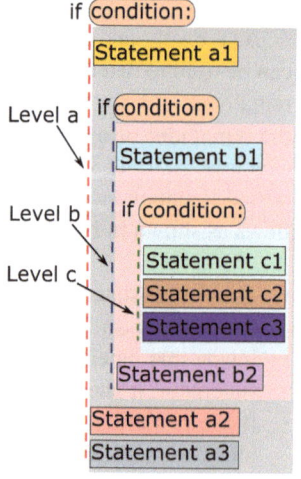

of which has a different color. The first (level a, with the gray background) occurs after the first if statement. In this block, there is one statement ("Statement a1"), followed by another "if" block (second "if"), then two statements ("Statement a2" and "Statement a3"). This block is executed if the condition in the outer if statement is true. In the second if statement, the scope is the one with the red background. In this scope, there is a statement ("Statement b1"), followed by another "if" (third "if"), and then another statement ("Statement b2"). In the third "if," if the condition is true, three statements ("Statement c1," "Statement c2," and "Statement c3") are executed, which are in the c indentation level (with the blue background). Thus, indentation helps us to understand which statements belong to which blocks and in which order they should be executed.

As we can see, the indentation gets deeper and deeper as we go into different sections of the program. The first "if" statement has three lines of code indented, the next "if" statement has two lines indented, and the third "if" statement has three lines of code indented.

If we do not use proper indentation, it can cause problems in the program. It may not work properly or even show errors. It is like using the blocks the wrong way, and it can change the meaning or order of the instructions in our program.

Here is a simple example that demonstrates different indentation levels in Python:

```python
1  x = 5
2
3  if x > 0: # first if
4      print("x is positive") # Indented at the if block level
5      if x % 2 == 0: # second if
6          print("x is even") # Indented at the nested if block level
7  else:
8      print("x is non-positive") # Indented at the else block level
9
10 print("End of program") # Not indented (outside any block)
```

In this example

- The first block of code is the first if block:
  - The line "if x > 0:" begins the "if" block, and the statement "print("x is positive")" is indented at the "if" block level, indicating that it will be executed if the condition "x > 0" is true.
- Inside the first if block, there is a nested if block (at line 5):
  - The line "if x % 2 == 0:" begins the nested "if" block, and the statement "print("x is even")" is indented at the level of the nested "if" block, meaning that it will be executed only if the condition "x % 2 == 0" is true.
- The second "if" block is followed by an "else" block; how do we know if this "else" statement belongs to the first or second if statements? This is where indentation can help. As we can see in the above code, the "else" in line 7 is indented with the first if. This means that in the first if, when the condition "x > 0:" is true, the program will print "x is positive" and then go to the second if, while if the condition is false, the code after the "else" statement will be executed. In other words, the else line starts the else block, and the print("x is not positive") statement is indented at the level of the else block, indicating that it will be executed if the "x > 0" condition in the if statement is False.
- The print("End of program") statement is not indented and is outside of any block. It will be executed regardless of the conditions in the if and else blocks.

In summary, by using different levels of indentation, we can clearly distinguish the different blocks and understand the hierarchical structure of the code. The levels of indentation ensure that the statements are executed based on the conditionals and maintain the intended logic of the program.

To see if you understand the idea of indentation, try to predict the correct output of the following program:

```
1  x = 5
2  y = 10
3
4  if x > 3:
5    print("Hello,")
6    if y < 15:
7      print("Python!")
8    else:
9      print("World!")
10 else:
11   print("Goodbye!")
12
13 print("End of program")
```

In the code above, we have two variables, "x" and "y," initialized with the values 5 and 10, respectively. The first if statement checks if "x" is greater than 3. If it is true, the code inside the first if block is executed. Inside the first if block is another if statement on line 6. It checks whether "y" is less than 15. If it is true, the code inside the nested if block is executed (line 7). Otherwise, if the condition (y < 15) is false, the code inside the else block is executed (line 9). After the code inside the nested if block or the else block is executed, the program continues to execute the code following the nested if statements (line 10), which is the else statement, and this will be executed if the condition in the first if (at line 4) is false. Finally, there is a print line at line 13, which is executed after the if statement. Thus, the following steps will produce the expected output:

> Hello,
> Python!
> End of program

Here is another example of more levels of indentation:

```
1  x = 25
2
3  if x > 10:
4    print("x is greater than 10.")
5
6    if x > 20:
7      print("x is also greater than 20.")
8
```

```
9    if x > 30:
10       print("x is even greater than 30.")
11    else:
12       print("x is not greater than 30.")
13
14   else:
15      print("x is not greater than 20.")
16
17 else:
18    print("x is not greater than 10.")
```

What is the expected output of this program?

Since "x" is greater than 10, the first if condition is true, and the code inside the first if block on line 3 is executed. It prints "x is greater than 10." Then, inside the first if block, the nested if condition is also true because "x" is greater than 20. Therefore, the code inside the nested if block, starting at line 7, is executed. It prints "x is also greater than 20." Inside the nested if block, at line 9, the deeply nested if condition is false because "x" is not greater than 30. Therefore, the code inside the else block is executed. It prints "x is not greater than 30." This is the expected output from the above program:

> x is greater than 10.
> x is also greater than 20.
> x is not greater than 30.

3.3   Solved Examples

In this section, we will try to solve and discuss some examples and write programs to practice what we have learned in this chapter and in the first two chapters.

3.3.1   Example 1: Even or Odd

Write a program that asks the user to enter a number. The program should then check whether the number is odd or even and print the result.

```
1  # Solved Example (1)
2  # Ask the user to enter a number
3  number = int(input("Enter a number: "))
4
5  # Check if the number is even or odd
6  if number % 2 == 0:
7     print(number, "is even.")
8  else:
9     print(number, "is odd.")
```

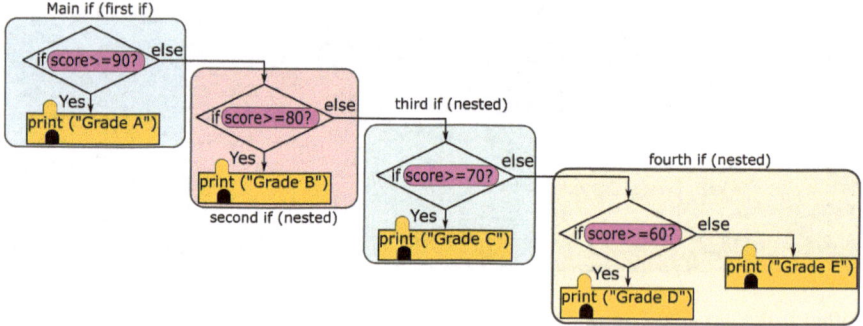

Figure 3-4. Visualization of the if-else statement of the grade calculator example

In this program, we use the input function to get user input and convert it to an integer using int(). Then we use the if statement to check if the number is divisible by 2 (number % 2 == 0). If the condition is true, this program prints that the number is even. If not, this program prints that the number is odd.

The output of the program in this example (Solved Example (1)) is as follows:

```
Enter a number: 7
The number 7 is odd.
```

3.3.2   Example 2: Grade Calculator

Write a program that asks the user to enter their score of a test. The program should check the score and print the corresponding grade based on the following criteria:

- Score ≥ 90: Grade A
- Score ≥ 80: Grade B
- Score ≥ 70: Grade C
- Score ≥ 60: Grade D
- Score < 60: Grade E

The output of the program of this example is as follows:

```
Enter your test score: 85
Your grade is B.
```

The code for this example is as follows:

```
1  # Solved Example (2): first version using if—else
2  # Ask the user to enter his/her score
3  score = int(input("Enter your score on the test: "))
4
5  # Check the score and print the corresponding grade
6  if score >= 90:
7    grade = "A"
8  else:
9    if score >= 80:
10     grade = "B"
11   else:
12     if score >= 70:
13       grade = "C"
14     else:
15       if score >= 60:
16         grade = "D"
17       else:
18         grade = "E"
19
20 print("Your grade is", grade)
```

In the program above, we use the input function to get the user's score and convert it to an integer using int(). Then we use the if and else statements to check the score against each condition. If the condition is true, we assign the grade to the score variable. Finally, the program prints out the score or grade. Instead of having many levels of the if-else statements, we can use another simple statement. Here, we want to introduce a new feature/option in the if statement, which is "**elif**". The elif statement is short for "else if," and it is used with an if statement and provides an additional condition to check if the previous if or elif conditions are not true. Thus, the elif statement allows us to test multiple conditions (as in this example) and execute different blocks of code. It can be used multiple times within a single if statement to check for different conditions in a structured and organized form. Additionally, when an elif condition evaluates to True, the block of code associated with that condition is executed, and the program skips the remaining elif and else parts. Finally, the elif statement is optional. It is not necessary to include an elif statement after every if statement. It depends on the specific logic and conditions you want to implement in your program.

Instead of "if" and "else," we can use "elif" to write the above code as follows:

```
1  # Solved Example (2): second version using elif
2  # Ask the user to enter his/her score
3  score = int(input("Enter your score on the test: "))
4
5  # Check the score and print the corresponding grade
6  if score >= 90:
7    grade = "A"
8  elif score >= 80:
9    grade = "B"
10 elif score >= 70:
```

```
11     grade = "C"
12  elif score >= 60:
13     grade = "D"
14  else:
15     grade = "E"
16
17  print("Your grade is", grade)
```

In the program above, as you can see, instead of using "else" and "if," we use the "elif" statement, which can do the same job as else if.

3.3.3   Example 3: Positive or Negative

Write a program that asks the user to enter a number. The program should check whether the number is positive, negative, or zero and print the result.

```
1   # Solved Example (3)
2   # Ask the user to enter a number
3   number = int(input("Enter a number: "))
4
5   # Check if the number is positive, negative, or zero
6   if number > 0:
7       print("The number is positive.")
8   elif number < 0:
9       print("The number is negative.")
10  else:
11      print("The number is zero.")
```

In this program, we use the input function to get user input and convert it to an integer using "int()." Then we use the if, elif, and else statements to check the number against the conditions. If the number is greater than zero, the program prints that it is positive. If the number is less than zero, the program prints that it is negative. Otherwise, the program prints that the number is zero. The output of the program in this example is shown below:

> Enter a number: -7
> The number -7 is negative.

3.3.4   Example 4: Simple Calculator

Write a program that acts as a simple calculator. The program should ask the user to enter two numbers and choose an operator from the available options (addition, subtraction, multiplication, or division). Based on the selected operator, the program should perform the corresponding operation and display the result.

```
1   # Solved Example (4)
2   # Prompt the user to enter two numbers
3   num1 = float(input("Enter the first number: "))
4   num2 = float(input("Enter the second number: "))
5
6   # Display the available operators
7   print("Available operators:")
8   print("1. Addition (+)")
9   print("2. Subtraction (−)")
10  print("3. Multiplication (∗)")
11  print("4. Division (/)")
12
13  # Prompt the user to choose an operator
14  operator_choice = int(input("Choose an operator (1−4): "))
15
16  # Perform the selected operation and display the result
17  if operator_choice == 1:
18      result = num1 + num2
19      operator = "+"
20  elif operator_choice == 2:
21      result = num1 − num2
22      operator = "−"
23  elif operator_choice == 3:
24      result = num1 ∗ num2
25      operator = "∗"
26  elif operator_choice == 4:
27      if num2 != 0:
28          result = num1 / num2
29          operator = "/"
30      else:
31          print("Error: Division by zero is not allowed.")
32          exit()
33  else:
34      print("Error: Invalid operator choice.")
35      exit()
36
37  print("Result:", num1, operator, num2, "=", result)
38  #print("Result: " + str(num1) + operator + str(num2), "=" + str(result))
```

The exit() function is used in this program to terminate the program execution. In the given context, it is used to stop the program if an error condition occurs, such as division by zero or an invalid operator choice.

The output of the program in this example is shown below:

```
Enter the first number: 5
Enter the second number: 3
Available operators:
1. Addition (+)
2. Subtraction (-)
3. Multiplication (*)
4. Division (/)
Choose an operator (1-4): 2

Result: 5 - 3 = 2
```

3.3.5 Example 5: Number Comparison

Write a program that asks the user to enter two numbers. The program should compare the numbers and print a message indicating which number is greater or if they are equal.

```python
1  # Solved Example (5)
2  # Prompt the user to enter the first number
3  num1 = float(input("Enter the first number: "))
4
5  # Prompt the user to enter the second number
6  num2 = float(input("Enter the second number: "))
7
8  # Compare the numbers and print the appropriate message
9  if num1 > num2:
10     print("The first number (" + str(num1)+") is greater than the second number (" + str(num2)+ ")")
11 elif num1 < num2:
12     print("The second number (" + str(num2)+") is greater than the first number (" + str(num1)+ ")")
13 else:
14     print("The two numbers are equal.")
```

The output of the program in this example is shown below:

```
Enter the first number: 10
Enter the second number: 15
The second number (15) is greater than the first number (10).
```

3.3.6 Example 6: Password Checker

Write a program that asks the user to enter a password. The program should check if the password matches a given password (e.g., "password123") and print a message indicating whether the password is correct or incorrect.

The program will be as follows:

```
1  # Solved Example (6)
2  # Predefined password
3  predefined_password = "password123"
4
5  # Ask the user to enter a password
6  user_password = input("Enter your password: ")
7
8  # Check if the entered password matches the predefined password
9  if user_password == predefined_password:
10    print("Correct password.")
11  else:
12    print("Incorrect password. Try again.")
```

The output of the above program is

```
Enter your password: secret123
Incorrect password. Try again.
```

3.4 Exercises

> ● **Exercise 1: Indentation output**
>
> What is the expected output of this program? [**Suggestion**: Read the indentation part first.]
>
> ```
> 1  temperature = 32
> 2
> 3  if temperature < 32:
> 4      print("It's freezing outside!")
> 5      print("Wear a warm coat.")
> 6  elif temperature < 65:
> 7      print("It's chilly today.")
> 8      print("You might need a jacket.")
> 9  else:
> 10     print("It's a nice day!")
> 11     print("Enjoy the weather!")
> 12
> 13 print("Have a great day!")
> ```

● Exercise 2: Indentation output

What is the expected output of this program? [**Suggestion**: Read the indentation part first.]

```
1  day = "Monday"
2  temperature = 72
3  rain_chance = 30
4
5  if day == "Monday":
6    print("It's the start of the week!")
7    if temperature < 50:
8      print("It's a bit chilly today.")
9      if rain_chance > 50:
10       print("Better bring an umbrella!")
11     else:
12       print("It should be a dry day.")
13   elif temperature < 70:
14     print("The temperature is pleasant.")
15   else:
16     print("It's a warm day today.")
17     if rain_chance > 20:
18       print("There's a chance of rain later.")
19     else:
20       print("It will be a sunny day.")
21 elif day == "Friday":
22   print("The weekend is almost here!")
23   if temperature < 60:
24     print("It's a bit cool for the end of the week.")
25   else:
26     print("The weather is great for the weekend.")
27 else:
28   print("It's a regular day.")
29   if rain_chance > 0:
30     print("There's a chance of rain today.")
31   else:
32     print("It should be a dry day.")
33
34 print("Have a wonderful day!")
```

● Exercise 3: Else if to elif

Rewrite the following program, and instead of using "else if," use "elif":

```
1  # Original code with if–else
2  day = input("Enter the day of the week: ")
3
4  if day == "monday":
5    print("It's the start of the work week.")
6  else:
7    if day == "tuesday":
```

```
 8     print("It's the second day of the week.")
 9   else:
10     if day == "wednesday":
11       print("It's the middle of the week.")
12     else:
13       if day == "thursday":
14         print("The weekend is almost here!")
15       else:
16         if day == "friday":
17           print("It's the end of the work week!")
18         else:
19           if day == "saturday":
20             print("It's the weekend!")
21           else:
22             if day == "sunday":
23               print("It's the start of the next week.")
24             else:
25               print("That's not a valid day of the week.")
```

● **Exercise 4: Elif to else if**

Rewrite the following program, and instead of using "elif," use "else if":

```
 1  # Original code with elif
 2  fruit = input("Enter a fruit: ")
 3
 4  if fruit == "apple":
 5    print("An apple a day keeps the doctor away.")
 6  elif fruit == "banana":
 7    print("Bananas are a great source of potassium.")
 8  elif fruit == "orange":
 9    print("Oranges are high in vitamin C.")
10  elif fruit == "strawberry":
11    print("Strawberries are sweet and juicy.")
12  else:
13    print("I don't have any information about that fruit.")
```

● **Exercise 5: Child or adult**

Write a program that asks the user to enter their age. If their age is greater than or equal to 18, print "You are an adult." Otherwise, print "You are a child."
    The output of this code should be

Enter your age: 40
You are an adult.

or

> Enter your age: 10
> You are a child.

● Exercise 6: Child, teenager, or adult

Write a program that asks the user to enter an age and determines whether the person is a child, teenager, or adult.
   The output of this code should be

> Enter your age: : 6
> You are a child.

   or

> Enter your age: : 50
> You are an adult.

● Exercise 7: Favorite fruit

Write a program that asks the user to enter their favorite fruit. If the fruit is "apple," print "Apples are delicious!" If the fruit is "banana," print "Bananas are a great choice!" For any other fruit, print "That's a nice fruit too!"
   The output of this code should be

> Enter your favorite fruit: apple
> Apples are delicious!

   What will be the output if the user enters "Apple" instead of "apple"?

● Exercise 8: Birth month

Write a program that asks the user to enter their birth month (as a number from 1 to 12). If the month is between 1 and 3, print "It is in the first quarter of the year." If the month is between 4 and 6, print "It is in the second quarter of the year." If the month is between 7 and 9, print "It is in the third quarter of the year." If the month is between 10 and 12, print "It is in the fourth quarter of the year."

The output of this code should be

> Enter your birth month (as a number from 1 to 12): 2
> It's in the first quarter of the year.

● Exercise 9: What school are you in?

Write a program that asks the user to enter their age. If their age is between 5 and 10 (inclusive), print "You are in elementary school." If their age is between 11 and 13 (inclusive), print "You are in middle school." If their age is between 14 and 18, print "You are in high school."

The output of this code should be

> Enter your age: 10
> You are in elementary school.

● Exercise 10: Favorite color

Write a program that asks the user to enter their favorite color. If the color is "red," print "Your favorite color is red." If the color is "blue," print "Your favorite color is blue." For any other color, print "Your favorite color is not red or blue."

The output of this code should be

> Enter your favorite color: blue
> Your favorite color is blue.

● Exercise 11: Multiple of a number

Write a program that asks the user to enter a number. If the number is a multiple of 4, print "The number is a multiple of 4." If the number is a multiple of 2 but not 4, print "The number is a multiple of 2 but not 4." Otherwise, print "The number is neither a multiple of 2 nor 4."

The output of this code should be

> Enter a number: 40
> The number is a multiple of 4.

● **Exercise 12: Maximum score calculation**

Write a program that asks the user to enter the scores of ten students. The program should then find and print the maximum score among all the students.
Example output:

Enter the score for student 1: 85
Enter the score for student 2: 72
Enter the score for student 3: 94
Enter the score for student 4: 88
Enter the score for student 5: 77
Enter the score for student 6: 90
Enter the score for student 7: 81
Enter the score for student 8: 95
Enter the score for student 9: 79
Enter the score for student 10: 83

The maximum score among all students is: 95

Note that in this example you have some variables and you want to find the maximum value, which is not an easy task. Because if we have numbers (e.g., 2, 3, 9, 7), we easily know that the maximum of these four numbers is 9, but we do not know how to find this maximum to explain this method (the way to find the maximum) in steps to the computer in our program. But, as you know, if we have some variables, each with a content, we can write a program to find the maximum of these variables. To do this, we define, for example, four variables V1, V2, V3, and V4 and set the maximum equal to the first variable (Max=V1). Next, we compare V2 to Max; if V2>Max, then Max is equal to V2; otherwise, Max is still equal to V1. Similarly, we compare V3 to Max and then V4 to Max. After that, the maximum variable is Max. Similarly, we can find the minimum value among some variables.

● **Exercise 13: Passing students**

Write a program that asks the user to enter the scores of ten students. The program should then determine and print the number of students who passed the test. Consider a passing score to be 60 or above.

Example output:

Enter the score for student 1: 85
Enter the score for student 2: 72
Enter the score for student 3: 45
Enter the score for student 4: 88
Enter the score for student 5: 77
Enter the score for student 6: 90
Enter the score for student 7: 52
Enter the score for student 8: 95
Enter the score for student 9: 79
Enter the score for student 10: 83
The number of students who passed the test: 8

Notice that in this exercise on counting the number of students passing, we should know how to create a counter. This counter is nothing more than a variable initialized to zero. For example, let us say we have a numeric variable called counter that is set to zero. After getting the score of each student, we should check if this score is below or above 60. If the score is greater than or equal to 60, it means that the student has passed, so the counter should be increased by one (counter=counter+1). The same step is done with the other students to get the final number. The number of students who have passed is stored in the variable counter.

● **Exercise 14: Area calculator**

Write a program that allows the user to calculate the area of different shapes (triangle, circle, square, rectangle). The program should provide a menu of options for the user to select the shape and then ask for the necessary inputs to calculate the area. Note that

- **Triangle**: The area of a triangle can be calculated using the formula $Area = 0.5 * base * height$.
- **Circle**: The area of a circle can be calculated using the formula $Area = \pi * radius^2$.
- **Square**: The area of a square can be calculated using the formula $Area = side^2$.

- **Rectangle**: The area of a rectangle can be calculated using the formula $Area = length * width$.

  Example output:

  ```
  — Area Calculator —
  1. Triangle
  2. Circle
  3. Square
  4. Rectangle
  5. Quit

  Enter your choice: 1
  Enter the base of the triangle: 5
  Enter the height of the triangle: 8
  The area of the triangle is: 20.0
  ```

● **Exercise 15: Average score calculation**

Write a program that asks the user to enter the scores of ten students. The program should then calculate and print the average score of all the students. Note: The average is the sum of all values or variables divided by the number of values. For example, the average of the four values 2, 4, 5, 9 is $\frac{2+4+5+9}{4} = 5$.

The expected output of this exercise is

```
Enter the score of student 1: 85
Enter the score of student 2: 90
Enter the score of student 3: 78
Enter the score of student 4: 92
Enter the score of student 5: 87
Enter the score of student 6: 80
Enter the score of student 7: 95
Enter the score of student 8: 89
Enter the score of student 9: 83
Enter the score of student 10: 91
The average score of all the students is: 87.0
```

● **Exercise 16: Weather display**

Write a program to read the temperature in Celsius and display a suitable message according to the temperature state below:

- Temp < 0, then Freezing weather
- Temp 0–10, then Very Cold weather
- Temp 10–20, then Cold weather
- Temp 20–30, then Normal in Temp
- Temp 30–40, then It's Hot
- Temp $\geq$ 40, then It's Very Hot

The expected output will be as follows:

> Enter the temperature : 42
> It's very hot.

● **Exercise 17: Print the day name**

Write a program to read any day number in integer and display the day name in word format.
The expected output will be as follows:

> Enter the number : 4
> Thursday

Write another version of this program to read any month number and displaying the month name as a word.

3.5   Glossary

Term	Definition
if	Used to perform conditional checks and execute specific code blocks based on the evaluation of a given condition.
elif	Used in conjunction with "if" statements to specify additional conditions to check whether the preceding "if" or "elif" condition evaluates to False, allowing multiple conditional branches in a block of code. See the second solved example for more details.
else	Used in conjunction with "if" statements to specify an alternate block of code to be executed if the condition of the "if" statement evaluates to False.
exit()	A command used to end the program execution. Please read Example 4 in the "Solved Examples" section to get more knowledge about how "exit()" works.

3.6   Our Next Adventure in Programming

In this chapter, Kai learned how to make decisions using the if statement. This will improve Kai's programming skills to create programs that react intelligently to different situations. Then, with the "if" statement, we could have two or more possible ways or routes for our programs, not just one.

In the next lesson, Kai realized that he was spending a lot of time and effort doing repetitive tasks. He then decided that it was important to explore the concept of loops and focus specifically on the "for loop." Loops are a powerful tool that allow us to efficiently repeat tasks. For example, the for loop in Python allows us to perform a task many times over. Imagine if you had to do something many times by hand – like making our calculator program, which we introduced in one of the solved examples, run many times. The for loop in Python makes it easy for us to do this automatically. In the next chapter, we will break down the syntax of the for loop, discuss its various uses, and show how it can be used to automate repetitive actions.

Repeating Actions with For Loops

4

In previous chapters, we have learned with Kai how to interact with programs using input and output statements, and we have discovered the wonders of variables and different variable types. We also explored the power of the if statement, which allows us to make decisions and control the flow of the code.

In this exciting chapter, Kai decided to make an adventure to discover the power of the for loop, which will help him perform repetitive tasks easily. As we dive into the world of programming, we should learn how to repeat actions and enhance our creativity through the magic of iteration. With this new programming tool, we can display a message for ten or more times. Another example is to give an order to the robot to move in a specific direction many steps, which is a repeated task. Get ready for this new and funny adventure.

4.1   The Power of Repetition

Imagine you have a task that you need to do many, many times. Let us say you need to print the numbers 1–100 on the screen. Without a special tool, you would have to write each number one by one, which would take a lot of time and effort. That is where the power of repetition comes in. In programming, we have some tools like the "for loop" that allow us to repeat a task as many times as we want without having to write it out again and again. To do such repetition, we can use the for loop statement.

The for loop is a basic control structure in Python that helps the programmer repeat a line or block of code a specified number of times. This means that we can execute a set of instructions repeatedly. It allows us to automate repetitive tasks by running the same block of code multiple times.

Figure 4-1 shows how the for statement can be used to repeat a block of code (or even a line of code) five times. As shown, the for loop has a block of code that consists of three statements; this block is repeated five times.

© Alaa Tharwat 2025
A. Tharwat, *Python Adventures for Young Coders*,
https://doi.org/10.1007/979-8-8688-1067-1_4

Figure 4-1. Visualization of the for statement; here, this block of code will be repeated for five times

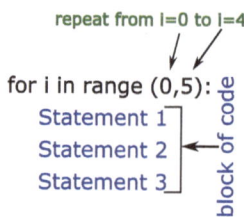

Here is an example that shows how we can use the for loop to print numbers from 0 to 4:

```
1  for i in range(0, 5):
2      print(i)
3  print("Good bye")
4
```

In this example:

- Step 1: We start by using a for loop to go through a range of numbers. In this case, the range is from 0 to 4 (5 is not included), so we will loop five times. To understand this, please try to print range(0, 5).
- Step 2: The loop starts with the first iteration. The variable i is assigned the value of 0, which is less than 5 (the end of the for loop).
- Step 3: Inside the loop, the print(i) statement is executed. Since the variable i is currently 0, the output will be "0."
- Step 4: The first iteration is now complete. The loop moves to the next iteration.
- Step 5: In the second iteration, the variable i is increased to be 1, which is also less than 5 (the end of the loop).
- Step 6: The print(i) statement is executed again. Now i is 1, the output will be "1."
- Step 7: The second iteration is complete. The loop moves to the next iteration.
- Step 8: This process is repeated for the remaining iterations of the loop, increasing i by one each time.
- Step 9: In the third iteration, i is 2, and the output will be "2."
- Step 10: Similarly, in the fourth iteration, i is 3, and the output will be "3."
- Step 11: Similarly, in the fifth iteration, i is 4, and the output will be "4." Then, increase i to 5, which is the end of the for loop.
- Step 12: The loop has finished iterating through all the numbers in the range. The program execution moves to the next line after the loop and prints "Good bye."

Overall, the code will print the numbers from 0 to 4 on separate lines because of the print(i) statement inside the loop.

As we can see in the code above, by using the for loop, we can repeat a specific set of statements for a defined range of values, making our code more efficient, readable, and able to handle repetitive tasks effectively.

Here is another example that uses the for loop to print a vertical line of ten stars.

```
1  for i in range(0, 10):
2      print("*")
```

The output of the above program will be as follows:

```
*
*
*
*
*
*
*
*
*
*
```

Since i in the above code is not used inside the loop, we can remove it from the header of the for loop and the program will be

```
1  for _ in range(0, 10):
2      print("*")
```

Sure, the for loop could be so helpful to solve some problems in our previous exercises and make the program more interactive. Also, we should think about how we can reduce the number of lines of our program by using the for statement. In the next section, we will try some more examples using the for loop statement to understand it better.

4.2   Solved Examples

In this section, we will try to solve and discuss some examples and write programs to practice what we have learned in this chapter and the first ones.

4.2.1   Example 1: Print Numbers with Different Sequences

Write a program that prints the numbers from 1 to 10:

```
1  # Solved example 1
2  for i in range(1, 11):
3      print(i)
```

The output of this code is

```
1
2
:
:
10
```

Here is a step-by-step explanation:

- The for keyword is used to start a loop in Python. It is followed by a loop variable, which in this case is i. The loop variable is typically used to iterate over a sequence of values.
- range(1, 11) is a built-in Python function that generates a sequence of numbers starting from the first argument (1 in this case) up to, but not including, the second argument (11 in this case). So, range(1, 11) will generate the sequence [1, 2, 3, 4, 5, 6, 7, 8, 9, 10].
- The for loop iterates over each value in the generated sequence. During each iteration, the loop variable "i" is assigned the current value from the sequence. The for loop cycles through each value in the generated sequence.
- The indented line print(i) is executed in each iteration of the loop. It prints the value of i.

Hence, when we run this code, it will print the numbers 1 to 10, each on a new line.

What about if we want to print the numbers from 10 to 0?

Instead of printing i, we can print 11-i; this will update the program as follows:

```
1  for i in range(1,11):
2      print(11−i)
```

The above code could also be written as follows:

```
1  for i in range(10, 0, −1):
2      print(i)
```

The code above uses the for loop and the range() function to iterate from 10 to 1. The range function allows us to specify a start point, an end point, and a step size. The step size determines how much the loop variable increases or decreases with each iteration. For example, using "range(3, 100, 4)" means that we will start counting from 3, and in each iteration or loop, the value will increase by 4. This will continue until we reach a number that is just before 100. Simply, this range function is like a staircase. We start at the bottom of the stairs (the starting point) and take steps of a fixed size (the step size) to go up. We keep climbing until we almost reach the top (the number just before the end point). By using this range function with a for loop, we can walk through a sequence of numbers, such as 3, 7, 11, ... This can be useful if we want to work with certain sequence of numbers.

We can also control this range function to start with a large number, and instead of increasing i, decrease it with a negative number (e.g., –2) to decrease the number by 2 at each iteration.

In the above code, the range() function takes three arguments: the starting number (10), the ending number (0, but not included), and the increment by –1, which means decrement by 1 each time.[1] Inside the loop, we simply print the current value of i, which counts down from 10 to 1.

4.2.2 Example 2: Average Score Calculation

Write a program that asks the user to enter the number of students and then asks for the scores of each student. The program should then calculate and print the average score of all the students.

```
1  # Solved example 2
2  # Prompt the user to enter the number of students
3  num_students = int(input("Enter the number of students: "))
4
5  # Initialize a variable to store the total score
6  total_score = 0
7
8  # Ask for the scores of each student and calculate the total score
9  for i in range(num_students):
10     score = float(input("Enter the score of student " + str(i + 1)))
11     total_score += score
12
13  # Calculate the average score
14  average_score = total_score / num_students
15
16  # Print the average score
17  print("The average score of all the students is:", str(average_score))
```

The output of this code will be as follows:

Enter the number of students: 4
Enter the score of student 1: 85
Enter the score of student 2: 90
Enter the score of student 3: 78
Enter the score of student 4: 92
The average score of all the students is: 86.25

From the example above, we can see that, first, the program asks the user to enter the number of students. The input function is used to get the input from the user, and

[1] "Increment" and "decrement" are fancy words for "counting up" and "counting down" in programming.

we convert it to an integer using int(). Then we initialize a variable "total_score" with zero to calculate the sum of all scores. Next, we use the for loop to ask for each student's score. The loop iterates "num_students" times, and in each iteration we ask the user to enter the score of the current student. Inside the loop, we add each score to the "total_score" variable. After the loop, we calculate the average score by dividing total_score by num_students. Finally, we use the print statement to display the average score.

As we can see, with this simple program we can calculate the average score of four students, and we can do this for any number of students. This could be considered as a solution for Exercise 15 in Chapter 3.

4.2.3 Example 3: Timetable Generator

Write a program that asks the user to enter a number. The program should then generate and print the timetable for that number, from 1 to 10. Do you remember the second solved example in Chapter 2? We solved this problem with a simple method, but now we want to do it again to show how the for loop makes the program simpler and shorter when we use the for loop.

```python
1   # Solved example 3
2   # Prompt the user to enter a number
3   number = int(input("Enter a number: "))
4
5   # Print the time table header
6   print("Time Table for", number, ":")
7
8   # Generate and print the time table
9   for i in range(1, 11):
10      result = number * i
11      print(number, "x", i, "=", result)
```

In this solution, we first ask the user to enter a number using the input function. We convert the input to an integer using int() and store it in the number variable. Next, we print the timetable header using the print statement, which includes the number entered by the user.

We use the for loop to iterate from 1 to 10 using range(1, 11). At each iteration, we calculate the result by multiplying the number by the current iteration value. Finally, we print each line of the timetable using the print statement, which displays the multiplication expression and the result. You can see how the for loop makes the repetition task easier, then we can print the timetable for a number from 1 to 100; to do this, we only need to change one number; what is that number?

4.2.4   Example 4: Number Guessing Game (Learning Break Statement)

Write a program that asks the user to guess the number between 1 and 100. The program should give the user feedback after each guess, telling them whether the guess was too high, too low, or correct. The program should run until the user guesses the correct number or until the user has made ten attempts.

```python
# Solved example 4
# Set secret_number to any number between 1 and 100
secret_number = 86

# Start the game
for attempts in range(1, 11): # only ten times
    # Ask the user to guess the number
    guess = int(input("Guess the number between 1 and 100: "))

    # Check if the guess is too high, too low, or correct
    if guess > secret_number:
        print("Too high! Try again.")
    elif guess < secret_number:
        print("Too low! Try again.")
    else:
        print("Congratulations! You guessed the correct number!")
        break

    # Check if the maximum number of attempts has been reached
    if attempts == 10:
        print("Game over! You have reached the maximum number of attempts.")
```

In the code above, Python's break statement is used to exit a loop earlier (i.e., before the normal end of the loop). As you can see, the break statement is used inside the else block of the if-else statement.

When the user guesses the correct number, the program prints a congratulatory message. Afterward, the break statement is executed, causing the loop to terminate immediately. This means that the program will exit the loop and continue executing the code that follows the loop, skipping any remaining iterations. In the context of the number guessing game, the break statement is used to stop the loop as soon as the player guesses the correct number, preventing unnecessary additional iterations and allowing the program to proceed to the end of the game.

4.2.5   Example 5: Infinite for Loop

In some cases, we need the for loop to continue for a long time, repeating a task over and over again. However, there is surely a specific condition at which the for loop should be stopped, and here we can use the "break" statement. For example, in the code below, the program will continue to print all numbers until the break condition, which is "i==1000," is met or until it reaches 100,000. This means that on each iteration, this condition is checked, and if it is false, the for loop will continue, but if it is true, the program will exit the loop.

```
1  # Solved example 5
2  for i in range(100000): # infinite loop
3      print(i)
4      if i==1000:
5          break
```

Let us try another example. In this example, we ask the user to enter the password. If the user enters the correct password, the program will print "That's the correct password!"; otherwise, it will continue trying forever or until the user decides to exit the program.

```
1  print("You can try to guess the password as many times as you want.")
2  print("If you want to give up, just type 'quit'.")
3
4  secret_password = "1234"
5
6  for _ in range(10**6): # This creates an infinite loop
7      password_guess = input("Please enter the password (or 'quit' to give up): ")
8
9      if password_guess == 'quit':
10         print("Good bye.")
11         break
12
13     if password_guess == secret_password:
14         print("That's the correct password!")
15         break
16     else:
17         print("Oops! That's not right. Try again!")
```

The above program shows a very long or approximately an "infinite loop." It is like a game that keeps going and going until we tell it to stop. Each time the loop runs, we ask the player or user to guess the password. If he types "quit," we say "Good bye" and exit the program and use "break" to stop the game. If the user guesses the correct password, we tell him that he got it right and use "break" to end the game. If his guess is wrong, we tell him to try again, and the loop continues.

4.3   Nested Loops

A nested for loop is when you have a loop inside another loop. This is similar to the nested concept that we have introduced in Chapter 3. It is like having a loop inside another loop. For example, let us say we have an outer loop that iterates from 1 to 3 and an inner loop that also iterates from 1 to 4. Each time the outer loop iterates, the inner loop completes a full iteration.

```
1  # Outer loop
2  for i in range(1, 4):
3      # Inner loop
4      for j in range(1, 5):
5          # Print the values of i and j
6          print("i =", i, " & j =", j)
```

Here is how the above code works:

- In the outer loop, i starts with the first value (1). Then, the inner loop starts and completes its full iteration (1, 2, 3, 4).
- In the outer loop, i increases to the next value (2). Again, the inner loop starts and completes its full iteration (1, 2, 3, 4).
- In the outer loop, i increases to the next value (3). The inner loop starts and completes a full iteration (1, 2, 3, 4).

The output of this program will be

```
i = 1 & j = 1
i = 1 & j = 2
i = 1 & j = 3
i = 1 & j = 4
i = 2 & j = 1
i = 2 & j = 2
i = 2 & j = 3
i = 2 & j = 4
i = 3 & j = 1
i = 3 & j = 2
i = 3 & j = 3
i = 3 & j = 4
```

Here is another example of using the nested loop to print the multiplication timetables from 1 to 4. The output of this program will be as follows:

$1 \times 1 = 1$
$1 \times 2 = 2$
$1 \times 3 = 3$
$1 \times 4 = 4$
$1 \times 5 = 5$
$\vdots$
$1 \times 10 = 10$

$2 \times 1 = 2$
$2 \times 2 = 4$
$2 \times 3 = 6$
$2 \times 4 = 8$
$2 \times 5 = 10$
$\vdots$
$2 \times 10 = 20$

$3 \times 1 = 3$
$3 \times 2 = 6$
$3 \times 3 = 9$
$3 \times 4 = 12$
$3 \times 5 = 15$
$\vdots$
$3 \times 10 = 30$

$4 \times 1 = 4$
$4 \times 2 = 8$
$4 \times 3 = 12$
$4 \times 4 = 16$
$4 \times 5 = 20$
$\vdots$
$4 \times 10 = 40$

The solution of this example will be

```
# Generate and print the multiplication time table
for i in range(1, 5):
    print()  # Print an empty line between each row for better readability
    for j in range(1, 11):
        result = i * j
        print(i, "x", j, "=", result)
```

In this solution, we use two nested for loops. The outer loop iterates from 1 to 4 using range(1, 5), representing the numbers for which we want to generate the timetable. Inside the outer loop, we print an empty line using print() to create a separation between each row of the timetable. Then, we have the inner loop, which also iterates from 1 to 10 using range(1, 11). This loop represents the multiplier for each row.

Inside the inner loop, we calculate the result by multiplying the current values of the outer and inner loops: i * j. Finally, we use the print statement to display each multiplication expression and its result.

When you run the program, it will generate and print the multiplication timetable from 1 to 4, just like the previous output. Try to modify the code to print the multiplication timetable from 1 to 100.

4.4 Exercises

● Exercise 1: Print output

What is the expected output of this program?

```
for i in range(1, 4):
    for j in range(1, 4):
        print(i, j)
```

● Exercise 2: Print output

What is the expected output of this program?

```
for i in range(1, 4):
    for j in range(1, i):
        print(i, "*", j, "=", i*j)
```

● Exercise 3: Print output

What is the expected output of this program?

```
for i in range(1, 100):
    if (i%3)==0:
        print(i)
```

● **Exercise 4: Print numbers**

Write a program that uses the for loop to iterate over the numbers from 1 to 10 (inclusive) and prints each number on a new line.
The output will be

```
1
2
3
4
5
6
7
8
9
10
```

● **Exercise 5: Print a pattern**

Write a program to display a pattern such as a right-angled triangle with a number.
Example of the output:

```
1
12
123
1234
```

Note: You can use "print(j, end="")" to print the number without a line break after it.

● **Exercise 6: Print a pattern**

Write a program to make a pattern like a right-angled triangle with a number that repeats a number in a row.
Example of the output:

```
1
22
333
4444
```

● Exercise 7: Sum of series

Write a program to display the sum of the series [9 + 99 + 999 + 9999 ...].
Example of the output:

Input the number or terms :5
Expected Output :
9 90 900 9000 90000
The sum of the series = 99999

● Exercise 8: Print numbers in descending order

Write a program that uses the for loop to iterate over the numbers from 10 to 1 (inclusive) in descending order and prints each number on a new line.
The output will be as follows:

10
9
8
7
6
5
4
3
2
1

● Exercise 9: Print text

Write a program that uses the for loop to print a word (e.g., "Hello") for ten times.
Example output:

Hello
Hello
Hello
Hello
⋮
Hello

● Exercise 10: Print numbers in a sequence

Write a program that uses the for loop to print a sequence of numbers 2, 4, 6, 8, ... or 3, 6, 9; also, try to print 100, 98, 96, 94, ..., 0.
Example of the output:

```
2
4
6
8
⋮
```

● Exercise 11: Sum of numbers

Write a program that takes a positive integer as input and uses the for loop to calculate the sum of all numbers from 1 to that integer. The program should print the sum.
Example of the output:

```
For input: 5
Sum: 15
```

● Exercise 12: Square a number

Write a program that uses the for loop to iterate over the numbers from 1 to 5 (inclusive). For each number, calculate and print its square.
The output will be

```
1
4
9
16
25
```

● **Exercise 13: Factorial**

Write a program that takes a positive integer as input and calculates its factorial using the for loop. The factorial of a number n is the product of all positive integers from 1 to n.

Example of the output:

> For input: 5
> Factorial of 5 is 120

● **Exercise 14: Sum of even numbers**

Write a program that takes as input two integers representing the starting and ending numbers of a range. The program should use a for loop to iterate over the numbers in the range (inclusive) and compute the sum of all even numbers in the range. Assume that the starting number is always less than or equal to the ending number.

Example of the output:

> Starting number: 1
> End number: 10
> Sum of even numbers: 30

● **Exercise 15: Password entry**

Write a program that asks the user to enter a password and continues to ask for the password until the correct password is entered. Once the correct password is entered, the program should display a success message and exit.

Example of the output:

> Enter the password: 12345
> Incorrect password. Please try again.
>
> Enter the password: password123
> Incorrect password. Please try again.
>
> Enter the password: 1234
> Success! You have entered the correct password.

4.5   Glossary

Term	Definition
for	This is used to repeat one line or many lines (block of code) a certain number of times.
break	This is used to exit a loop early and stop the execution of the loop.
nested for	Nested for loops refer to using a for loop inside another for loop. This allows you to iterate over two or more sequences simultaneously.

4.6   Our Next Adventure in Programming

In this chapter, Kai learned how to perform repetitive tasks using the for loop statement. This will help Kai's programming skills to do repeated tasks quickly without having to do them manually, saving time and effort and making the program shorter and easier to understand.

In the next chapter, Kai feels a bit confused about all the topics he has learned in the previous chapters. Therefore, he decides to make a checkpoint and review and solidify his understanding of the key programming concepts covered in the first four chapters. In the next chapter, we will briefly introduce some new topics with Kai, such as break and continue statements, Python casting, assignment operators, and logical operators, but the main focus of this chapter will be to reinforce the core programming constructs we have learned. We will also see examples of how for and if can be used together, how an "if statement" works inside the for loop, and how a "for statement" can work inside the if statement. We will also look at some other ideas for dealing with counters and finding the maximum or minimum of a variable. At the end of the next chapter, we will introduce three simple projects to practice what we have learned and to make sure that we know how the first four chapters relate to each other.

Checkpoint: Strengthening Your Programming Skills

5

In the previous chapters, we learned with Kai several basic programming topics that allow us to interact with programs using input and output statements, and we discovered the wonders of variables and different variable types. We also explored the powerful decision-making that is possible with the if statement. Finally, we discovered how to use the for loop to perform repetitive tasks easily and in a short amount of time.

In this chapter, Kai decided to take a break from learning new concepts and instead focus on reviewing and reinforcing what he has learned so far. Think of this chapter as a checkpoint – a moment to reflect on the knowledge and skills we gained in the previous chapters. We will revisit the important topics we have explored, giving us an opportunity to solidify our understanding and address any questions or confusion we may have. We will also try to tie all of the previous chapters together so that we can see how everything fits together. Finally, we will conclude this chapter with a series of solved examples and exercises designed to test our knowledge from the previous chapters. These worked examples will not only reinforce our understanding of the concepts but will also develop our problem-solving skills and creativity. In addition, in this chapter, we will introduce three exciting projects. Our goal with Kai is to work on these projects step by step, which means that we will take them one at a time and improve them as we progress through the next chapters. This allows us to practice what we have already learned and understand what we need to learn next. Furthermore, with each chapter, as we learn new topics, we can improve these projects and make them better as we continue to learn. This helps us learn new things in a fun and organized way. Remember that programming is not just about learning syntax, it is also about solving problems and using your imagination.

© Alaa Tharwat 2025
A. Tharwat, *Python Adventures for Young Coders*,
https://doi.org/10.1007/979-8-8688-1067-1_5

5.1   Python Assignment Operators

Assignment operators in Python are symbols or combinations of symbols that are used to assign values to variables. They allow you to store data in variables for later use or manipulation. Here are some commonly used assignment operators:

Operator	Example	Same As
=	x = 5	x = 5
+=	x += 3	x = x + 3
-=	x -= 3	x = x - 3
*=	x *= 3	x = x * 3
/=	x /= 3	x = x / 3

Here is an example to explain how the assignment operators are working in programming:

```
1  # Assign a value using the = operator
2  x = 10
3  print("x =", x)  # Output: x = 10
4
5  # Compound assignment operators
6  x += 5  # Equivalent to x = x + 5
7  print("x += 5 =>", x)  # Output: x += 5 => 15
8
9  x -= 3  # Equivalent to x = x - 3
10  print("x -= 3 =>", x)  # Output: x -= 3 => 12
11
12  x *= 2  # Equivalent to x = x * 2
13  print("x *= 2 =>", x)  # Output: x *= 2 => 24
14
15  x /= 4  # Equivalent to x = x / 4
16  print("x /= 4 =>", x)  # Output: x /= 4 => 6.0
```

Let us go through the example step by step:

- $x = 10$: This assigns the value 10 to the variable x.
- $x+ = 5$: This is a compound assignment operator, equivalent to x = x + 5. It takes the current value of x (10), adds 5 to it, and then assigns the result (15) back to x.
- $x- = 3$: This is a compound assignment operator, equivalent to x = x - 3. It takes the current value of x (15), subtracts 3 from it, and then assigns the result (12) back to x.
- $x* = 2$: This is a compound assignment operator, equivalent to x = x * 2. It takes the current value of x (12), multiplies it by 2, and then assigns the result (24) back to x.

- $x/=4$: This is a compound assignment operator, equivalent to $x = x / 4$. It takes the current value of x (24), divides it by 4, and then assigns the result (6.0) back to x.

In Python also, we can assign the same value to many variables in a single line; this is called "chained assignments," and it will be as follows:

```
x = y = z = 4
```

The above code means that we assign the same value 4 to three variables x, y, and z in a single line.

5.2 Looping Using While

In the previous chapter, we introduced the for loop as a tool for repeating tasks. In Python, there is another tool that can make a loop; this is the while loop statement. With the while loop, we can execute a set of statements as long as a condition is true. It is like playing a game where you keep doing something until you reach a certain goal. So in programming, a while loop has a condition that you check before each iteration of the loop. If the condition is true, you continue to execute the instructions inside the loop. If the condition becomes false, you stop and move on to the next part of your program. Let us print the numbers from one to five using the for loop and the while statement and compare both.

Using a for loop:

```
for num in range(1, 6):
    print(num)
```

Using a while loop:

```
num = 1
while num <= 5:
    print(num)
    num += 1
```

In both cases, we are printing the numbers from 1 to 5.

In the for loop, we use the range(1, 6) function to generate a sequence of numbers from 1 to 5. The loop iterates over each number in the sequence and prints it. In the while loop, we initialize the variable num to 1. The loop continues as long as num is less than or equal to 5 (the condition in the while statement). Inside the loop, we print the current value of num and then increment it by 1 using num += 1. This way, we keep printing the numbers until num reaches 6, at which point the condition becomes false, and the loop stops.

Both the for loop and the while loop achieve the same result of printing the numbers from 1 to 5. However, the for loop is more concise and often used when we know the number of iterations in advance. The while loop is more flexible and useful when the number of iterations depends on a specific condition.

Let us have another example to know how the while statement is used to do repeated tasks. Let us write a program that asks the user to enter a number and then generate and print the timetable for that number, from 1 to 10. This example was solved in the last chapter using a for loop. To solve it using while, the code will be

```
1  # Prompt the user to enter a number
2  number = int(input("Enter a number: "))
3
4  # Print the time table header
5  print("Time Table for", number, ":")
6
7  # Generate and print the time table
8  i = 1
9  while i <= 10:
10     result = number * i
11     print(number, "x", i, "=", result)
12     i += 1
```

As you can see in the above code, the variable "i" is initialized with 1, and at the header of the while statement (line 9), a condition is checked to make sure that if i is lower than or equal to 10 (i≤10), if the condition is true, the result variable will be calculated and then print a line from the timetable. After that, i will be increased by one; this ensures that on the next iteration of the loop, i will have the next value. The loop will continue executing as long as the condition $i \leq 10$ is true. Once i becomes greater than 10, the loop will terminate.

5.3   The Break and Continue Statements

In Python, the break statement (we have explained this in Chapter 4) is used to end a loop earlier, regardless of whether the condition of the loop is still fulfilled or not. If the break statement occurs within a while loop or for loop, it ends the loop immediately and transfers control to the next statement that follows the loop block.

Here is an example to illustrate how the break statement works within a while loop:

```
1  while True:
2     name = input("What is your name? ")
3     if name == "quit":
4        print("Exiting...")
5        break
6     print("Hello,", name)
```

In the above example, the while loop runs infinitely because its condition is set to True. Inside the loop, the user is asked to enter their name. If the user enters the word "quit," the break statement is executed, and the loop is terminated. The program then prints "Exiting..." and continues with the next statement after the loop.

The break statement allows you to control the flow of your program and exit a loop based on certain conditions. It can be useful when you want to exit a loop early, skip the remaining iterations, or terminate a loop based on specific criteria.

Another example is as follows:

```
1  i = 1
2  while i < 6:
3    print(i)
4    if i == 3:
5      break
6    i += 1
7
```

The above program initializes the variable i to the value 1. Start the while loop, which will continue executing as long as the condition i < 6 is true. If the condition is true, the program will print the current value of i and then check if the value of i is equal to 3. If i is indeed equal to 3 in line 4, the break statement is executed and terminates the loop immediately, regardless of whether the condition i < 6 is still true. Program execution continues with the next statement outside the loop.

Here is the output of the above code program:

```
1
2
3
```

The continue statement is used in Python to skip the remaining code within a loop iteration and move on to the next iteration. When the continue statement occurs in a while loop or for loop, the program immediately jumps back to the condition check of the loop (the beginning of the loop) and continues with the next iteration, skipping any code that follows the continue statement within the loop block.

Here is an example to illustrate how the continue statement works within a while loop:

```
1  i = 0
2  while i < 5:
3    i += 1
4    if i == 3:
5      continue
6    print(i)
```

In this example, the while loop runs as long as i is less than 5. Within the loop, i is increased by 1 with each iteration. When i reaches the value 3, the continue statement is executed. As a result, the program skips the print(i) statement for this iteration and jumps back to the condition check of the loop (line 2). The loop then continues with the next iteration. The output of this program would be

```
1
2
4
5
```

As you can see, the value 3 is skipped because of the continue statement. The loop continues execution, printing the values 1, 2, 4, and 5.

5.4   Python Casting

In Python, casting is the process of converting one data type to another. It allows you to change the type of a variable or value to perform specific operations or assignments that require a different data type. Python provides several built-in functions for casting, including int(), float(), and str().

Here are some examples:

```
1  x = int(1) # x will be 1
2  y = int(2.8) # y will be 2
3  z = int("3") # z will be 3
4
5  x = float(1) # x will be 1.0
6  y = float(2.8) # y will be 2.8
7  z = float("3") # z will be 3.0
8
9  x = str("s1") # x will be 's1'
10 y = str(2) # y will be '2'
11 z = str(3.0) # z will be '3.0'
```

Here is an explanation of the above examples:

1. x = int(1): The int() function is used to convert a value to an integer. In this case, the value 1 is already an integer, so the result is 1. The variable x is assigned the value 1.
2. y = int(2.8): The int() function converts the floating-point number 2.8 to an integer. When you convert a float to an integer using int(), the decimal part is truncated. Therefore, the result is 2, and the variable y is assigned the value 2.
3. z = int("3"): The int() function converts the string "3" to an integer. Since the string represents a valid integer, the result is 3, and the variable z is assigned the value 3.
4. x = float(1): The float() function converts the integer 1 to a floating-point number. The result is 1.0, and the variable x is assigned the value 1.0.
5. y = float(2.8): The float() function is used to convert the float 2.8 to a float (which is already a float). The result is 2.8, and the variable y is assigned the value 2.8.

6. z = float("3"): The float() function converts the string "3" to a floating-point number. The result is 3.0, and the variable z is assigned the value 3.0.

7. x = str("s1"): The str() function converts the value "s1" to a string. Since it is already a string, it remains unchanged. The variable x is assigned the value "s1."

8. y = str(2): The str() function converts the integer 2 to a string. The result is "2," and the variable y is assigned the value "2."

9. z = str(3.0): The str() function converts the float 3.0 to a string. The result is "3.0," and the variable z is assigned the value "3.0."

5.5   Logical Operators

Logical operators are used in conditional statements (such as if statements) to combine and evaluate conditions. They allow you to make decisions based on multiple conditions or to specify how conditions should be combined. Therefore, you can use these logical operators to create more complex conditions that handle different scenarios and make decisions based on multiple factors.

Suppose we want to write a program that prints all the numbers from 1 to 100 that are divisible by 5, for example, 5, 10, 15, 20, and so on. In simple terms, the program will look like this:

```
# Divisible by 5

for num in range(1, 101):
    if num % 5 == 0:
        print(num)
```

This program uses the for loop to iterate through the numbers from 1 to 100 using the range() function, and for each number num, the program checks if it is divisible by 5 using the modulo operator %. If num % 5 == 0, it means that num is divisible by 5. If the condition is true, the program prints the number num using the print() function. The loop continues to the next number, and the process is repeated until all numbers from 1 to 100 have been checked.

What about if we want to write a program that prints all numbers from 1 to 100 that are divisible by 5, by 7, or by 9, for example, 5, 7, 9, 10, 14, 18, and so on. Then, we can write three separate if statements as follows:

```
# Divisible by 5, 7, and 9

for num in range(1, 101):
    if num % 5 == 0:
        print(num)
    if num % 7 == 0:
        print(num)
    if num % 9 == 0:
        print(num)
```

As we can see, the code uses the for loop to iterate over numbers from 1 to 100 (inclusive), and for each number num in the loop, the code checks three conditions using separate if statements:

- The first if statement checks if "num" is divisible by 5 using the condition num % 5 == 0.
- The second if statement checks if "num" is divisible by 7 using the condition num % 7 == 0.
- The third if statement checks if "num" is divisible by 9 using the condition num % 9 == 0.

If any of the three conditions is true for the variable called num, the code prints the value of num. The loop continues to the next number, and the process is repeated until all numbers from 1 to 100 have been checked.

If you run the above program, you will find that some numbers are printed twice; guess why? Because there are some numbers, for example, 35, that are divisible by 5 and 7. Hence, these numbers will be printed twice. To avoid this, we can modify the code as follows:

```python
# Divisible by 5, 7, and 9
for num in range(1, 101):
    if num % 5 == 0:
        print(num)
        continue
    if num % 7 == 0:
        print(num)
        continue
    if num % 9 == 0:
        print(num)
```

But, did you know that we can combine the three if statements in one using the **logical operators**? Table 5-1 shows the logical operators that we can use to combine two or more conditions. This is instead of writing many if statements.

For example, in the previous code, we wrote three if statements, each checking one condition. Instead, we can combine the three conditions as follows: if (num % 5 == 0) or (num % 7 == 0) or (num % 9 == 0).

Table 5-1. Python logical operators

Operator	Explanation	Example
and	Returns True if both statements are true	if (x <5) and (x >-5)
or	Returns True if one of the conditions is true	if (x <5) or (y <8)
not	Reverses the result, returns False if the result is true	not(x <5)

```
1  # Divisible by 5, 7, and 9
2
3  for num in range(1, 101):
4      if (num % 5 == 0) or (num % 7 == 0) or (num % 9 == 0):
5          print(num)
```

The output will be as follows:

```
5
7
9
10
14
⋮
```

As you can see, we used "or" to combine the three if statements, and the program will print the number if the first condition (num % 5 == 0) is true "or" the second condition (num % 7 == 0) is true "or" the third condition (num % 9 == 0) is true. Therefore, if any of the three conditions is true, the number will be printed.

What about if we replace "or" with "and," what will happen? As mentioned in Table 5-1, if we have two conditions, the "or" of them will be true if at least one of them is true or both, while with the "and" operator, both conditions should be true to get true output. Therefore, if we change the above program to "if (num % 5 == 0) and (num % 7 == 0) and (num % 9 == 0)," what will be the output? The answer is nothing, because there is no number divisible by 5, 7, and 9.

5.6   Making Counters

In some exercises, we found that we should make a counter to count, for example, the number of students, count the numbers that are divisible by five, or count passing students. To do this, the counter is nothing more than a variable with any name, we prefer to call it counter, and initially it will be zero (counter=0). At each time a specific condition is achieved, the counter is increased by one as follows: counter=counter+1.

Do you remember Exercise 13 in Chapter 3? This exercise tells us to write a program that asks the user to enter the scores of ten students. The program should then determine and print the number of students who passed the test. Consider a passing score to be 60 or above. In this example, we should use a counter to count the number of passing students. As you can see in the code below, the counter is called num_passed and initialized to zero. As you can also see in the code, when the score of any student is more than or equal to 60, the counter will be increased by one as follows:

```
1   # Initialize a variable to keep track of the number of students who passed
2   num_passed = 0
3
4   # Prompt the user to enter the scores of ten students
5   score_1 = int(input("Enter the score for student 1: "))
6   score_2 = int(input("Enter the score for student 2: "))
7   score_3 = int(input("Enter the score for student 3: "))
8   score_4 = int(input("Enter the score for student 4: "))
9   score_5 = int(input("Enter the score for student 5: "))
10  score_6 = int(input("Enter the score for student 6: "))
11  score_7 = int(input("Enter the score for student 7: "))
12  score_8 = int(input("Enter the score for student 8: "))
13  score_9 = int(input("Enter the score for student 9: "))
14  score_10 = int(input("Enter the score for student 10: "))
15
16  # Check if each student's score is above or equal to 60
17  if score_1 >= 60:
18      num_passed = num_passed+ 1
19  if score_2 >= 60:
20      num_passed = num_passed+ 1
21  if score_3 >= 60:
22      num_passed = num_passed+ 1
23  if score_4 >= 60:
24      num_passed = num_passed+ 1
25  if score_5 >= 60:
26      num_passed = num_passed+ 1
27  if score_6 >= 60:
28      num_passed = num_passed+ 1
29  if score_7 >= 60:
30      num_passed = num_passed+ 1
31  if score_8 >= 60:
32      num_passed = num_passed+ 1
33  if score_9 >= 60:
34      num_passed = num_passed+ 1
35  if score_10 >= 60:
36      num_passed = num_passed+ 1
37
38  # Print the number of students who passed the test
39  print("The number of students who passed the test:", num_passed)
```

The above code could be simpler using the for loop statement, as follows:

```
1   # Initialize a variable to keep track of the number of students who passed
2   num_passed = 0
3
4   # Prompt the user to enter the scores of ten students using for loop
5   for i in range(1, 11):
6       score = int(input(f"Enter the score for student {i}: "))
7       if score >= 60:
8           num_passed += 1  # or num_passed = num_passed+ 1
9
10  # Print the number of students who passed the test
11  print("The number of students who passed the test:", num_passed)
```

Can you write the above program using the while statement?

The answer will be as follows:

```
1  # Initialize a variable to keep track of the number of students who passed
2  num_passed = 0
3
4  # Initialize a variable to keep track of the current student number
5  student_num = 1
6
7  # Use a while loop to prompt the user for the scores of 10 students
8  while student_num <= 10:
9      score = int(input(f"Enter the score for student {student_num}: "))
10     if score >= 60:
11         num_passed += 1
12     student_num += 1
13
14 # Print the number of students who passed the test
15 print("The number of students who passed the test:", num_passed)
```

5.7   Calculating Total (or Sum) and Product

In other exercises, we want to find the total (or the sum) of some variables. For example, if we want to find the total of four variables (V1, V2, V3, and V4), how to do this? Let us call the variable by "total", and it will be initialized by zero. The total could be directly calculated as follows, total=V1+V2+V3+V4. Instead of this, we can do this also by adding one variable by one variable as follows, total=total+V1, then total=total+V2, and so on.

Do you remember Exercise 11 in Chapter 4? This exercise was telling us to write a program that takes a positive integer as input and uses the for loop to calculate the sum of all numbers from 1 to that integer. The program should print the sum. As you can see, the sum variable is called "sum_numbers", and it was initialized to zero. Next, to get the total of all numbers from 1 to num+1, in the for loop, the sum will be increased iteratively as follows, sum_numbers = sum_numbers + i.

```
1  # Take input for the number
2  num = int(input("Enter a positive integer: "))
3
4  # Initialize the sum variable
5  sum_numbers = 0
6
7  # Calculate the sum using for loop
8  for i in range(1, num+1):
9      sum_numbers = sum_numbers + i
10
11 # Print the sum
12 print("Sum:", sum_numbers)
```

In another exercise, Exercise 14 in Chapter 4 was telling us to write a program that takes two integers as input, representing the starting and ending numbers of a range. The program should use the for loop to iterate over the numbers in the range (inclusive) and calculate the sum of all even numbers within that range. Assume that the starting number is always less than or equal to the ending number. As we can see below, the sum variable is called sum_even and initialized to zero. Next, inside the for loop, if the number is even, the number will be added to the sum_even variable as follows, sum_even = sum_even+ num.

```
1  # Take input for the starting and ending numbers
2  start = int(input("Enter the starting number: "))
3  end = int(input("Enter the ending number: "))
4
5  # Initialize the sum variable
6  sum_even = 0
7
8  # Iterate over the range and calculate the sum of even numbers
9  for num in range(start, end+1):
10     if num % 2 == 0:
11        sum_even = sum_even+ num
12
13 # Print the sum of even numbers
14 print("Sum of even numbers:", sum_even)
```

The output of the above program is as follows:

```
Enter the starting number: 2
Enter the ending number: 6
Sum of even numbers: 12
```

Similarly, to calculate the product of some variables, we can do also the same steps, but there is an important difference between calculating the sum and calculating the product of some variables. The main difference is that the total variable is initialized with zero, while the product should be initialized by one. For example, in Exercise 13 in Chapter 4, the goal was to write a program to print the factorial of a number if the number is only positive. As you can see in the code below, to calculate the factorial of a number, the variable that is called "factorial" is initialized with one. Next, in the for loop, in each iteration, the product of factorial with i will be calculated. This will continue until the end of this loop. The final product value is in the factorial variable.

```
1  # Printing the factorial of a number, but only if the number is positive
2
3  num = int(input("Enter a number "))
4  factorial = 1
5
6  if num > 0:
7     for i in range(1, num + 1):
8        factorial *= i
9
10    print("The factorial of", num, "is:", factorial)
11 else:
12    print("The number must be positive.")
```

The output of the above program is as follows:

Enter a number: 5
The factorial of 5 is: 120

5.8 Calculating Maximum and Minimum

In some exercises, the goal was to find the maximum or the minimum value among many variables. Assume that we have four variables, V1, V2, V3, and V4. To find the maximum value, we should compare all these variables. This could be achieved by first assigning the first variable V1 to a variable called Max (Max=V1). This means that we consider that the first variable V1 is the maximum. Then, we will compare V2 with Max as follows: if V2>Max, hence, the second variable (V2) is now the maximum (if the condition is true); otherwise, the Max will still be the same without any change. After that, we should compare Max with all the rest of the variables. After doing this with all variables, the maximum value will be in Max.

This was clear in Exercise 12 in Chapter 3, where the program asks the user to enter the scores of ten students. The program should then find and print the maximum score among all the students' scores. As we can see in the code below, the maximum variable is initialized with the first score as follows: max_score = score1. Next, using an if statement, the score of the second student will be compared with max_score; if score2>max_score, the maximum will be the score2 as follows: max_score = score2. This process will continue to compare the maximum score with the other scores. After comparing all scores with the max_score, one by one, the final line in the code prints the maximum score.

Using the same steps, we can also calculate the minimum score.

```python
# Prompt the user to enter the scores for all ten students
score1 = int(input("Enter the score for student 1: "))
score2 = int(input("Enter the score for student 2: "))
score3 = int(input("Enter the score for student 3: "))
score4 = int(input("Enter the score for student 4: "))
score5 = int(input("Enter the score for student 5: "))
score6 = int(input("Enter the score for student 6: "))
score7 = int(input("Enter the score for student 7: "))
score8 = int(input("Enter the score for student 8: "))
score9 = int(input("Enter the score for student 9: "))
score10 = int(input("Enter the score for student 10: "))

# Initialize the maximum score with the first score
max_score = score1

# Compare the remaining scores with the current maximum score
if score2 > max_score:
    max_score = score2
if score3 > max_score:
    max_score = score3
```

```
21  if score4 > max_score:
22      max_score = score4
23  if score5 > max_score:
24      max_score = score5
25  if score6 > max_score:
26      max_score = score6
27  if score7 > max_score:
28      max_score = score7
29  if score8 > max_score:
30      max_score = score8
31  if score9 > max_score:
32      max_score = score9
33  if score10 > max_score:
34      max_score = score10
35
36  # Print the maximum score
37  print("\nThe maximum score among all students is:", max_score)
```

Using the for loop statement, the code is simpler, like this:

```
1   # Prompt the user to enter the scores for all ten students using for loop
2   # Initialize the maximum score with zero
3   max_score = 0
4   for i in range(0, 10):
5       score = int(input("Enter the score for student " + str(i + 1) + ": "))
6       if score > max_score:
7           max_score = score
8
9   # Print the maximum score
10  print("The maximum score among all students is:", max_score)
```

The output of the above code will be

```
Enter the score for student 1: 85
Enter the score for student 2: 72
Enter the score for student 3: 94
Enter the score for student 4: 88
Enter the score for student 5: 77
Enter the score for student 6: 90
Enter the score for student 7: 81
Enter the score for student 8: 95
Enter the score for student 9: 79
Enter the score for student 10: 83
The maximum score among all students is: 95
```

5.9   Nested Conditional Statements and Loops

In this section, we present some solved examples to illustrate how the looping statements (for example, the for loop or while statement) and the conditional statement (if statement) can be used inside each other (nested). This means that some examples may have a for loop inside if or if inside the for loop.

5.9.1   Solved Example 1: Print Numbers Divisible by a Number

Write a program to print all numbers from 1 to 100 that are divisible by 5, for example, 5, 10, 15, 20, ...

```python
# Solved example 1

for num in range(1, 101):
    if num % 5 == 0:
        print(num)
```

The above code works as follows:

- The program uses the for loop to iterate through the numbers from 1 to 100 using the range() function.
- For each number "num", the program checks if it is divisible by 5 using the modulo operator %. If num % 5 == 0, it means that num is divisible by 5.
- If the condition is true, the program prints the number "num" using the print() function.
- The loop continues to the next number, and the process is repeated until all numbers from 1 to 100 have been checked.

Can you write the above code using while instead of the for loop?

5.9.2   Solved Example 2: Find Average, Maximum, and Minimum Score

Write a program that asks the user to enter the number of students and then asks for the scores of each student. The program should then calculate and print the average, maximum, and minimum scores of all the students.

```python
# Solved example 2

num_students = int(input("Enter the number of students: "))

total_score = 0
max_score = float('−inf')  # Initialize with negative infinity
min_score = float('inf')   # Initialize with positive infinity

for i in range(1, num_students + 1):
```

```
10    score = float(input(f"Enter the score for student {i}: "))
11    total_score += score
12
13    # Update maximum score
14    if score > max_score:
15        max_score = score
16
17    # Update minimum score
18    if score < min_score:
19        min_score = score
20
21  average_score = total_score / num_students
22
23  print("Average score:", average_score)
24  print("Maximum score:", max_score)
25  print("Minimum score:", min_score)
```

The output of this code is

Enter the number of students: 4
Enter the score of student 1: 85
Enter the score of student 2: 90
Enter the score of student 3: 78
Enter the score of student 4: 92
The average score of all the students is: 86.25
The maximum score of all the students is: 92
The minimum score of all the students is: 78

From the above code and output, the program steps are as follows:

- The program asks the user to enter the number of students using the input() function and stores it in the variable called "num_students".
- Variables "total_score", "max_score", and "min_score" are initialized. As shown, "max_score = float('-inf')." The float('-inf') value represents negative infinity. This means that "max_score" will be set to the smallest possible floating-point number, effectively making it the lowest possible value to start with. As the program runs and scores are processed, max_score will be updated to the highest score encountered. Similarly, "min_score" will be initialized with positive infinite number or the largest possible floating-point number.
- The for loop is used to iterate from 1 to "num_students". Inside the loop, the program asks the user to enter the score for each student and converts it to a float. The score is then added to the "total_score" variable.
- The if statements inside the loop check if the current score is greater than the current maximum score (max_score) or less than the current minimum score (min_score) and update the respective variables accordingly.
- After the loop, the program calculates the average score by dividing the "total_score" by "num_students" and stores it in the variable called "average_score".
- Finally, the program prints the average, maximum, and minimum scores.

Can you modify the above code to know which person obtains the maximum score? And try to use while.

The program will be as follows:

```
# Student Scores

num_students = int(input("Enter the number of students: "))

total_score = 0
max_score = float('-inf')  # Initialize with negative infinity
min_score = float('inf')   # Initialize with positive infinity
max_score_student = None
min_score_student = None

i = 1
while i <= num_students:
    score = float(input(f"Enter the score for student {i}: "))
    total_score += score

    # Update maximum score
    if score > max_score:
        max_score = score
        max_score_student = i

    # Update minimum score
    if score < min_score:
        min_score = score
        min_score_student = i

    i += 1

average_score = total_score / num_students

print("Average score:", average_score)
print("Maximum score:", max_score, "obtained by student", max_score_student)
print("Minimum score:", min_score, "obtained by student", min_score_student)
```

In the code above, we found a new word, that is, "None." None is a special value in Python that represents the absence of a value or a nonexistent value. It is a built-in constant in Python and is often used to initialize variables that will later be assigned a value. Also, if score > max_score: is like asking, "Did this student jump higher than our current record?" If the answer is yes, max_score = score is like updating the variable named "max_score" with the new high score. It is like saying "Wow! This is our new high score." max_score_student = i is like writing down which student number or index made this amazing jump. The variable "i" tells us which student we are looking at.

5.9.3   Solved Example 3: Calculating Factorial

Write a program to print the factorial of a number if the number is only positive.

```
1  # Solved example 3
2
3  num = int(input("Enter a number "))
4  factorial = 1
5
6  if num > 0:
7      for i in range(1, num + 1):
8          factorial *= i
9
10     print("The factorial of", num, "is:", factorial)
11 else:
12     print("The number must be positive.")
```

Here are some examples of the output of this program:

```
Enter a number: 5
The factorial of 5 is: 120
```

```
Enter a number: -9
The factorial of -9 is: The number must be positive.
```

5.9.4   Solved Example 4: Repeating a Word

Write a program to ask the user to enter a number (call it x). If the number (x) is positive, print "Hello" x times. If the number is negative, print "Good bye."

```
1  # Solved example 4
2  x = int(input("Enter a number: "))  # Ask the user to enter a number
3
4  if x > 0:  # Check if the number is positive
5      for _ in range(x):  # Loop x times
6          print("Hello")  # Print "Hello" x times
7  else:
8      print("Goodbye")  # Print "Goodbye"
```

Here is the output of this program:

```
Enter a number: 5
Hello
Hello
Hello
Hello
Hello
```

Or, with a negative number, the output will be

Enter a number: -6
Good bye

5.9.5 Solved Example 5: Print Divisible Numbers by a Number

Write a program that prints all the numbers from 1 to 100 that are divisible by 5, 3, and 7. Then, if the number is divisible by 5, count and print the odd and even numbers. Use while to perform this repetitive task.

```python
# Solved example 5
# Initialize counters
num_even = 0
num_odd = 0
num = 1

while num <= 100:
    if num % 5 == 0 or num % 3 == 0 or num % 7 == 0:
        print(num)

        # Check if the number is divisible by 5
        if num % 5 == 0:
            # Check if the number is even or odd
            if num % 2 == 0:
                num_even += 1
            else:
                num_odd += 1

    num += 1

print("Even numbers divisible by 5:", num_even)
print("Odd numbers divisible by 5:", num_odd)
```

Example output:

3
5
6
:
100
Even numbers divisible by 5: 11
Odd numbers divisible by 5: 7

5.9.6   Solved Example 6: Simple Calculator

Write a program that acts as a simple calculator. The program should prompt or ask the user to enter two numbers and choose an operator from the available options (addition, subtraction, multiplication, or division). Based on the selected operator, the program should perform the corresponding operation and display the result. This calculator should work for only five times.

```python
1  # Solved example 6
2  for _ in range(5):  # Loop for a maximum of five iterations
3      # Prompt the user to enter two numbers
4      num1 = float(input("Enter the first number: "))
5      num2 = float(input("Enter the second number: "))
6
7      # Display the available operators
8      print("Available operators:")
9      print("1. Addition (+)")
10     print("2. Subtraction (−)")
11     print("3. Multiplication (∗)")
12     print("4. Division (/)")
13
14     # Prompt the user to choose an operator
15     operator_choice = int(input("Choose an operator (1−4): "))
16
17     # Perform the selected operation and display the result
18     if operator_choice == 1:
19         result = num1 + num2
20         operator = "+"
21     elif operator_choice == 2:
22         result = num1 − num2
23         operator = "−"
24     elif operator_choice == 3:
25         result = num1 ∗ num2
26         operator = "∗"
27     elif operator_choice == 4:
28         if num2 != 0:
29             result = num1 / num2
30             operator = "/"
31         else:
32             print("Error: Division by zero is not allowed.")
33             break
34     else:
35         print("Error: Invalid operator choice.")
36         exit()
37
38     print("Result:", num1, operator, num2, "=", result)
```

The exit() function is used to terminate the program execution.

Here is an example of the output of the above program:

Enter the first number: 5
Enter the second number: 3
Available operators:
1. Addition (+)
2. Subtraction (-)
3. Multiplication (*)
4. Division (/)
Choose an operator (1-4): 1
Result: 5.0 + 3.0 = 8.0
Enter the first number: 10
Enter the second number: 2
Available operators:
1. Addition (+)
2. Subtraction (-)
3. Multiplication (*)
4. Division (/)
Choose an operator (1-4): 5
Error: Invalid operator choice.

5.10 Exercises

● Exercise 1: Print the output

Write the output of this program:

```
1  # Integer to other types
2  i = 42
3  print("Integer i =", i)
4  print("Integer to float:", float(i))
5  print("Integer to string:", str(i))
6
7  # Float to other types
8  f = 3.14
9  print("\nFloat f =", f)
10 print("Float to integer:", int(f))
11 print("Float to string:", str(f))
12
13 # String to other types
14 s1 = "12"
15 s2 = "3.45"
16 s3 = "hello"
17 print("\nStrings:")
18 print("s1 =", s1)
```

```
19  print("s2 =", s2)
20  print("s3 =", s3)
21  print("String to integer:", int(s1))
22  print("String to float:", float(s2))
23  # print("String to float:", float(s3)) # ValueError: could not convert string to float: 'hello'
```

Note that with the code "print("String to integer:", int(s3))", an error will occur when trying to convert the string "hello" to an integer, because the int() function in Python can only convert strings that represent valid integer numbers. Similarly, with "print("String to float:", float(s3))" there will be an error because the string "hello" cannot be converted to a valid floating-point number.

● Exercise 2: Print the output

Write the output of this program:

```
1   small_basket_size = 10
2   medium_basket_size = 15
3   large_basket_size = 20
4
5   small_basket = 0
6   medium_basket = 0
7   large_basket = 0
8
9   while True:
10    produce_size = int(input("Enter the size of the produce (1—20): "))
11
12    if produce_size >= 1 and produce_size <= 10:
13      small_basket += 1
14      print("Small basket now has", {small_basket}, " items.")
15      if small_basket == small_basket_size:
16        print("The small basket is full!")
17        small_basket = 0
18    elif produce_size >= 11 and produce_size <= 15:
19      medium_basket += 1
20      print("Medium basket now has", {medium_basket}, " items.")
21      if medium_basket == medium_basket_size:
22        print("The medium basket is full!")
23        medium_basket = 0
24    elif produce_size >= 16 and produce_size <= 20:
25      large_basket += 1
26      print("Large basket now has", {large_basket}, " items.")
27      if large_basket == large_basket_size:
28        print("The large basket is full!")
29        large_basket = 0
30    else:
31      print("Invalid produce size. Please enter a number between 1 and 20.")
```

• Exercise 3: Print the output

Write the output of this program:

```
1  total_cost = 0
2  item_count = 0
3
4  while item_count < 5:
5      item_price = float(input("Enter the price of item", item_count + 1)
6      total_cost += item_price
7      item_count += 1
8
9      if item_count == 5:
10         print("The total cost of the purchase is: ",total_cost)
11         break
12     else:
13         print("The current total cost is:", total_cost)
```

• Exercise 4: Print the output

Write the output of the two programs below:

```
1  for i in range(10):
2      if i == 5:
3          print("Breaking the loop at i =", i)
4          break
5      print("Iteration", i)
```

```
1  for i in range(10):
2      if i == 5:
3          print("Skipping iteration at i =", i)
4          continue
5      print("Iteration", i)
```

What is the difference between the two programs?

• Exercise 5: Print the output

Write the output of this program:

```
1  # Initialize some variables
2  a = 10
3  b = 5
4  c = 20
5
6  print("Initial values:")
7  print("a =", a)
8  print("b =", b)
9  print("c =", c)
10
```

```
11  # Compound assignment operators
12  a += 3  # a = a + 3
13  b -= 2  # b = b - 2
14  c *= 4  # c = c * 4
15  print("\nAfter compound assignment:")
16  print("a =", a)
17  print("b =", b)
18  print("c =", c)
19
20  # Chained assignments
21  x = y = z = 15
22  print("\nChained assignment:")
23  print("x =", x)
24  print("y =", y)
25  print("z =", z)
26
27  # Augmented assignments with various operators
28  x += 2   # x = x + 2
29  y -= 3   # y = y - 3
30  z *= 4   # z = z * 4
31  c /= 2   # c = c / 2
32  print("\nAugmented assignments:")
33  print("x =", x)
34  print("y =", y)
35  print("z =", z)
36  print("c =", c)
```

● Exercise 6: Convert for to while

Write the following program using a while statement instead of using the for loop:

```
1  for i in range(1, 4):
2    for j in range(1, 4):
3      print(i, j)
```

Note: This is nested for, so you may need nested while.

● Exercise 7: Print numbers in descending order

Write a program that uses the while statement to iterate over the numbers from 10 to 1 (inclusive) in descending order and prints each number on a new line (this exercise was in Chapter 4, but using the for loop).

The output will be as follows:

```
10
9
8
7
6
5
4
3
2
1
```

5.11   Project A: Math Test

In this project, our goal is to create a program that tests students' or users' understanding of the Math topic by asking the user some questions and checking their answers. The program will have various types of exercises, such as multiplication, addition, division, and subtraction, among others. Each exercise type will have multiple levels. Each level will contain a set of questions that the student needs to answer. After completing a level, if the student scores 60% or more on that level, they can progress to the next level, which will be slightly more challenging.

Simply, in the code below (the code of this project is in this link: https://github.com/Eng-Alaa/Programming_4_Kids/blob/main/Project_A.py), we can write a program that presents a simple multiplication test to a student. The program should ask the student to answer a series of multiplication questions and provide feedback on their performance.

```python
1   print("Welcome to the multiplication test!")
2   print("Please answer the following questions:\n")
3
4   Score = 0
5
6   question1 = "2x3"
7   question1_ans = 6
8   question2 = "5x6"
9   question2_ans = 30
10  question3 = "7x8"
11  question3_ans = 56
12  question4 = "8x8"
13  question4_ans = 64
14  question5 = "9x6"
15  question5_ans = 54
16
17  print(question1, " = ")
18  answer = int(input(""))
19
```

```
20  if answer == question1_ans:
21      Score = Score + 1
22
23  print(question2, " = ")
24  answer = int(input(""))
25
26  if answer == question2_ans:
27      Score = Score + 1
28
29  print(question3, " = ")
30  answer = int(input(""))
31
32  if answer == question3_ans:
33      Score = Score + 1
34
35  print(question4, " = ")
36  answer = int(input(""))
37
38  if answer == question4_ans:
39      Score = Score + 1
40
41  print(question5, " = ")
42  answer = int(input(""))
43
44  if answer == question5_ans:
45      Score = Score + 1
46
47  print("\nTest Results:")
48  print("You answered " + str(Score) + " out of five questions correctly.")
```

The expected output is

Welcome to the multiplication test! Please answer the following questions:
2x3 = 6
5x6 = 30
7x8 = 56
8x8 = 64
9x6 = 54
Test Results: You answered 3 out of five questions correctly.

We should think about how to improve this program or project by

- Adding many levels (e.g., three levels); these levels are different in their difficulties. The user can start and reach a specific level and then quit, and the program will save their score and the level they reached.
- Allowing many users to use the program. Hence, when a user starts the program, their details will be loaded (not other users' details).
- Trying to make the number of questions flexible.
- Allowing the questions to be selected randomly from a large pool of questions.
- Trying to make the program more short and simple.

5.12   Project B: The Game of Guessing a Number

In this project, our aim is to create a number guessing game program. As in the code below (the code of this project is in this link: https://github.com/Eng-Alaa/ Programming_4_Kids/blob/main/Guess_number_1.py), the game will ask the user to guess a number within a given range. The program will have multiple levels, each with its own range, rules, and difficulty. At the start of each level, there will be instructions explaining the objective of guessing the number. The user's performance will be evaluated based on their score, which depends on how quickly and accurately they guess the number. Upon completing a level, if the user's score is sufficient, they can progress to the next level, which will present a slightly more challenging task.

```python
secret_number = 84

for _ in range(10):
    guess = int(input("Enter your guess (between 1 and 100): "))

    if guess == secret_number:
        print("Congratulations! You guessed correctly.")
        break
    elif guess < secret_number:
        print("Too low. Try again.")
    else:
        print("Too high. Try again.")
```

The expected output is as follows:

Enter your guess (between 1 and 100): 50
Too low. Try again.
Enter your guess (between 1 and 100): 80
Too low. Try again.
Enter your guess (between 1 and 100): 90
Too high. Try again.
Enter your guess (between 1 and 100): 85
Too high. Try again.
Enter your guess (between 1 and 100): 84
Congratulations! You guessed correctly.

We should think about how to improve this program or project by

- Add multiple levels (e.g., three levels) to the game, each varying in difficulty. This could include differences in the number of attempts allowed and/or the time available for the user. The user can start and reach a specific level and then quit, and the program will save their score and the level they reached.
- Allowing many users to use the program. Hence, when a user starts the program, their details will be loaded (not other users' details).

- By randomly selecting the number we need to guess for each run; this will make the program more challenging and reliable.
- Trying to make the program more short, simple, and flexible.

5.13   Project C: Question Bank

The objective of this program is to create a question bank that can be used for testing and training students across various subjects. The program consists of different levels, each offering a set of questions with specific difficulty levels (the code of this project is in this link: https://github.com/Eng-Alaa/Programming_4_Kids/blob/main/Project_C.py). The question bank covers a wide range of topics, including English, Math, Science, and general information. After answering the questions in each level, if the student achieves a good score, they can progress to the next level. Alternatively, they have the option to repeat the current level to further enhance their understanding and knowledge. A simple example of this program will be as in project A.

We should think about how to improve this program or project by

- Introducing multiple levels (e.g., three levels) with varying difficulties can enhance the experience. These levels could include more challenging questions, shorter answer times, or a reduced number of attempts to find the correct answer. The user can start and reach a specific level and then quit, and the program will save their score and the level they reached.
- Allowing many users to use the program. Hence, when a user starts the program, their details will be loaded (not other users' details).
- Trying to make the program more short and flexible.
- Trying to make the program select the questions randomly; this is to solve the problem of memorizing the answers of the questions.
- Display the names of the top five scores achieved using this program.

5.14   Glossary

Term	Definition
while	This is used to repeat one line or many lines (block of code) a certain number of times (similar to a for loop).
break	This is used within a loop (such as for or while) to exit a loop early and stop the execution of the loop.
continue	This statement is used within a loop to skip the current iteration of the loop and move on to the next one.
logical operators	These operators are used with conditional statements (like the if statement) to combine two or more conditions.
inf	In Python, inf is a special constant that represents positive infinity (a value greater than any finite number).

5.15   Our Next Adventure in Programming

In this chapter, Kai successfully connected all the concepts he had learned earlier, discovered new ideas, and filled in some missing information from the previous chapters. This process helped him improve his programming skills and explore the world of Python more efficiently. Kai engaged in extensive practice through various solved examples, clever exercises, and projects that simulated real-world problems.

Through this practice, Kai realized the need for a new data structure beyond the use of single variables. He searched the books around him in the giant robot and found information about a feature called "lists" that could help him store collections of items in a particular order and access them easily. In the next chapter, we will dive into the world of Python lists with Kai. We will start by learning how to access individual items within a list, using indices to access specific items. We will then explore the various ways to modify existing items in a list, whether it is changing a single item or replacing a section of the list altogether. Next, we will look at how to add new items to a list, either by appending them to the end of the list or by inserting them at specific positions within the list. Deleting items from a list will also be a focus, as we will learn the different methods available for removing items based on their values or indices. Throughout the next chapter, we will highlight the benefits of using lists in Python programming, such as their flexibility, versatility, and ability to store collections of related data. By the end of the next chapter, we will have a solid understanding of how to effectively use lists in our Python programs and unlock their full potential to enhance our coding abilities.

Exploring Lists: Operations and Manipulations 6

In the last chapter, we worked with Kai to reinforce the concepts covered in the previous chapters and to introduce new ideas and information to fill in the knowledge gaps. In addition, Kai worked really hard and practiced extensively through various solved examples, clever exercises, and projects that simulated real-world problems. This practice helped him to better explore and discover new programming topics. As a result, this practice will improve his communication with the robot and his ability to control the robot to do what Kai needs it to do.

Building on this foundation, Kai discovered a new tool that could help him store and manage data more effectively: Python lists. Lists are a fundamental data structure in Python, allowing us to store collections of items in a particular order and access them easily. In this chapter, we will explore the rich world of lists with Kai. We will begin by learning how to perform basic operations on lists, such as updating values, adding or removing items, and more. By highlighting the benefits of using lists in Python programming, such as their flexibility, versatility, and ability to store collections of related data, we will help Kai unlock the power of lists and expand his programming skills. Get ready to dive into the world of lists and improve your coding skills.

6.1 Definition of the Lists

We can think of the list as a container that holds multiple objects or values. For example, you can think of it as a shopping list or a list of objects, where each item has a position or index.

Here is an example that shows how to create a list using square brackets []:

```
Fruits = ["apple", "banana", "cherry", "Melon"]
```

In the code above, we define a list named "Fruits" that contains four elements: "apple," "banana," "cherry," and "Melon." Each item is a string, and they are

© Alaa Tharwat 2025
A. Tharwat, *Python Adventures for Young Coders*,
https://doi.org/10.1007/979-8-8688-1067-1_6

enclosed in square brackets [ ], separated by commas. By assigning this list to the variable called "Fruits", we can now use this collection of fruits and perform various operations on it (see Figure 6-1). Some of these operations are described in the following subsections.

> **➡ List**
>
> The list is a container that can hold a collection of different items of data, such as numbers, strings, or even other lists, that are stored in a particular order.

6.1.1   List of Anything

We can say that the list could be a list of numbers, as follows:

```
list = [1, 5, 7, 9, 3]
```

or list of strings:

```
list = ["Ali", "Ahmed", "Tom", "Georg", "Mona"]
```

or a mix between numbers and strings, as follows:

```
list = ["abc", 34, 40.5, "male"]
```

6.1.2   Access List Items Using Indices

Each item in the list has an index, where the first item has index 0, and the second one has index 1, and so on. Indices are important because they allow us to access or refer to specific items in the list by using their corresponding index numbers. We can use the indices to retrieve, modify, or perform operations on individual items in the list.

For example, if we have the list as in the following code, the print command prints "banana" which has index 1:

```
Fruits = ["apple", "banana", "cherry", "Melon"]
print(Fruits[1])
```

Figure 6-1. Visualization of how each item in the list has an index to access it. Further, a negative index could be also used to access items at the end of the list

Negative index:	-4	-3	-2	-1
Fruits	"apple"	"banana"	"cherry"	"Melon"
Positive index:	0	1	2	3
	Fruits [0]	Fruits [1]	Fruits [2]	Fruits [3]

In the fruit list above, "apple" is at index 0, "banana" is at index 1, and "cherry" is at index 2, as shown in Figure 6-1. To demonstrate accessing list items by index:

```
Fruits = ["apple", "banana", "cherry", "Melon"]
print(Fruits[0])  # Output: apple
print(Fruits[1])  # Output: banana
print(Fruits[2])  # Output: cherry
print(Fruits[3])  # Output: Melon
```

Now, think of this line of fruits in two ways:

- Counting from the front (positive indices): Fruits[0], Fruits[1], Fruits[2], and Fruits[3], then we will get apple, banana, cherry, and Melon.
- Counting from the back (negative indices): Fruits[-4], Fruits[-3], Fruits[-2], and Fruits[-1], then we will get apple, banana, cherry, and Melon.

Negative indices are like counting backward from the end of the line. It is as if you are standing at the end of the line and counting the fruits from right to left. Hence, when we say print(Fruits[-2]), it means "Start at the end of the line, move two steps to the left, and tell me what fruit you see." In this case, Fruits[-2] would give us "cherry."

6.1.3 Check of an Item Within the List

We can also search within the list to know if an item is already within the list or not, as follows:

```
Fruits = ["apple", "banana", "cherry"]
if "apple" in Fruits:
    print("Yes, 'apple' is in the fruits list")
```

The "in" operator is used to check whether the string "apple" is present in the list called "Fruits". In this case, the condition "apple" in Fruits evaluates to True because the list Fruits contains the string "apple."

6.1.4 Modifying List Items

Each item in a list can be modified using

- **Updating the list contents**: This is done by assigning a new value to a specific index. For example:

```
1  Fruits = ["apple", "banana", "cherry"]
2  Fruits[1] = "grape"
3  print(Fruits)  # Output: ["apple", "grape", "cherry"]
```

- **Adding new items to the list**: We can add new items to a list using the append() method. The append() method adds an item to the end of the list. For example:

```
1  Fruits = ["apple", "banana", "cherry"]
2  Fruits.append("orange")
3  print(Fruits) # Output: ["apple", "banana", "cherry", "orange"]
```

This will add the item at the end of the list. However, if we want to add an item at a specific index, we can use the "insert" command as follows:

```
1  Fruits.insert(2, "watermelon")
```

The above code adds a new element "watermelon" to the third position (after the item "banana").

We can also add multiple items to a list with a single command using the extend() method, as follows:

```
1  my_list = [1, 2, 3]
2  my_list.extend([4, 5, 6])
3  print(my_list)  # Output: [1, 2, 3, 4, 5, 6]
```

- **Removing items**: We can remove items from a list using the remove() method. The remove() method takes the value of the item you want to remove. For example:

```
1  Fruits = ["apple", "banana", "cherry"]
2  Fruits.remove("banana")
3  print(Fruits) # Output: ["apple", "cherry"]
```

The del statement can be used to remove an item from a list by specifying its index. Here is an example:

```
1  Fruits = ["apple", "banana", "cherry"]
2  del Fruits[1]
3  print(Fruits) # Output: ["apple", "cherry"]
```

Another option is to remove all items from the list; in other words, to empty the list. This could be done as follows:

```
Fruits.clear()
```

Finally, we can also remove the whole list called "Fruits" as follows:

```
del Fruits
```

Below is an example of the above list operations:

```
# Updating the list contents
Fruits = ["apple", "banana", "cherry"]
Fruits[1] = "grape"
print(Fruits)  # Output: ["apple", "grape", "cherry"]

# Adding new items to the list
Fruits.append("orange")
print(Fruits)  # Output: ["apple", "grape", "cherry", "orange"]

Fruits.insert(2, "watermelon")
print(Fruits)  # Output: ["apple", "grape", "watermelon", "cherry", "orange"]

my_list = [1, 2, 3]
my_list.extend([4, 5, 6])
print(my_list)  # Output: [1, 2, 3, 4, 5, 6]

# Removing items
Fruits.remove("grape")
print(Fruits)  # Output: ["apple", "watermelon", "cherry", "orange"]

del Fruits[1]
print(Fruits)  # Output: ["apple", "cherry", "orange"]

Fruits.clear()
print(Fruits)  # Output: []

# Removing the whole list
my_list = [1, 2, 3]
del my_list
print(my_list)  # NameError: name 'my_list' is not defined
```

In the example above, we first update the contents of the list by changing the value at index 1 from "banana" to "grape." Then, we add new items to the list using the append() and insert() methods, as well as the extend() method to add another list. Next, we show different ways to remove items from the list, using the remove() method, the del statement, and the clear() method. Finally, we will show how to remove the entire list by using the del statement on the list variable itself.

6.1.5   List Operations

There are various operations, such as concatenation (+), repetition (*), and slicing:

- **Concatenation (+):** This operation combines two or more lists into a single list. Here is an example:

```
# Concatenation
Fruits1 = ["apple", "banana"]
Fruits2 = ["cherry", "orange"]
combined_fruits = Fruits1 + Fruits2
print(combined_fruits) # Output: ["apple", "banana", "cherry", "orange"]
```

This combines the "Fruits1" and "Fruits2" lists using the + operator to create "combined_fruits", which contains all items from both lists in the order they appear.

- **Repetition (*):** This operation repeats a list a specified number of times. For example:

```
Fruits = ["apple", "banana"]
repeated_fruits = Fruits * 3
print(repeated_fruits) # Output: ["apple", "banana", "apple", "banana", "apple", "banana"]
```

The * operator is used to repeat the "Fruits" list three times, creating a new list called "repeated_fruits" with the original elements repeated.

- **Slicing:** This operation allows you to extract a portion of a list. For example:

```
Fruits = ["apple", "banana", "cherry", "orange"]
sliced_fruits = Fruits[1:3]
print(sliced_fruits) # Output: ["banana", "cherry"]
```

Slicing uses the syntax list[start:end]. In this case, Fruits[1:3] extracts elements from index 1 (inclusive) to index 3 (exclusive), resulting in a new list called "sliced_fruits" containing "banana" and "cherry."

6.1.6   Benefits of Using Lists

Before we go to the solved examples, let us discuss the advantages of using lists in programming:

- **Collection of items**: Lists allow you to store and organize multiple items of different types in a single data structure. This makes it easier to manage and work with groups of related data.
- **Sorted items**: Lists maintain the order of items as they are added. This means that you can access and manipulate items based on their position or index in the list. The ability to maintain order is critical in scenarios where order is important, such as keeping track of events or processing data in a particular order.

- **Mutable and flexible**: Lists are mutable, meaning that you can modify, add, or remove items after the list is created. This flexibility allows you to dynamically update lists as your program progresses or as new data becomes available.
- **Iteration and looping**: Lists work seamlessly with loops, making it easy to iterate over each item in the list and perform operations on it. This is especially useful when you want to apply the same logic to each item in a collection. We will learn more about this in the next chapter.

6.2 Solved Examples

6.2.1 Example 1: Adding (Appending) Items

Write a program that asks the user to enter a list of four numbers. The program should then add the numbers to a list. Finally, print the resulting list.

```
1  numbers = []
2  num = int(input("Enter a number: "))
3  numbers.append(num)
4  num = int(input("Enter a number: "))
5  numbers.append(num)
6  num = int(input("Enter a number: "))
7  numbers.append(num)
8  num = int(input("Enter a number: "))
9  numbers.append(num)
10
11 print("Resulting list:", numbers)
```

The steps of the above code are as follows:

- numbers = []: This line initializes an empty list called "numbers" to store the numbers entered by the user.
- num = int(input("Enter a number: ")): This line asks the user to enter a number, which is then converted to an integer using the int() function and stored in the variable called "num".
- numbers.append(num): This line adds the value of "num" (the number entered by the user) to the end of the list of numbers using the append() method. This process is repeated for the next three lines to enter four numbers and append them to the list.
- print("Resulting list:", numbers): This line prints the resulting list containing all the numbers entered by the user.

The output of this program will be

Enter a number: 5
Enter a number: 8
Enter a number: 3
Enter a number: 9
Resulting list: [5, 8, 3, 9]

The code above adds numbers to a list one at a time. But this is not very flexible, because you can only add a few numbers at a time. It would be better to use a loop, which allows you to add as many numbers as you want. With a loop, you can ask the user "How many numbers do you want to add?" and then let the user type in all the numbers they want. The computer can then take those numbers and add them to the list instead of having to do it step by step. This makes the code more flexible because you can add as many numbers as you want instead of being limited to a few. It is a more efficient and user-friendly way to build the list of numbers. Therefore, the above code could be modified as follows:

```
1  numbers = []
2  list_size = int(input("Enter the number of numbers: "))
3
4  for i in range(0,list_size):
5    num = int(input("Enter a number: "))
6    numbers.append(num)
7
8  print("Resulting list:", numbers)
```

As you can see, the program is shorter when we use the for loop.
In the code above, after initializing the list, the following steps are performed:

- list_size = int(input("Enter the number of numbers: ")): This line asks the user to enter the number of numbers they want to input. The input is converted to an integer using the int() function and stored in the variable called "list_size".
- for i in range(0, list_size): This line sets up a loop that will iterate list_size number of times. The loop variable "i" takes on values from 0 to list_size – 1.
- num = int(input("Enter a number: ")): This line prompts the user to enter a number, which is then converted to an integer using the int() function and stored in the variable called num.
- numbers.append(num): This line adds the value of num (the number entered by the user) to the end of the numbers list using the append() method. This process is repeated "list_size" number of times, as controlled by the for loop.
- print("Resulting list:", numbers): This line prints the resulting list containing all the numbers entered by the user.

6.2.2 Example 2: Removing Items

Write a program that removes all occurrences of a specific element from a list. The program should ask the user to enter some items, one at a time, and add these elements or items to a list. Then, ask the user to enter the element to be removed and remove this item from the list. Finally, print the updated list.

The expected code will be

```
numbers = []
num = int(input("Enter a number: "))
numbers.append(num)
num = int(input("Enter a number: "))
numbers.append(num)
num = int(input("Enter a number: "))
numbers.append(num)
num = int(input("Enter a number: "))
numbers.append(num)

element_to_remove = int(input("Enter the number/element to remove: "))

numbers.remove(element_to_remove)

print("Updated list:", numbers)
```

In the above code, after adding elements as in the previous example, the program will work as follows:

1. element_to_remove = int(input("Enter the number/element to remove: ")): This line prompts the user to enter a number or element to remove, which is then converted to an integer using the int() function and stored in the variable called "element_to_remove".
2. numbers.remove(element_to_remove): This line removes the first occurrence of element_to_remove from the numbers list using the remove() method. If there are multiple occurrences, only the first one encountered will be removed.
3. print("Updated list:", numbers): This line prints the updated list after removing the specified element.

The output of this program will be

```
Enter a number: 10
Enter a number: 5
Enter a number: 7
Enter a number: 2
Enter the number/element to remove: 5
Updated list: [10, 7, 2]
```

To remove all occurrences of a specific element from the list, you can use a loop instead of the remove() method, which only removes the first occurrence. Here is the modified code:

```
numbers = []

# Prompt the user to enter 4 numbers and add them to the list
for i in range(4):
    num = int(input(f"Enter number {i+1}: "))
    numbers.append(num)

print("The current list is:", numbers)

element_to_remove = int(input("Enter the number/element to remove: "))

# Remove all occurrences of the element_to_remove
while element_to_remove in numbers:
    numbers.remove(element_to_remove)

print("Updated list:", numbers)
```

In the above code, the program uses a while loop to remove all occurrences of the "element_to_remove" from the numbers list. The while loop continues as long as the "element_to_remove" is present in the numbers list. Inside the loop, the remove() method is used to remove the first occurrence of the "element_to_remove" at each iteration.

We can also write the above program using the for loop as follows:

```
numbers = []

# Ask the user to enter 4 numbers and add them to the list
for i in range(4):
    num = int(input(f"Enter number {i+1}: "))
    numbers.append(num)

print("The numbers in the list are:", numbers)

# Ask the user which number they want to remove
number_to_remove = int(input("Which number do you want to remove? "))

# Create a new list with all the numbers that are not the same as the number to remove
new_numbers = []
for num in numbers:
    if num != number_to_remove:
        new_numbers.append(num)

print("The updated list is:", new_numbers)
```

In the code above, the program creates a new list called "new_numbers". It iterates through the list of numbers and adds each number to the "new_numbers" list, but only if it is not the same as the number the user wants to remove.

6.2.3   Example 3: Modifying or Updating Items

Write a program that asks the user to enter a list of words or names one by one and append these names to a list. The program should then replace the second item with another word entered by the user. Finally, print the updated list.

```
1  names = []
2  name = input("Enter a new name: ")
3  names.append(name)
4  name = input("Enter a new name: ")
5  names.append(name)
6  name = input("Enter a new name: ")
7  names.append(name)
8  name = input("Enter a new name: ")
9  names.append(name)
10
11 replacement_word = input("Enter the replacement word: ")
12
13 names[1] = replacement_word
14
15 print("Updated list:", names)
```

In the above code, after creating the list and adding elements to it, the program will work as follows:

- replacement_word = input("Enter the replacement word: "): This line asks the user to enter the replacement word, which will be used to replace the second item in the names list. The input is stored in the variable called "replacement_word".
- names[1] = replacement_word: This line replaces the value at index 1 (the second item) in the names list with the "replacement_word". The list index starts at 0, so names[1] refers to the second item in the list.
- print("Updated list:", names): This line prints the updated list of names after modifying the second item.

The output of this program will be

Enter a new name: John
Enter a new name: Alice
Enter a new name: Bob
Enter a new name: Sarah
Enter the replacement word: Kate
Updated list: ["$John$", "$Kate$", "Bob", "$Sarah$"]

6.2.4   Example 4: Even and Odd Numbers

Write a program that takes a list of numbers as inputs and separates them into two lists: one for even numbers and one for odd numbers. To do this, try the following steps:

- Ask the user to enter the number of numbers they want to input.
- Create two new lists: one for even numbers and one for odd numbers.
- Use a loop to ask the user to enter each number one by one and store or append them in a list.
- Iterate through the input list, checking each number. If the number is even, add it to the even numbers list. If the number is odd, add it to the odd numbers list.
- Calculate and display the sum of the even numbers and the sum of the odd numbers.
- Display the list of even numbers and the list of odd numbers.

```python
num_numbers = int(input("Enter the number of numbers: "))

numbers = []
even_numbers = []
odd_numbers = []
even_sum = 0
odd_sum = 0

for i in range(num_numbers):
    new_num = int(input(f"Enter number {i+1}: "))
    numbers.append(new_num)

for i in range(num_numbers):

    if numbers[i] % 2 == 0:
        even_numbers.append(numbers[i])
        even_sum += numbers[i]
    else:
        odd_numbers.append(numbers[i])
        odd_sum += numbers[i]

print("\nEven numbers:", even_numbers)
print("Odd numbers:", odd_numbers)

print("Sum of even numbers:", even_sum)
print("Sum of odd numbers:", odd_sum)
```

In the above code, simply, we have used the first for loop to enter numbers into the list called "numbers," and in the second for loop, we have checked each element or number in the list called "numbers"; if the number is even, we add it to the even_numbers list; otherwise, we add this element to the odd_numbers list.

The output of this program will be

Enter the number of numbers: 7
Enter number 1: 12
Enter number 2: 7
Enter number 3: 9
Enter number 4: 4
Enter number 5: 15
Enter number 6: 6
Enter number 7: 7
Even numbers: [12, 4, 6]
Odd numbers: [7, 9, 15, 7]
Sum of even numbers: 22
Sum of odd numbers: 38

6.3   Exercises

● **Exercise 1: The output of the program**

Write the output of the following program:

```python
# Create a list of numbers
numbers = [10, 20, 30, 40, 50, 60, 70, 80, 90, 100]

print("Original list of numbers:")
print(numbers)

# Remove a specific number
num_to_remove = int(input("Enter the number you want to remove: "))
if num_to_remove in numbers:
    numbers.remove(num_to_remove)
    print(f"{num_to_remove} has been removed from the list.")
else:
    print(f"{num_to_remove} is not in the list.")

print("\nUpdated list of numbers:")
print(numbers)

# Remove a number at a specific index
index_to_remove = int(input("\nEnter the index of the number you want to remove: "))
if index_to_remove >= 0 and index_to_remove < len(numbers):
    removed_num = numbers.pop(index_to_remove)
    print(f"{removed_num} has been removed from the list.")
else:
    print("Invalid index.")

print("\nUpdated list of numbers:")
```

```
27  print(numbers)
28
29  # Clear the entire list
30  clear_list = input("\nDo you want to clear the entire list of numbers? (y/n) ")
31  if clear_list == 'y':
32      numbers.clear()
33      print("The list of numbers has been cleared.")
34  else:
35      print("The list of numbers remains unchanged.")
36
37  print("\nThe final list of numbers:")
38  print(numbers)
```

● Exercise 2: Months

Write a program that asks the user to create a list called "Month_list" and asks the user to enter the names of the months and put them into the list.
   Example output:

> Let's make a list of the 12 months
> Enter the name of month 1: January
> Enter the name of month 2: February
> Enter the name of month 3: March
> Enter the name of month 4: April
> Enter the name of month 5: May
> Enter the name of month 6: June
> Enter the name of month 7: July
> Enter the name of month 8: August
> Enter the name of month 9: September
> Enter the name of month 10: October
> Enter the name of month 11: November
> Enter the name of month 12: December
> Great! Here is the list of months you entered:
> ['January', 'February', 'March', 'April', 'May', 'June', 'July', 'August', 'September', 'October', 'November', 'December']

● Exercise 3: Favorite colors

Write a program that asks the user to create a list called "Color_list" and enter their favorite color. The program will first ask how many favorite colors the user has.

Example output:

How many colors do you want to add? 5
Enter color 1: Blue
Enter color 2: Green
Enter color 3: Red
Enter color 4: Yellow
Enter color 5: Purple
Great! Here is your list of favorite colors: ['Blue', 'Green', 'Red',
'Yellow', 'Purple']

● Exercise 4: Remove a fruit

The following program has a list of fruits as in the code below. Write a
program that asks the user which item in the list to remove. If the item is
in the list, remove it and print the list; otherwise, print "This fruit is not in the
list."

```
# Create a list of fruits
fruits = ['apple', 'banana', 'cherry', 'date', 'elderberry', 'fig']
```

Example output:

Here is the current list of fruits:
'apple', 'banana', 'cherry', 'date', 'elderberry', 'fig'
Which fruit do you want to remove? date
date has been removed from the list.
Here is the updated list of fruits: ['apple', 'banana', 'cherry', 'elderberry', 'fig']

Try to write the same program, but try to remove a fruit at a specific index.

● Exercise 5: Update a fruit

The following program has a list of fruits as in the code below. Write a
program that asks the user which item in the list to update. If the item is
in the list, update it and print the list; otherwise, print "This fruit is not in the
list."

```
# Create a list of fruits
fruits = ['apple', 'banana', 'cherry', 'date', 'elderberry', 'fig']
```

Example output:

Here is the current list of fruits:
['apple', 'banana', 'cherry', 'date', 'elderberry', 'fig']
Which fruit do you want to update? date
What do you want to update 'date' to? peach
'date' has been updated to 'peach'.

● **Exercise 6: Sum of numbers**

Write a program that asks the user to enter five numbers and stores them in a list. Then, print the sum of the numbers.
Example output:

2
4
6
8
10
The sum of the numbers is: 30

● **Exercise 7: Largest and smallest numbers**

Write a program that takes a list of five numbers as input and prints the largest and smallest numbers in the list. Example output:

2
8
9
1
4
Largest number: 9
Smallest number: 1

● Exercise 8: Positive and negative numbers

Write a program that asks the user to enter a number of items and separates them into two lists: one for positive numbers and one for negative numbers. To do this:

1. Ask the user to enter the number of numbers they want to input.
2. Create two new lists: one for positive numbers and one for negative numbers.
3. Use a loop to ask the user to enter each number one by one.
4. Iterate over the input list and check each number. If the number is positive, add it to the list of positive numbers. If the number is negative, add it to the negative numbers list.
5. Display the positive numbers list and the negative numbers list.

Example output:

```
Enter the number of items: 5
Enter a number: 10
Enter a number: -5
Enter a number: 7
Enter a number: -3
Enter a number: 8
Positive numbers: [10, 7, 8]
Negative numbers: [−5, −3]
```

● Exercise 9: Shopping list organizer

Write a program that allows the user to create and organize a shopping list. To do this:

1. Start by creating an empty list called shopping_list to store the items.
2. Ask the user if they want to add items to the shopping list. If they answer "yes," proceed to the next step. If they answer "no," skip to step 5.
3. Inside a loop, ask the user to enter a new item to add to the shopping list. Append each item to the shopping_list list.
4. After adding the item, ask the user if they want to add more items. If they answer "yes," go back to step 2. If they answer "no," proceed to step 5.
5. Display the final shopping list to the user.
6. After displaying the final shopping list, ask the user if they want to remove any items. If they answer "yes," ask them to enter the name of the item they want to remove. Remove the item from the shopping_list if it exists.

Example output:

Would you like to add items to the shopping list? (yes/no): yes
Enter a new item to add: Apples
Do you want to add more items? (yes/no): yes
Enter a new item to add: Bread
Do you want to add more items? (yes/no): yes
Enter a new item to add: Milk
Do you want to add more items? (yes/no): no
Shopping List:
- Apples
- Bread
- Milk
Would you like to remove any items from the shopping list? (yes/no):
yes
Enter the name of the item to remove: Bread
Item "Bread" removed from the shopping list.
Updated Shopping List:
- Apples
- Milk

● **Exercise 10: Positive number sum**

Write a program that prompts the user to enter a series of positive numbers and stores them in a list. The program should continue to ask for numbers until the user enters a negative number. Afterward, it should calculate and display the sum of all the positive numbers entered. To do this:

- Create an empty list called number_list to store the positive numbers.
- Ask the user to enter a positive number.
- Check whether the number is positive.
  - If the number is positive, append it to number_list.
  - If the number is negative, break (or exit) the loop and proceed to the next step.
- Keep asking the user to enter positive numbers until they enter a negative number.
- Calculate the sum of all the positive numbers in number_list.
- Display the sum to the user.

Example output:

```
Enter a positive number (or a negative number to quit): 5
Enter a positive number (or a negative number to quit): 3
Enter a positive number (or a negative number to quit): 8
Enter a positive number (or a negative number to quit): -2
Sum of positive numbers: 16
```

● **Exercise 11: Temperature converter**

Write a program that prompts the user to enter a series of temperatures in Celsius and stores them in a list. The program should then convert each temperature to Fahrenheit and display both the Celsius and Fahrenheit temperatures side by side. To do this:

- Create an empty list called celsius_temperatures to store the temperatures in Celsius.
- Create a new list called fahrenheit_temperatures that contains the Fahrenheit equivalents of the temperatures in celsius_temperatures. The conversion formula is $Fahrenheit = Celsius * 9/5 + 32$.
- Ask the user to enter a series of temperatures in Celsius, one at a time.
- For each temperature entered by the user, append it to the celsius_temperatures list.
- Convert the celsius_temperatures into fahrenheit_temperatures and add it to the fahrenheit_temperatures list.
- Continue asking the user to enter temperatures until they choose to stop; display the temperatures side by side.

Example output:

```
Enter a temperature in Celsius (or 'q' to quit): 20
Enter a temperature in Celsius (or 'q' to quit): 10
Enter a temperature in Celsius (or 'q' to quit): 30
Enter a temperature in Celsius (or 'q' to quit): q
Temperature Conversion:
Celsius  Fahrenheit
20          68.0
10          50.0
30          86.0
```

6.4   Glossary

Term	Definition
append	This is a function or instruction in Python that is used to add a new element to the end of a list. The syntax is "list_name.append(element)".
insert	This is a function in Python that is used to insert an element at a specific index within a list. The syntax is "list_name.insert(index, element)".
remove	This is a function in Python that is used to remove the first occurrence of a specified element from a list. The syntax is "list_name.remove(element)".
extend	This is a function in Python that is used to append multiple elements to the end of a list. The syntax is "list_name.extend(list)".
del	The del statement in Python is used to delete objects, such as variables or list elements. The syntax is "del object_name".
clear	This is a function in Python that is used to remove all elements from a list, effectively emptying the list. The syntax is "list_name.clear()".

6.5   Our Next Adventure in Programming

In this chapter, Kai learned about a new data container called lists, which allows us to store collections of items in a particular order and access them easily. With Kai, we covered how to perform basic operations on lists, such as updating values, adding or removing items, and more. We also found that lists offer a new advantage over using variables in certain scenarios.

Kai feels that his knowledge of lists was still lacking, and he wants to explore the topic in more depth, using his previous knowledge to make efficient use of lists. Therefore, in the next chapter, we will dive deeper into advanced list operations and techniques. We will learn how to use looping statements such as for and while to iterate over the elements of a list, allowing us to access and manipulate individual elements. Beyond basic element access, we will explore more complex list operations, including finding the intersection of two lists, sorting, inverting, and decomposing lists to extract specific pieces of data. Through practical examples and exercises, our goal is to build on Kai's basic knowledge of lists and equip him with the skills to use lists as a powerful data structure in his Python programs.

Using Loop Statements for Searching, Removing, and Updating Lists

7

In the last chapter, we worked with Kai to discover the new "list" data container and how this container can store collections of items in a specific order and provide easy access to them. We covered the basics of lists, such as updating values, adding or removing items, and more, and highlighted the benefits of using lists.

Kai, on the other hand, still feels that his knowledge of lists was not enough, and he wanted to delve deeper into the topic by using his knowledge from the previous chapters to use lists efficiently. In this chapter, then, we will build on Kai's knowledge from the previous chapter and explore how we can use the powerful for loop and if statement to perform various operations on lists. Previously, we have learned how to add, delete, and modify list items using direct indexing and special list methods. By using loops (from Chapter 4) and conditional statements such as the if statement (from Chapter 3) with lists, we can automate processes and make our code more efficient and flexible.

7.1   Loop Through the List

7.1.1   Each Item Has an Index

Imagine that you have a list of several items that you need to buy. Each item in the list has a number assigned to it, and this number is called an **index**. The index helps you identify the position or location of each item on the list. Think of the list as a series of boxes, and each box contains an item. The first box is labeled (or has an index) zero, the second box is labeled one, the third box is labeled two, and so on (see Figure 7-1). Each box represents one item in your list. For example:

```
1  Fruits = ["apple", "banana", "cherry", "Melon"]
2  print(Fruits[1])
```

© Alaa Tharwat 2025
A. Tharwat, *Python Adventures for Young Coders*,
https://doi.org/10.1007/979-8-8688-1067-1_7

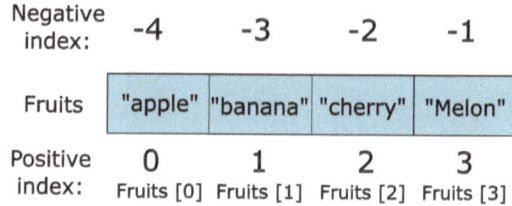

Figure 7-1. Visualization of how items are sorted in the list. Additionally, each item has an index to access it. Also, a negative index could be used to access items at the end of the list

Hence, when we say that each item in the list has an index, we mean that each item has a unique number assigned to it based on its position in the list. The index is like an address that tells us exactly where to find the item in the list.

In the "Fruit" list above, "apple" is at index 0, "banana" is at index 1, "cherry" is at index 2, and so on, as shown in Figure 7-1. The following code explains how to access list items by index:

```
Fruits = ["apple", "banana","cherry", "Melon"]
print(Fruits[0]) # Output: apple
print(Fruits[1]) # Output: banana
print(Fruits[2]) # Output: cherry
print(Fruits[3]) # Output: Melon
```

7.1.2   For Loop, Revision

As mentioned in Chapter 4, the for loop is used for making repetitive tasks. For example, the for loop could be used to print numbers from 1 to 5, as follows:

```
for i in range(0, 5):
    print(i)
print("Good bye")
```

The above code prints 0, 1, 2, 3, and 4 and then Good bye.

7.1.3   Iterate over the List

To iterate over the list (search element by element), we can use the for loop statement as mentioned earlier to use "i" (as in the example above) to access each element in the list. This means that "i" represents the indices of the elements, and changing "i" allows us to access different elements in the list.

Let us have the above list (Fruits list); we can use the for loop to access each element and print it; the for loop will be

```
Fruits = ["apple", "banana", "cherry", "Melon"]

for i in range(len(Fruits)):
    print(Fruits[i])
```

Figure 7-2. Visualization of
how the items in the list could
be accessed using the indices
using the for loop statement

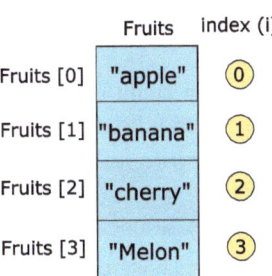

Figure 7-2 shows how the items in the list are accessed using the for loop. The
for loop is set up to iterate over the range of indices of the "Fruits" list using the
range(len(Fruits)) expression. The len(Fruits) function returns the length of the list,
which in this case is 4. Hence, the range will be from 0 to 3.

During each iteration of the loop, the index variable "i" takes on the values of 0,
1, 2, and 3, representing the indices of the elements in the "Fruits" list. Inside the
loop, we access each element of the "Fruits" list using Fruits[i]. With each iteration,
the value of "i" changes, allowing us to access a different element from the list. The
print() function is used to display the value of Fruits[i], which corresponds to the
current element being accessed in each iteration. In more detail:

- The loop begins its first iteration at i = 0.
- Inside the loop, we execute the print(Fruits[i]) statement. Since "i" is 0, it
  accesses the element at index 0 in the "Fruits" list, which is "apple," and this
  will be printed.
- The loop proceeds with the next iteration, incrementing "i" to 1.
- Now, the print(Fruits[i]) statement accesses the element at index 1 in the "Fruits"
  list, which is "banana," and this will be printed.
- The loop continues with the third iteration, incrementing "i" to 2.
- The print(Fruits[i]) statement accesses the element at index 2 in the "Fruits" list,
  which is "cherry," and this will be printed.
- The loop proceeds to the fourth and final iteration, incrementing "i" to 3.
- The print(Fruits[i]) statement accesses the element at index 3 in the "Fruits" list,
  which is "Melon," and this will be printed.
- The loop completes its iterations because there are no more elements to iterate
  over.
- The program execution ends.

7.1.4   Iterate Without Indices

The loop could directly iterate over the elements of the list itself, without using indices, as follows:

```
1  List = ["apple", "banana", "cherry"]
2  for x in List:
3    print(x)
```

In the above code, we have a list called List that contains three items: "apple," "banana," and "cherry." The code uses the for loop to iterate over each item in the List (without using indices). Instead of doing this, we can also use indices as follows:

```
1  List = ["apple", "banana", "cherry"]
2  for i in range(len(List)):
3    print(List[i])
```

7.2   Solved Examples

7.2.1   Example 1: Score Analysis

Write a program that allows the user to enter scores into a list and performs some analysis on the scores.

- Ask the user to enter the number of scores he wants to input.
- Using a loop, prompt the user to enter each score one by one and store them in a list.
- Calculate and display the average score, maximum score, and minimum score.
- Optionally, you can provide additional analysis such as the range of scores (the difference between the maximum and minimum) or the number of scores above a certain value.

The solution will be as follows:

```
1   num_scores = int(input("Enter the number of scores: "))
2
3   scores = []
4   total_score = 0
5   max_score = float('-inf')  # Initialize with negative infinity
6   min_score = float('inf')   # Initialize with positive infinity
7
8   for i in range(num_scores):
9     score = int(input(f"Enter score {i+1}: "))
10    scores.append(score)
11    total_score += score
12
13    if score > max_score:
14      max_score = score
```

```
15
16    if score < min_score:
17       min_score = score
18
19  average_score = total_score / num_scores
20
21  print("\nScore Analysis")
22  print("——————————————")
23  print(f"Average score: {average_score}")
24  print(f"Maximum score: {max_score}")
25  print(f"Minimum score: {min_score}")
```

In the code above, the program first asks the user how many scores he wants to enter. Then create an empty list to store the scores, and define variables to keep track of the total score, the highest score, and the lowest score. For each score the user wants to enter, ask the user to enter a score, add the score value to the list, and add the score to the total. Also, check if it is the new highest or lowest score. Then calculate the average score by dividing the total score by the number of scores, and then print a summary showing the average score, the highest score, and the lowest score.

The output of this program will be

Enter the number of scores: 5
Enter score 1: 85
Enter score 2: 92
Enter score 3: 78
Enter score 4: 95
Enter score 5: 88

Average score: 87.6
Maximum score: 95
Minimum score: 78

We can modify this exercise by incorporating another list of names and finding the student's name who has the maximum and minimum scores. Here is the updated solution:

```
1   num_scores = int(input("Enter the number of scores: "))
2
3   names = []
4   scores = []
5   total_score = 0
6   max_score = float('-inf')
7   min_score = float('inf')
8   max_name = ""
9   min_name = ""
10
11  for i in range(num_scores):
12     name = input("Enter name " + str(i+1) + ": ")
13     score = int(input("Enter score " + str(i+1) + ": "))
```

```
14
15      names.append(name)
16      scores.append(score)
17      total_score += score
18
19      if score > max_score:
20          max_score = score
21          max_name = name
22
23      if score < min_score:
24          min_score = score
25          min_name = name
26
27   average_score = total_score / num_scores
28
29   print("\nScore Analysis")
30   print("––––––––––––––––")
31   print("Average score: "+ str(average_score))
32   print("Maximum score: " + str(max_score) + " Student: " + str(max_name))
33   print("Minimum score: " + str(min_score) + " Student:" + str(min_name))
```

7.2.2   Example 2: List Intersection

Write a program that prompts the user to enter elements for two separate lists. The program should then find and display the common elements that are present in both lists. To do this:

- Create two empty lists called list1 and list2 to store the elements.
- Ask the user to enter items for list1, one at a time. Continue until the user chooses to stop.
- Prompt the user to type items for list2, one at a time. Continue until the user chooses to stop.
- Create a new empty list called intersection to store the common elements.
- Iterate over each item in list1 and check if it exists in list2. If so, append it to the intersection list.
- Show the user the elements in the intersection list.

```
1   # Create two empty lists to store the elements
2   list1 = []
3   list2 = []
4
5   # Ask the user to enter elements for list1
6   for i in range(0,1000):
7       element = input("Enter elements for list1 (or 'q' to quit): ")
8       if element == 'q':
9           break
10      list1.append(element)
11
```

```
12  # Ask the user to enter elements for list2
13  for i in range(0,1000):
14      element = input("Enter elements for list2 (or 'q' to quit): ")
15      if element == 'q':
16          break
17      list2.append(element)
18
19  # Find the common elements between list1 and list2
20  intersection = []
21  for element in list1:
22      if element in list2:
23          intersection.append(element)
24
25  # Display the common elements
26  print("Common Elements:", intersection)
```

The program starts by initializing two empty lists, list1 and list2, which will be used to store items entered by the user. Next, the first for loop is used to repeatedly ask the user to enter items for list1. The loop continues until the user enters "q" to exit. Each item entered by the user is appended to list1 using the append() method. Similarly, the second loop prompts the user to enter items for list2. The loop continues until the user enters "q" to exit. The items entered are appended to list2.

After creating and initializing both lists, we create an empty list called intersection to store the common elements between list1 and list2. We iterate over each element in list1 using a for loop. For each element, we check if it exists in list2 using the in operator. If an element is found in both lists, it is appended to the intersection list. Finally, we print the common elements found in both list1 and list2, which are stored in the intersection list.

Example output:

```
Enter elements for list1 (or 'q' to quit): 5
Enter elements for list1 (or 'q' to quit): 10
Enter elements for list1 (or 'q' to quit): 15
Enter elements for list1 (or 'q' to quit): q

Enter elements for list2 (or 'q' to quit): 10
Enter elements for list2 (or 'q' to quit): 15
Enter elements for list2 (or 'q' to quit): 20
Enter elements for list2 (or 'q' to quit): q

Common Elements: [10, 15]
```

7.3   Exercises

● Exercise 1: Questions and answers

The program below has two lists, one for questions and one for answers. Write a program that asks the user a question from the question list, compares their answer with the correct answer in the answer list, keeps track of the score, and prints the score. [Note: This exercise should help in enhancing projects A and C previous chapters.]

```
1   # List of questions and answers
2   questions = [
3     "What is the capital of France?",
4     "What is the largest ocean on Earth?",
5     "Who wrote the novel 'To Kill a Mockingbird'?",
6     "What is the symbol for the chemical element gold?",
7     "What is the tallest mountain in the world?" ]
8
9   answers = ["paris", "pacific","harper lee", "au","mount everest"]
```

● Exercise 2: Unique names

Write a program that prompts the user to enter a list of names and then removes any duplicate names from the list. To do this:

- Ask the user to enter the number of names they want to enter.
- Using a loop, prompt the user to enter each name one by one and store them in a list.
- Remove any duplicate names from the list.
- Display the final list of unique names.

  Example output:

  Enter the number of names: 4
  Enter name 1: John
  Enter name 2: John
  Enter name 3: Mary
  Enter name 4: Mary

  Unique names: ['John', 'Mary']

● Exercise 3: Unique number list

Write a program that allows the user to enter a series of numbers and stores them in a list. The program should store only unique numbers and discard duplicates. To do this:

- Create an empty list called number_list to store the unique numbers.
- Ask the user to enter a series of numbers, one after the other.
- For each number the user enters, check to see if it already exists in number_list.
  - If the number is not in the list, append it to number_list.
  - If the number is already in the list, ignore it and go to the next number.
- Continue asking the user to enter numbers until they choose to stop.
- Show the user the final list of unique numbers.

Example output:

```
Enter a number (or 'q' to quit): 5
Enter a number (or 'q' to quit): 3
Enter a number (or 'q' to quit): 8
Enter a number (or 'q' to quit): 5
Enter a number (or 'q' to quit): 2
Enter a number (or 'q' to quit): q

Unique Number List:
[5, 3, 8, 2]
```

● Exercise 4: List merger

Write a program that prompts the user to enter a series of elements and stores them in three separate lists. The program should then merge the three lists into a single list, remove any duplicates, and display the merged list. To do this:

- Create three empty lists called list1, list2, and list3 to store the elements.
- Ask the user to enter elements for each list, one at a time.
- For each element entered by the user, append it to the corresponding list.
- Continue to ask the user to enter items for each list until the user chooses to stop.
- Create a new list called merged_list by concatenating the three lists together.
- Try to remove any duplicates from merged_list.
- Display the merged list to the user.

Example output:

Enter elements for list 1 (or 'q' to quit): 5
Enter elements for list 1 (or 'q' to quit): 10
Enter elements for list 1 (or 'q' to quit): q

Enter elements for list 2 (or 'q' to quit): 10
Enter elements for list 2 (or 'q' to quit): 15
Enter elements for list 2 (or 'q' to quit): 20
Enter elements for list 2 (or 'q' to quit): q

Enter elements for list 3 (or 'q' to quit): 5
Enter elements for list 3 (or 'q' to quit): 20
Enter elements for list 3 (or 'q' to quit): 25
Enter elements for list 3 (or 'q' to quit): q

Merged List: [5, 10, 15, 20, 25]

● Exercise 5: Score frequencies

Write a program that prompts the user to enter a series of scores and stores them in a list. The program should then count the frequencies of each score and display the results. To do this:

- Create an empty list called scores to store the scores.
- Prompt the user to enter scores, one at a time. Continue until the user chooses to stop.
- Create an empty list called frequency to store the frequencies of each score.
- Iterate over each score in the scores list. Check if the score is already within the list. If it is, increment the corresponding value by 1. If it is not, add a new key-value pair with the score as the key and an initial value of 1.
- Display the frequencies of each score to the user.

Here, in this exercise, we can explain what is a dictionary in programming. A dictionary is like a real dictionary, where you look up a word and find its meaning. In programming, a dictionary helps us store information in pairs: a key and a value. Key: This is like the word you are looking up. It is unique and helps you find the information you need. Value: This is the information or meaning associated with the key.

Imagine you have a box of toys. You want to keep track of how many of each toy you have. You could use a dictionary like this:

- **Key:** The name of the toy (e.g., "Teddy Bear")
- **Value:** The number of this toy you have (e.g., 3)

So your dictionary might look like this:

```
{
  "Teddy Bear": 3,
  "Car": 5,
  "Doll": 2
}
```

Suppose you want to count the scores of your friends in a game:

- **Key:** The score (such as 10, 20, or 30)
- **Value:** How often that score was achieved

If your friends have the following scores – Alice: 10, Bob: 20, Carol: 10, and Dave: 30 – you can create a dictionary to count the scores:

```
{
  10: 2, # two friends scored 10
  20: 1, # One friend scored 20
  30: 1 # One friend scored 30
}
```

This idea about the dictionary might help you find the solution to this exercise, where the key is the score and the value is the number of times that key appears in the list.

Example output:

```
Enter a score (or 'q' to quit): 85
Enter a score (or 'q' to quit): 90
Enter a score (or 'q' to quit): 85
Enter a score (or 'q' to quit): 80
Enter a score (or 'q' to quit): q

Score Frequencies:
85: 2
90: 1
80: 1
```

● **Exercise 6: List reversal**

Write a program that prompts the user to enter a list of numbers and then reverses the order of the elements in the list. The program should display the reversed list to the user. To do this:

- Create an empty list called numbers to store the numbers entered by the user.
- Prompt the user to enter numbers, one at a time. Continue until the user chooses to stop.
- Reverse the order of the elements in the numbers list.
- Display the reversed list to the user.

Example output:

Enter a number (or 'q' to quit): 5
Enter a number (or 'q' to quit): 10
Enter a number (or 'q' to quit): 15
Enter a number (or 'q' to quit): q

Reversed List: [15, 10, 5]

● **Exercise 7: Number sorter**

Write a program that prompts the user to enter a series of numbers and stores them in a list. The program should then sort the numbers in ascending order and display the sorted list. To do this:

- Create an empty list called number_list to store the numbers.
- Ask the user to enter a series of numbers, one at a time.
- Append each number the user enters to the number_list.
- Continue asking the user to enter numbers until they choose to stop.
- Sort the number_list in ascending order. Assign the sorted list to a new variable called sorted_numbers.
- Display the sorted list to the user.

Example output:

Enter a number (or 'q' to quit): 5
Enter a number (or 'q' to quit): 10
Enter a number (or 'q' to quit): 2
Enter a number (or 'q' to quit): 7
Enter a number (or 'q' to quit): q

Sorted Numbers: [2, 5, 7, 10]

7.4   Glossary

There are no new programming commands in this chapter.

7.5   Our Next Adventure in Programming

In this chapter, Kai has learned more about working with lists professionally by combining the knowledge he learned in the first five chapters, such as the for loop and the if statement, to control the lists and extract the required information from these lists. Now he can perform a variety of list operations, such as searching, sorting, merging, adding, updating, and deleting items.

Kai found that there were a lot of repetitive parts in his programs, and even when he copied and pasted these parts, it was still confusing to him, and the programs became longer. This makes it even more difficult to read his code, update it, and find bugs if there are any. Then Kai had an idea: he could package the repeated parts of his code and use that package whenever needed. He searched the books around inside the robot and found something that could work similarly, called a "function." In the next chapter, we will read and learn more about functions, including what they are, how to define them, and the benefits of using them. Several examples will be given to illustrate the benefits of using functions.

Exploring Functions: Building Blocks of Code

In the last two chapters, we explored the new "list" data container with Kai and covered not only the basics of lists but also some professional topics to handle lists professionally.

Kai noticed that there were a lot of repetitive parts in his programs, which made it difficult to read, update, or trace the code. Then Kai had an idea to put all the repeated parts of the code into a package and use that package whenever needed. He searched the books around inside the robot and found something that could work similarly, called a "function." Functions take an input, such as a number or piece of information, and perform a specific task or calculation to give you an output. Functions are like magic tools that turn inputs into desired outputs. This new tool is super helpful because it saves us time. Instead of writing the same steps over and over again, we can put those repetitive parts into a function and just call it whenever we need it, saving us time and effort. Let us explore this new adventure of exploring functions together with Kai.

8.1   What Are Functions

Functions are magical tools that help us perform certain tasks in our programs. They are a collection of instructions that we can reuse over and over again. Figure 8-1 shows that the function has an input, an output, and a name. Let us call this function "f." When we want to use this function, we "call" it by using its name, providing the necessary input, and getting the desired output. This is like asking the function to do something for us.

Imagine you have a special robot that can make coffee for you every day or even several times a day. To make a cup of coffee, you usually have to follow several steps. First, you heat the water. Then you crush or ground the coffee beans. Finally, you mix the hot water with the crushed or ground coffee. To make sure there are no solids, you strain or filter the mixture. Finally, you pour the coffee into

© Alaa Tharwat 2025
A. Tharwat, *Python Adventures for Young Coders*,
https://doi.org/10.1007/979-8-8688-1067-1_8

Figure 8-1. Visualization of a function that takes an input, performs some operations on that input, and then produces or generates an output

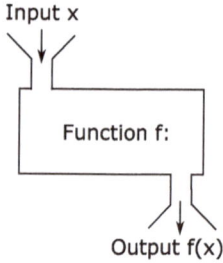

Input x

Function f:

Output f(x)

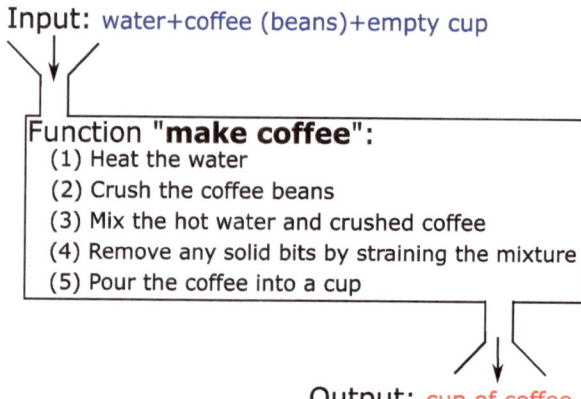

Input: water+coffee (beans)+empty cup

Function "**make coffee**":
(1) Heat the water
(2) Crush the coffee beans
(3) Mix the hot water and crushed coffee
(4) Remove any solid bits by straining the mixture
(5) Pour the coffee into a cup

Output: cup of coffee

Figure 8-2. Visualization of the "make coffee" function, which takes inputs (water, crushed coffee, and an empty cup) and, based on these inputs, makes or performs some processes or steps and then produces or generates an output, which is a cup of coffee

a cup. But instead of telling the robot each step every time, you can create a "make coffee" function. Therefore, when you want the robot to make coffee, you just say "make coffee." The robot will know to perform all the necessary actions within this function, such as heating the water, grinding the coffee, mixing, straining, and pouring (see Figure 8-2). So, by calling the "make coffee" function and giving it the inputs like water, coffee beans, and empty cup, implicitly all the instructions or steps within that function will be executed, and the function will return some outputs like the cup of coffee as in our example. Therefore, we can say that functions make our lives easier because they save us from repeating the same instructions and help us keep our code organized.

Another numerical example is shown in Figure 8-3, which shows that the function called "Multiply" has two inputs and one output. The goal of this function is to multiply two numbers (x and y) together, such as 3 and 5. Therefore, we can call the function called "Multiply" which takes two numbers as input and gives you the result or the multiplication.

Figure 8-3. Visualization of the "Multiply" function, which takes two input numbers and multiplies those two numbers and gives the output, which is the multiplication

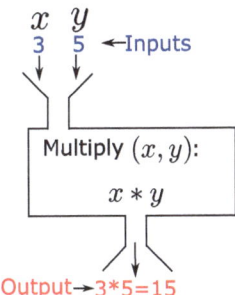

From all the previous examples, we can now define the function as follows:

> **➡ The function**
>
> In programming, a function is a named block of code made of a set of steps that performs a single specific task or action. It is like a mini-program within a larger program. Functions are used to organize and reuse code, making it easier to manage and understand.

Let us introduce another example to show how using functions reduces the length of the program, especially for repetitive tasks. In this example, suppose we have a program that draws shapes on the screen many times for many reasons. Specifically, we want to draw a square and a triangle. Without using functions to draw three squares and three triangles, the program might look something like this:

```
1   # program #1
2   Draw the first square:
3   — Draw a line
4   — Draw another line
5   — Draw another line
6   — Draw another line
7
8   Draw the first triangle:
9   — Draw a line
10  — Draw another line
11  — Draw another line
12
13  Draw the second square:
14  — Draw a line
15  — Draw another line
16  — Draw another line
17  — Draw another line
18
19  Draw the second triangle:
20  — Draw a line
21  — Draw another line
22  — Draw another line
23
24  Draw the third square:
```

```
25  — Draw a line
26  — Draw another line
27  — Draw another line
28  — Draw another line
29
30  Draw the third triangle:
31  — Draw a line
32  — Draw another line
33  — Draw another line
```

As you can see, by repeating the drawing of the two shapes only three times, the program reached 33 lines, and certainly more drawings or repetitions need more lines and make the program very long.

Now let us test how using functions can help. First, we can define a "DrawSquare" function that contains the instructions to draw a square and a "DrawTriangle" function that contains the instructions to draw a triangle:

```
1   DrawSquare:
2   — Draw a line
3   — Draw another line
4   — Draw another line
5   — Draw another line
6
7   DrawTriangle:
8   — Draw a line
9   — Draw another line
10  — Draw another line
```

After defining these two functions, in our program, to draw a shape, we do not need to write all the instructions, but only "call" the appropriate function. For example, to draw three squares and three triangles, as we did in the program above, the program might look like this:

```
1   # program #2
2   Functions:
3   —DrawSquare:
4   —— Draw a line
5   —— Draw another line
6   —— Draw another line
7   —— Draw another line
8
9   —DrawTriangle:
10  —— Draw a line
11  —— Draw another line
12  —— Draw another line
13
14  Main program:
15  Call the DrawSquare function # to draw the first square
16  Call the DrawTriangle function # to draw the first triangle
17  Call the DrawSquare function # to draw the second square
18  Call the DrawTriangle function # to draw the second triangle
19  Call the DrawSquare function # to draw the third square
20  Call the DrawTriangle function # to draw the third triangle
```

As you can see in the above code, the difference between the main program in program #1 and the one above (program #2) that uses the function, is that using functions reduces the length of the program. This enhances clarity and makes the code easier to read. The next sections explain how to define and call a function.

From all of the previous examples, we can say that using functions saves our time and effort by automating repetitive tasks or complex calculations. Therefore, functions allow us to break down large problems into smaller, more manageable parts.

8.2   Why Do We Need Functions?

Functions are incredibly useful for many reasons:

- **Code reusability**: Instead of writing the same code over and over again, we can define a function once and use it multiple times, saving us time and effort.
- **Modularity**: Functions allow us to break our program into smaller, more manageable pieces. This makes our code easier to understand, debug, and update.
- **Abstraction**: Functions allow us to hide complex code behind a simple interface. It is like having a magic box that performs complicated tasks, but we only need to know how to use it, not how it works internally.

8.3   How to Define a Function and Pass Parameters to It?

To create a function, we need to do the following:

- **Define the function**: Use the keyword "def" to define a function.
- **Give the function a name**: This will help us remember and refer to the function later. Let us define the "Multiply" function we discussed earlier (see Figure 8-4).
- **Define the inputs (inputs also called as parameters or arguments) of the function**: These inputs are like parameters or variables that will hold the actual values when we use the function. In our example, let us only have two inputs, x and y, as shown in Figure 8-4.
- **Write the statements inside the function**: This is called the "body" of the function. This is where we can perform operations or calculations on the inputs that the function receives. In our example, the function takes the inputs "x" and "y," calculates their product, and stores it in a variable called "z."
- **Return the output**: After performing the necessary operations, we can use the "return" keyword to return the results. In our example, we return the value of "z," which represents the product of "x" and "y."

In the given example, we have created a function called "Multiply" that helps us calculate the product of two numbers and gives us the result. Now, let us learn how

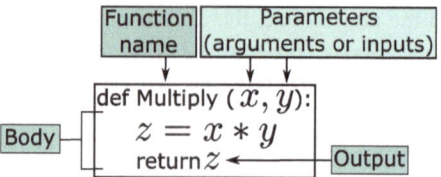

Figure 8-4. Visualization of the function called "Multiply" which takes two inputs (x and y), and based on these inputs, the function calculates the product and returns it as output

Figure 8-5. Visualization of how the function is called

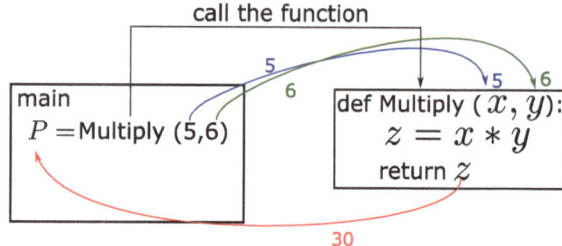

to use this function (or call it) in our main program. To use a function, we need to follow these steps. In the code below (see also in Figure 8-5), you can see how we call a function:

```
1  # Call the Multiply function
2  P=Multiply(5,6)
```

In our main program, if we want to find the product of two numbers, say 5 and 6, we call the "Multiply" function we created earlier. To do this, we write the function name followed by parentheses, as in the code above. Inside the parentheses, we specify the values we want to multiply, in this case 5 and 6. When we call the function, these values are sent to the "x" and "y" parameters of the function. This explains how we call the function and send inputs to it (see Figure 8-5).

As shown in Figure 8-5, inside the "Multiply" function, the product of the two numbers "x" and "y" is calculated and stored in another variable called "z." This product is then returned to the main program. Hence, in our main program, if we print the variable "P," it will display the product of 5 and 6.

The complete program of the "main" and "Multiply" functions is as follows:

```
1  # program #3
2  def Multiply(x,y):
3      z=x+y
4      return z
5
6  # Main program
7  # Call the Multiply function
8  P=Multiply(5,6)
9  print(P)
```

In this example, we start with two pieces of information (two parameters). But remember that a function can have lots of different pieces of information or even no information at all. Moreover, when we use a function, it can give us one answer (i.e., return one value) or more than one answer, or sometimes it can give us no answer at all. Therefore, the number of things we put into the function (inputs) and the number of things we get out of it (outputs) depends on what we want the function to do.

Another important point we can learn from our example: No matter how long or short the function is (i.e., how many statements it contains), we only need one line to call or use it. This one line causes the function to do everything it is supposed to do. Also, we can use the function multiple times in our main program if we want to do that. This is one of the biggest advantages of functions – they give us the ability to simply do things over and over again. The following program shows how the function can be called many times to perform the multiplication many times:

```
# program #4
def Multiply(x,y):
    z=x*y
    return z

# Main program
# Call the Multiply function
P1=Multiply(5,6)
P2=Multiply(2,3)
P3=Multiply(10,20)
print(P1)
print(P2)
print(P3)
```

In the above code, we can shorten the function by directly returning the value of "x*y" without saving it into another variable, as follows:

```
# program #4
def Multiply(x,y):
    return x*y

# Main program
# Call the Multiply function
P1=Multiply(5,6)
print(P1)
```

8.3.1 Function Without Inputs

Our Multiply function had two inputs. However, we can do it with no inputs as follows:

```
# program #5
def Multiply():
    x=int(input("Enter the first number: "))
    y=int(input("Enter the second number: "))
```

```
5    z=x*y
6      return z
7
8  # Main program
9  # Call the Multiply function
10 P1=Multiply()
11 print(P1)
```

As we can see in the code above, this function does not have any inputs inside the brackets, which means that in the main program, when we call this function, there are no input parameters required, and as you can see, we call the function as follows, "Multiply()." However, inside the function there are two input statements to get the numbers from the user and multiply them and return the result back to the main program.

8.3.2   Function Without Return

In the previous Multiply functions, the function returns a value that is the result of multiplying two numbers that we sent to it. We can also return nothing; this can happen with other functions that are supposed to perform an action on their own without returning a value to the main program. Here is the modified version of the Multiply function that returns nothing:

```
1  # program #5
2  def Multiply():
3    x = int(input("Enter the first number: "))
4    y = int(input("Enter the second number: "))
5    z = x * y
6    print(z)
7
8  # Main program
9  # Call the Multiply function
10 Multiply()
```

In this modified version, when we call the multiply function, the function still takes two numbers from the user, multiplies them together, and stores the result in the variable "z." However, instead of returning the value of "z" to the main program using the return statement, the function now simply prints the value of "z" using the print(z) statement. Thus, the function returns nothing; that is, we do not need the returned value in our main program. Therefore, when we call the Multiply() function, we no longer store the result in a variable. Instead, we simply call the function, and it will print the result directly.

8.3.3   Function with Many Returns

In functions, we can return nothing, return one value, or return many values. This gives functions more flexibility in programming. The code below shows an example:

```
1   # program #5
2   def Multiply():
3     x = int(input("Enter the first number: "))
4     y = int(input("Enter the second number: "))
5     z = x * y
6     return x, y, z
7
8   # Main program
9   # Call the Multiply function
10  first_number, second_number, result = Multiply()
11  print(f"The first number is: {first_number}")
12  print(f"The second number is: {second_number}")
13  print(f"The result is: {result}")
```

In this Multiply() function, it now returns three values: "x," "y," and "z." These represent the first number, the second number, and the result of multiplying them. When we call the Multiply() function in our main program, we assign the three returned values to three separate variables: "first_number," "second_number," and "result," respectively.

8.4   Solved Examples

8.4.1   Example 1: Area of Rectangle

Let us write a program that uses a function called **calculate_area** that takes the length and width of a rectangle and returns its area. With this function, we can easily calculate the area of any rectangle just by providing the length and width values.

The program will be

```
1   # Solved example 1
2
3   def calculate_area(length, width):
4     area = length * width
5     return area
6
7   # Main program
8   # Prompt the user for the length and width of the rectangle
9   length = float(input("Enter the length of the rectangle: "))
10  width = float(input("Enter the width of the rectangle: "))
11
12  # Call the calculate_area function and store the result in a variable
13  rectangle_area = calculate_area(length, width)
14
15  # Print the calculated area
16  print("The area of the rectangle is:", rectangle_area)
```

In the above program, to use the function, in the main program, we prompt the user to enter the length and width of the rectangle using input and store the values in the length and width variables. We then call the calculate_area function with length and width as arguments in the function, and then the function calculates the area and returns the area. This area or the returned value will be stored in the rectangle_area variable. An example of the output of this program is

```
Enter the length of the rectangle: 5
Enter the width of the rectangle: 3
The area of the rectangle is: 15.0
```

8.4.2 Example 2: Area of Different Shapes

In this example, we will try to create functions to calculate the area of different shapes. In this example, we will create three functions, the first one will calculate and return the area of a rectangle, the second one will calculate and return the area of a square, and the third and last one will calculate and return the area of a triangle.

The program will be

```
1  # Solved example 2 (version #1)
2
3  def calculate_rectangle_area(length, width):
4      area = length * width
5      return area
6
7  def calculate_square_area(side):
8      area = side ** 2
9      return area
10
11 def calculate_triangle_area(base, height):
12     area = 0.5 * base * height
13     return area
14
15 # Main program
16 # Prompt the user to choose a shape
17 print("Choose a shape:")
18 print("1. Rectangle")
19 print("2. Square")
20 print("3. Triangle")
21
22 shape_choice = int(input("Enter the number corresponding to your choice: "))
23
24 if shape_choice == 1:
25     length = float(input("Enter the length of the rectangle: "))
26     width = float(input("Enter the width of the rectangle: "))
27     area = calculate_rectangle_area(length, width)
28     print("The area of the rectangle is:", area)
29
30 elif shape_choice == 2:
31     side = float(input("Enter the length of a side of the square: "))
32     area = calculate_square_area(side)
33     print("The area of the square is:", area)
```

```
34
35  elif shape_choice == 3:
36      base = float(input("Enter the base of the triangle: "))
37      height = float(input("Enter the height of the triangle: "))
38      area = calculate_triangle_area(base, height)
39      print("The area of the triangle is:", area)
40
41  else:
42      print("Invalid choice. Please try again.")
```

In the above program, we define three functions: calculate_rectangle_area, calculate_square_area, and calculate_triangle_area.

- The calculate_rectangle_area function takes length and width as parameters and calculates the area of a rectangle using the formula length * width.
- The calculate_square_area function takes the side as a parameter and calculates the area of a square using the formula side ** 2.
- The calculate_triangle_area function takes base and height as parameters and calculates the area of a triangle using the formula (1/2) * base * height.

In the main program, we prompt the user to select a shape from a menu by entering an appropriate number. Based on the user's choice, we prompt for the required inputs and call the appropriate area calculation function. Finally, we print the calculated area of the selected shape.

This problem could also be solved as follows:

```
1   # Solved example 2 (version #2)
2
3   def calculate_rectangle_area():
4       length = float(input("Enter the length of the rectangle: "))
5       width = float(input("Enter the width of the rectangle: "))
6       area = length * width
7       return area
8
9   def calculate_square_area():
10      side = float(input("Enter the length of a side of the square: "))
11      area = side ** 2
12      return area
13
14  def calculate_triangle_area():
15      base = float(input("Enter the base of the triangle: "))
16      height = float(input("Enter the height of the triangle: "))
17      area = 0.5 * base * height
18      return area
19
20  # Main program
21  # Prompt the user to choose a shape
22  print("Choose a shape:")
23  print("1. Rectangle")
24  print("2. Square")
25  print("3. Triangle")
```

```
26
27 shape_choice = int(input("Enter the number corresponding to your choice: "))
28
29 if shape_choice == 1:
30     area= calculate_rectangle_area()
31     print("The area of the rectangle is:", area)
32 elif shape_choice == 2:
33     area= calculate_square_area()
34     print("The area of the square is:", area)
35 elif shape_choice == 3:
36     area=calculate_triangle_area()
37     print("The area of the triangle is:", area)
38 else:
39     print("Invalid choice. Please try again.")
```

The previous program (# Solved example 2 (version #2)) does the same task as program version #1. The only difference is that in program version #2, all the steps are inside the functions. Depending on the shape_choice value we get from the input command, we will call a specific function without giving it any information. Within each function, we ask the user for certain values (e.g., the length and the width in the function called calculate_rectangle_area), then we use those values to calculate the area of the shape. Finally, each function sends the calculated area back to the main program for printing or further processing.

Here is an example of the output of the code:

```
Choose a shape:
1. Rectangle
2. Square
3. Triangle
Enter the number corresponding to your choice: 1
Enter the length of the rectangle: 5
Enter the width of the rectangle: 3
The area of the rectangle is: 15.0
```

8.4.3   Example 3: Finding Power of a Number

Write a program that asks the user to enter a number and uses a function to calculate the power of that number:

```
1 # Solved example 3
2
3 def calculate_power(base, exponent):
4     power = base ** exponent
5     return power
6
7 # Main program
8 # Prompt the user to enter a number
```

```
9  number = float(input("Enter a number: "))
10
11 # Prompt the user to enter the exponent
12 exponent = float(input("Enter the exponent: "))
13
14 # Calculate the power using the calculate_power function
15 result = calculate_power(number, exponent)
16
17 # Print the result
18 print(number, "raised to the power", exponent, "is:", result)
```

In this program, we define a function called calculate_power that takes a base and an exponent as parameters and calculates the power of the base raised to the exponent.

In the main program, we prompt the user to enter a number and store it in a variable called "number". Next, we prompt the user for the exponent and store it in the variable called "exponent". Using the calculate_power function, we pass the "number" and the "exponent" as arguments to calculate the power. The function, as in the code above, calculates the result and sends it back to the main program. Finally, we print the result by concatenating the appropriate values.

8.4.4   Example 4: Creating a Simple Calculator

In this example, we want to create a calculator as we did before in solved example 3 in Chapter 3. The program in this example uses four functions to add, subtract, multiply, and divide. The program will be

```
1  # Solved example 4
2
3  def add(x, y):
4      """Function to add two numbers"""
5      return x + y
6
7  def subtract(x, y):
8      """Function to subtract two numbers"""
9      return x − y
10
11 def multiply(x, y):
12     """Function to multiply two numbers"""
13     return x * y
14
15 def divide(x, y):
16     """Function to divide two numbers"""
17     if y != 0:
18         return x / y
19     else:
20         print("Error: Cannot divide by zero")
21
22 # Main program
23 # Prompt the user to enter two numbers
24 num1 = float(input("Enter the first number: "))
```

```
25  num2 = float(input("Enter the second number: "))
26
27  # Perform the arithmetic operations using the defined functions
28  sum_result = add(num1, num2)
29  difference_result = subtract(num1, num2)
30  product_result = multiply(num1, num2)
31  quotient_result = divide(num1, num2)
32
33  # Print the results
34  print("Sum:", sum_result)
35  print("Difference:", difference_result)
36  print("Product:", product_result)
37  print("Quotient:", quotient_result)
```

In this program, we define four functions: add, subtract, multiply, and divide. Each function takes two numbers as input parameters and performs the corresponding arithmetic operation on these numbers.

The add function adds the two numbers, the subtract function subtracts the second number from the first, the multiply function multiplies the two numbers, and the divide function divides the first number by the second. In the main function, we then ask the user to enter two numbers, which are stored in the variables num1 and num2.

In the main program, we use the defined functions to perform the arithmetic operations, passing the entered numbers as arguments to the functions. The called functions calculate the outputs and send them back to the main program, and the results are stored in the variables sum_result, difference_result, product_result, and quotient_result. Finally, the program prints the results of these operations.

We can combine all these functions into a single function that returns four values instead of one. This means that we can send many parameters or arguments to the function and also return many values, as follows:

```
1   def perform_arithmetic(x, y):
2     """Function to perform arithmetic operations on two numbers"""
3     return x + y, x - y, x * y, x / y
4
5   # Main program
6   # Prompt the user to enter two numbers
7   num1 = float(input("Enter the first number: "))
8   num2 = float(input("Enter the second number: "))
9
10  # Perform the arithmetic operations using the defined function
11  Addition, Subtraction, Multiplication, Division = perform_arithmetic(num1, num2)
12
13  # Print the results
14  print("Sum:", Addition)
15  print("Difference:", Subtraction)
16  print("Product:", Multiplication)
17  print("Quotient:", Division)
```

8.5   Exercises

● **Exercise 1: Print line of stars**

Write a program that uses a function to print a line of stars.
   Example output:

```
**********
```

● **Exercise 2: Print line of stars**

Modify the program from the first exercise that prints a row of stars. In this exercise, the user passes or sends a number to a function that prints a row of stars with the number entered by the user.
   Example output:

```
Enter the number of stars: 10
**********
```

Modify this program again by adding arguments to control the character used for the line. Hence, we can print a line of stars ("******") or other characters, for example, "#########."
   We can also add another option to this program by giving it the ability to print several lines instead of one line.
   Example of the output:

```
Enter the number the character you want to repeat: #
Enter the number of repetitions: 5
Enter the number of lines: 3
#####
#####
#####
```

● **Exercise 3: Celsius to Fahrenheit**

Write a program that uses a function to convert the temperature from Celsius to Fahrenheit.
   Example output:

```
Enter the temperature in Celsius: 25
The temperature in Fahrenheit is: 77.0
```

● Exercise 4: Find maximum

Write a program that uses a function to find the maximum of two numbers.
   Example output:

> Enter the first number: 7
> Enter the second number: 12
> The maximum number is: 12

● Exercise 5: Find average

Write a program that uses a function to calculate the average of three numbers.
   Example output:

> Enter the first number: 7
> Enter the second number: 12
> Enter the third number: 5
> The average of the three numbers is: 8

● Exercise 6: Even or odd

Write a program that uses a function to determine whether a number is even
or odd. The program should take a number as input from the user and call the
function to check whether the number is even or odd. Display an appropriate
message indicating whether the number is odd or even.
   Example output:

> Enter a number: 9
> The number is odd.

● Exercise 7: Leap year

Write a program that uses a function to determine whether or not a year is a
leap year. The program should take a year as input from the user and call the
function to check if it is a leap year. Display an appropriate message indicating
whether the year is a leap year or not.
   Example output:

> Enter a year: 2020
> The year is a leap year.

● Exercise 8: Multiplication table

Write a program that uses a function to display the multiplication table of a given number. The program should take a number as input from the user and call the function to display the multiplication table up to a certain limit (e.g., up to 10).

Example output:

Enter a number: 5
Multiplication Table:
5 × 1 = 5
5 × 2 = 10
5 × 3 = 15
...
5 × 10 = 50

● Exercise 9: Factorial calculation

Write a program that uses a function to calculate the factorial of a given number. The program should prompt the user to enter a number and call the function to calculate and display its factorial.

Example output:

Enter a number: 5
The factorial of 5 is 120.

● Exercise 10: Calorie calculator

Write a program that uses a function to calculate the calories because our user is on a diet to lose some weight. Tell the user that an apple has 49 calories, a banana has 95 calories, and an orange has 37 calories. Ask the user to enter the number of apples, bananas, and oranges they eat and calculate the number of calories consumed (this exercise is similar to Exercise 7 in Chapter 2).

The expected output of this program is

Enter the number of apples you ate: 2
Enter the number of bananas you ate: 1
Enter the number of oranges you ate: 3
You consumed a total of 304 calories.

● Exercise 11: Square a number

Write a program to find the square of any number using a function. The expected output of this program is

> Enter a number: 2
> The square of 2 is 4

● Exercise 12: Swap two numbers

Write a program to swap two numbers using a function. For example, to swap two numbers, if x=2 and y=3, after the swap, the two variables will exchange their contents, so x will be 3 and y will be 2. The expected output of this program is

> Enter the first number: 2
> Enter the second number: 5
> Before swapping: x=2, y=5
> After swapping: x=5 and y=2

● Exercise 13: Print numbers in a range

Write a program that uses a function to print all the numbers in a given range. The expected output of this program is

> Enter the starting number: 1
> Enter the end number: 100
> The numbers are:
> 1
> 2
> 3
> :
> 100

Modify the function to include another parameter to print the numbers in a sequence or with a step, for example, 2, 4, 6, ...

> ● **Exercise 14: Seconds to minutes**
>
> Write a program that uses a function to convert seconds to minutes. In the program, ask the user for a number of seconds and print the equivalent in minutes. You know that 1 minute equals 60 seconds.
>
> The expected output of this program is as follows:
>
> Enter a number of seconds: 180
> 180 seconds is equal to 3 minutes.

8.6   Glossary

Term	Definition
def fn_name(x,y)	This command defines a function with the name, for example, "Multiply," and with the input parameters x and y.
return	The "return" statement is used within a function to return a value from the function. When the function is called, it executes the code it contains until it reaches the "return" statement and then sends the specified value back to the part of the code that originally called the function.

8.7   Our Next Adventure in Programming

In this chapter, Kai learned how to use functions to make the code not only shorter but also more flexible. As Kai learned, by using functions, he could encapsulate repeated lines of code into a single function and then call that function with just one line whenever he needed to use that code in his program.

Kai still had some unanswered questions about functions, such as whether a function could call another function or even itself. Therefore, Kai decides to read on and learn more about functions. In the next chapter, we will dive deep into the world of functions to answer Kai's questions. We will also learn about some built-in functions – these are special functions that are available to all programmers. These built-in functions can be used to perform complex tasks without requiring a deep understanding of their inner workings.

Coding at an Advanced Level with Functions

9

In the previous chapter, Kai and we have learned about the power of functions and how they can help organize our code and make it simple.

Kai still had some gaps in his knowledge about functions, such as whether a function can call another function or even itself. Therefore, in this chapter, we will learn about the scope of variables and how functions can call other functions. These tools can perform complex tasks with a single command, saving us time and effort. Further, by exploring Python's built-in functions, which are like the superheroes of the programming world, we will use these prebuilt tools to perform incredible tasks in our programs, simplifying our code and making it more powerful.

9.1 Scope and Variable Access

Imagine that you have a big house with different rooms. In each room, there are different things – toys, books, clothes, and so on. The things or items in one room are different from the things in another room, right? Similarly, in programming, we have something similar called "scope." Scope is like the different rooms in a house (different functions in the main program), and the "things" in each room (function) are the variables. The variables that are defined in function "A" are different from the variables in function "B," and both are different from the variables in the main program.

Let us explain this in the following program:

```python
# Global scope
favorite_color = "blue"

def change_favorite_color():
    # Local scope inside the function
    favorite_color = "green"
    print("Inside the function, my favorite color is:", favorite_color)

```

A. Tharwat, *Python Adventures for Young Coders*,
https://doi.org/10.1007/979-8-8688-1067-1_9

```
9   # main program
10  print("Outside the function, my favorite color is:", favorite_color)
11  change_favorite_color()
12  print("Outside the function, my favorite color is still:", favorite_color)
```

As we can see from the code above, the program starts with a variable called "favorite_color" in the global scope, which means it can be accessed anywhere in our program, regardless of the main function or the other functions. We set it to the value of this variable with "blue." Then we define a function called "change_favorite_color()." Inside this function, we have a variable also called "favorite_color," but it is in the local scope of the function. Inside the function, we print the value of "favorite_color," which is "green," because that is the value we set it to inside the function.

In the main program, we print the value of "favorite_color" outside the function (in the main function), which is still "blue" because the global variable has not been changed. Then we call the "change_favorite_color()" function, which changes the value of the local "favorite_color" variable inside the function to green. Finally, we print the value of "favorite_color" again outside the function, and it is still "blue" because the global variable was not affected by the changes made inside the function. This example shows that variables inside a function (local scope) are separate or different from variables outside the function (global scope). The local variables can only be accessed within the function, while the global variable can be accessed anywhere in the program.

This is the output of the above program:

> Outside the function, my favorite color is: blue
> Inside the function, my favorite color is: green
> Outside the function, my favorite color is still: blue

Here is what the output shows:

- "Outside the function, my favorite color is: blue": This prints the value of the global "favorite_color" variable, which is "blue."
- "Inside the function, my favorite color is: green": This prints the value of the local variable "favorite_color" inside the function called "change_favorite_color()," which is "green." This means that only the local variable can be changed inside the function.
- "Outside the function, my favorite color is still: blue": This prints the value of the global variable called "favorite_color" again, which is still "blue" because the function call only changed the local variable, not the global one.

Here is another example in the program below:

```python
# Global variable
score = 0

def increase_score():
    # Local variable inside the function
    score = score + 1
    print("Inside increase_score(), the score is:", score)

def set_score():
    # Local variable inside the function
    score = 5
    print("Inside reset_score(), the score is:", score)

def reset_score():
    # Local variable inside the function
    score = 0
    print("Inside reset_score(), the score is:", score)

# main program
print("In the main program, the initial score is:", score)
increase_score()
print("In the main program, the score is now:", score)
reset_score()
print("In the main program, the score is now:", score)
set_score()
print("In the main program, the score is now:", score)
```

If we trace the above code, we will see that the program starts with a global variable called "score" and sets it to zero. We define three functions: "increase_score()," "set_score()," and "reset_score()."

- Inside the "increase_score()" function, we have a local variable also called "score." We increment this local score variable by one and print its value.
- Inside the "reset_score()" function, we have another local variable also called "score." We set this local score variable to zero and print its value.
- Inside the "set_score()" function, we have another local variable also called "score." We set this local score variable to five and print its value.

In the main program, we print the initial value of the global score variable, which is zero. Then we call the "increase_score()" function, which changes the local score variable inside the function to one, but does not affect the global score variable. We then print out the global score, which is still zero. We call the "reset_score()" function, which changes the local score variable inside the function to zero, but does not affect the global score variable. Finally, we call the "set_score()" function, which changes the local score variable inside the function to five, but does not affect the global score variable. We then print out the global score, which is still zero.

Therefore, the output of the above program is

> In the main program, the initial score is: 0
> Inside increase_score(), the score is: 1
> In the main program, the score is now: 0
> Inside reset_score(), the score is: 0
> In the main program, the score is now: 0
> Inside set_score(), the score is: 5
> In the main program, the score is now: 0

Again, as we can see, the changes made to the local score variables within the functions did not affect the global score variable. This is the key concept of variable scope – local variables are only accessible within the function in which they are defined, while the global variable can be accessed throughout the entire program.

9.2   Function Calling Another Function

Let us try an example where one function calls another function, and the second function uses the input from the first function to do some calculations. In the following example, we want to multiply some numbers, so let us break it down step by step as follows:

```python
def get_numbers():
    print("Let's multiply some numbers!")
    num1 = int(input("Enter the first number: "))
    num2 = int(input("Enter the second number: "))
    return num1, num2

def multiply_numbers():
    a, b = get_numbers()
    result = a * b
    print("The result is:", result)

# main program
multiply_numbers()
```

In the code above, we have two functions. In the "multiply_numbers()" function, instead of taking "a" and "b" as parameters, the function now calls the "get_numbers()" function directly. This is done with the line "a, b = get_numbers()." The "get_numbers()" function still does the same thing – it asks the user for two numbers and returns them to the "multiply_numbers()" function. Hence, the "multiply_numbers()" function calls the "get_numbers()" function itself and stores the returned values in the "a" and "b" variables. Finally, in the main part of the program, we just call the "multiply_numbers()" function, and it takes care of everything else.

The main advantage of this version is that the main program is even simpler – it just calls the "multiply_numbers()" function, and this function takes care of getting the numbers from the user by calling the "get_numbers()" function and performing the multiplication. This means that we can break the function down into smaller and simpler functions.

Let us have another advanced example as follows:

```
 1  def show_menu():
 2    while True:
 3      print("Welcome to the Shape Area Calculator!")
 4      print("Please choose an option:")
 5      print("1. Calculate the area of a circle")
 6      print("2. Calculate the area of a rectangle")
 7      print("3. Quit")
 8
 9      choice = int(input("Enter your choice (1−3): "))
10
11      if choice == 1:
12        radius = float(input("What is the radius of the circle? "))
13        calculate_circle_area(radius)
14      elif choice == 2:
15        length = float(input("What is the length of the rectangle? "))
16        width = float(input("What is the width of the rectangle? "))
17        calculate_rectangle_area(length, width)
18      elif choice == 3:
19        print("Goodbye!")
20        break
21      else:
22        print("Invalid choice. Please choose again.")
23
24
25  def calculate_circle_area(radius):
26    print("Okay, let's calculate the area of a circle!")
27    area = 3.14 * radius * radius
28    print("The area of the circle is ", area, " square units.")
29
30  def calculate_rectangle_area(length, width):
31    print("Okay, let's calculate the area of a rectangle!")
32    area = length * width
33    print(f"The area of the rectangle is ", area, " square units.")
34
35
36  # main program
37  show_menu()
```

As we can see in the code above, there are three functions. First, the "show_menu()" function, which is responsible for displaying the main menu options to the user. It displays a welcome message and the available options (calculate the area of a circle, calculate the area of a rectangle, or quit). It then prompts the user to make a choice (1, 2, or 3). Based on the choice, one of the other two functions is called. If the user enters 1 (first choice), the program will ask the user for the radius of the circle and then call the second function, which is called the "calculate_circle_area(radius)" function. This function takes the radius of a circle as an argument and prints a message that the area of the circle is being calculated. It then calculates the area of the circle using the formula area = 3.14 * radius * radius. Finally, it prints the calculated area. If the user chooses 2, the program will first ask the user for the length and width of the rectangle and then call the third function, which is called "calculate_rectangle_area(length, width)." This function takes as arguments the length and width of a rectangle. It then calculates the area of the rectangle using the formula area = length * width. Finally, it returns the calculated area.

The main program starts only by calling the "show_menu()" function, which shows the main menu and then calls the other functions according to the user's choice.

9.3   Function Calling Itself (Recursive Function)

In some cases, one of the solutions of some problems is when the function calls itself; this is called a recursive function. This adds another way to solve some problems. Let us try to write a program that calculates the factorial of a number. For example, the factorial of 5 is $5 \times 4 \times 3 \times 2 \times 1 = 120$. Hence, we can use the for loop to solve this problem as follows:

```
1  def factorial(n):
2      # Initialize the result to 1
3      result = 1
4
5      # Iterate from 1 to n, multiplying the result by each number
6      for i in range(1, n+1):
7          result *= i
8
9      return result
10
11  # main program
12  result = factorial(5)
13  print(result) # Output: 120
```

In the program above, we define a function called "factorial()" which takes a number "n" as an argument. Inside the function, we initialize a variable called result to 1. This will be the variable we use to store the final result. We then use a for loop to iterate from 1 to "n" (inclusive). On each iteration, we multiply the current value of the variable called result by the current value of "i" (which will be 1, 2, 3, 4, 5 if "n" is 5). After the loop completes, the function returns the final value of result. Therefore, when we call factorial(5), the variable "result" is initialized to 1. The for loop iterates five times, with "i" taking the values 1, 2, 3, 4, and 5. On the first iteration, the variable "result" is multiplied by 1, so "result" becomes 1. On the second iteration, the "result" variable is multiplied by 2, so "result" becomes 2, and so on.

Instead of using the iterative for loop method to calculate the factorial, the recursive method could be used. Thus, instead of using the for loop, the function calls itself. The code is as follows:

```
1  def factorial(n):
2      # Base case: the factorial of 0 is 1
3      if n == 0 or n==1:
4          return 1
5      # Recursive case: the factorial of n is n * the factorial of n−1
6      else:
7          return n * factorial(n−1)
8
9  # main program
10 result = factorial(5)
11 print(result)  # Output: 120
```

In the code above, the program defines a function called "factorial()," which takes a number "n" as an argument. Inside the function, we have an if statement with "**a base case**": if "n" is 0 or "n" is 1, the function returns 1; this is called the "base case" which is the stopping condition for the function. This is because the factorial of 0 and 1 is defined as 1. If $n > 0$, in the "**recursive case**," we return the product of "n" and the factorial of "n-1" (e.g., factorial(5)=$5 \times factorial(4)$). This means that in the "recursive case" the function calls itself with a smaller number. We call the "factorial()" function with the argument 5, and the function calculates the factorial of 5 by calling itself with smaller and smaller numbers until it reaches the base case of 0. Here is how the function call would work step by step:

- factorial(5) is called; then, 5 * factorial(4).
- factorial(4) is called; then, 4 * factorial(3).
- factorial(3) is called; then, 3 * factorial(2).
- factorial(2) is called; then, 2 * factorial(1).
- factorial(1) is called; this is the base case and the function returns 1. This means that factorial(1)=1.
- The final result will be calculated as $5 \times 4 \times 3 \times 2 \times 1 = 120$ and returns this value to the main program.

This recursive approach to calculate the factorial is a classic example of a function calling itself to solve a problem (see Figure 9-1). The key is to have a well-defined base case to stop the recursion and prevent an infinite loop.

Recursion can be a powerful technique, but it is important to use it carefully and make sure you fully understand the base case and the recursive case. In some cases, an iterative approach (using a loop) may be more efficient or easier to understand.

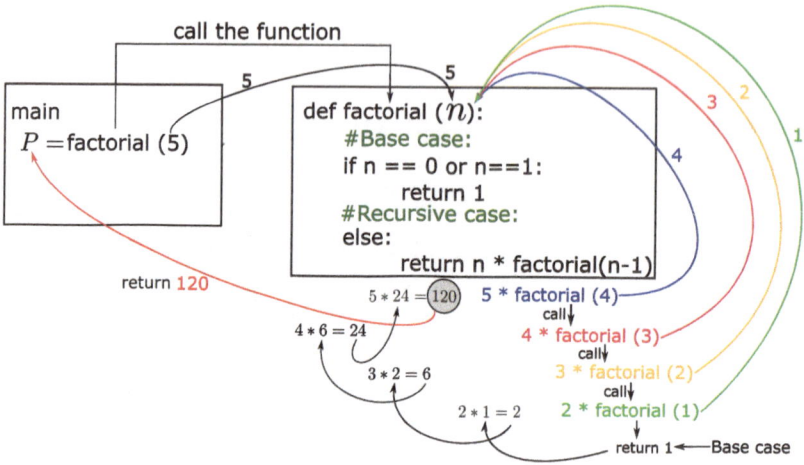

Figure 9-1. The steps of how the function recursively calls itself to calculate the factorial of 5

To improve your knowledge of recursive functions, here is another example to calculate the sum of numbers from 1 to n. This "n" will be the input to the function as in the following program:

```python
def sum_numbers(n):
    # Base case: if n is 1, return 1
    if n == 1:
        return 1
    # Recursive case: add n to the sum of the numbers from 1 to n—1
    else:
        return n + sum_numbers(n—1)

# main program
result = sum_numbers(10)
print(result) # Output: 55
```

Try to trace the above code and think about what the output of this program is.

In the above program, we have a special function called "sum_numbers()." The task of this function is to calculate the sum of all numbers from 1 to the given number. For example, if we want to find the sum of the numbers from 1 to 10, the answer would be $1 + 2 + 3 + 4 + 5 + 6 + 7 + 8 + 9 + 10 = 55$. The sum_numbers() function uses a "base case" and a "recursive case" to calculate the sum. The base case is when the number (n) is 1. In this case, the function simply returns 1, because the sum of the numbers from 1 to 1 is just 1. The recursive case is when the number (n) is greater than 1. In this case, the function adds the current number "n" to the sum of the numbers from 1 to n-1.

Suppose we want to find the sum of the numbers from 1 to 5 as in Figure 9-2. We will use the "sum_numbers()" function to do this. The "sum_numbers()" function is started when we call it, and inside it, n is 5. Since 5 is greater than 1, the

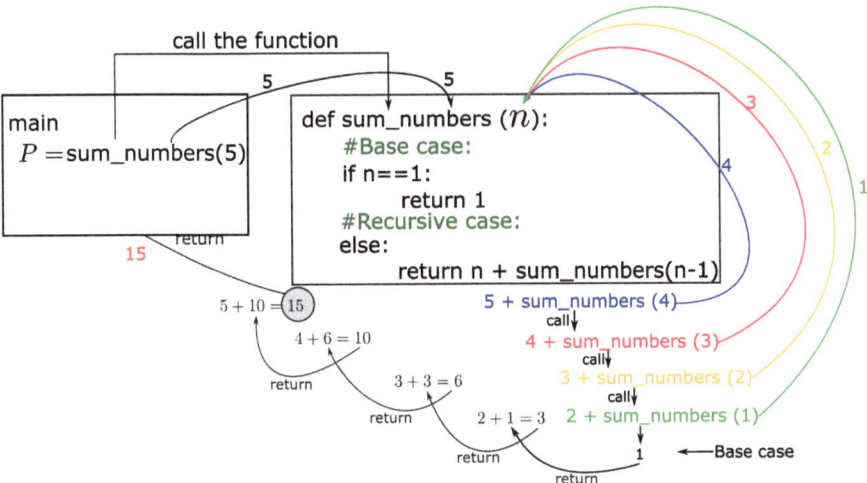

Figure 9-2. The steps of how the function recursively calls itself to calculate the sum of 5 (5 + 4 + 3 + 2 + 1 = 15)

function uses the "recursive case." In the recursive case, the function adds 5 to "sum_numbers(4)," which is the sum of the numbers from 1 to 4. To find the sum of the numbers from 1 to 4 ("sum_numbers(4)"), the function calls itself again, but this time with the number 4. Since 4 is greater than 1, the function again uses the recursive case. In the recursive case, the function adds 4 to "sum_numbers(3)," which is the sum of the numbers from 1 to 3. To evaluate "sum_numbers(3)," the function calls itself again, but this time with the number 3. Since 3 is greater than 1, the function again uses the recursive case, and the function adds 3 to the sum of the numbers from 1 to 2 ("sum_numbers(2)"). To find the sum of the numbers from 1 to 2, the function calls itself again, but this time with the number 2. Since 2 is greater than 1, the function uses the recursive case again, and the function adds 2 to "sum_numbers(1)." Now the function has reached the "base case" because n is equal to 1 and simply returns the number 1. Now the function can go back through the previous steps and add up all the numbers, as shown in Figure 9-2.

9.4   Built-In Functions

Instead of writing each function and understanding exactly how it works, as we did before, we have a magic solution in Python called "built-in functions." These functions are like little helpers that are already available for us to use without any extra work. They are super useful because they come built-in with Python or whatever programming language you are using. So why are these built-in functions so great? Well, they make life a lot easier for programmers. Instead of spending a lot of time and effort writing long, complicated functions to solve certain problems, we can just use these built-in functions. They are like shortcuts that allow us to do our tasks quickly and easily.

Let us take a simple example. Imagine we have a list of numbers and we want to find the smallest number in the list. Without built-in functions, we would have to write many lines of code to find that out. But with built-in functions, we can get the same result with just one simple command. We can use a special built-in function designed specifically for finding the minimum value in a list. We call this function and it magically gives us the answer without having to do all the hard work inside the function. Hence, again, built-in functions save us time, effort, and headaches by providing ready-made solutions to common problems. We can use them simply without worrying about how they work behind the scenes.

> ### Built-in functions
> Built-in functions, also known as predefined functions, are functions that are provided as part of a programming language's standard library. They are ready-to-use functions that come combined with the programming language itself and are immediately available to programmers without the need for additional setup or installation.

Built-in functions are often grouped into libraries, which are collections of related functions and modules that provide additional functionality beyond the programming language's basic functions. Here are some examples of popular libraries in Python:

- **Math library**: The math library is a specialized library that provides a range of mathematical functions. It allows us to perform complex mathematical calculations without having to write the code from scratch. For example, if we need to calculate square roots, trigonometric functions like sine or cosine, or logarithms, we can use the functions provided by the math library. These functions are designed to perform mathematical operations accurately and efficiently.
- **Graphics library (graphics.py)**: The graphics.py library is a popular library for creating graphics and animations. It provides an easy and beginner-friendly way to draw shapes, colors, and images on the screen. Using this library, we can bring our programs to life by adding visual elements and interactivity. We can create games, design user interfaces, or even visualize data in a graphical form.
- **NumPy library**: Just like the math library, the NumPy library is a special tool that helps us with math and science in programming. NumPy stands for "Numerical Python," and it is a powerful library that gives us access to many of advanced mathematical functions and data structures. With NumPy, we can work with arrays, which are like collections of numbers or data that are organized in rows and columns. These arrays allow us to perform complex calculations and transformations on large amounts of data really quickly and efficiently.
- **Pygame**: Pygame is a library that provides tools for creating games and interactive applications. We can use Pygame to build our own games, add graphics and sound effects, handle user input, and create a fun gaming experience.

When we want to use a group of useful functions that are stored together in a library, we use a special word called "import." This word helps us to bring the whole library or just the specific functions we need into our code.

Here is an example of using the import and one function within the math library:

```
1  # Import the math module
2  import math
3
4  # Get two numbers from the user
5  num1 = int(input("Enter the first number: "))
6  num2 = int(input("Enter the second number: "))
7
8  # Find the maximum of the two numbers using the math.max() function
9  biggest_number = math.max(num1, num2)
10
11 # Print the result
12 print("The biggest number is:", biggest_number)
```

In the code above, we first import the math module or library using the import statement. This gives us access to all the functions and tools provided by the math module. Next, we prompt the user to enter two numbers and convert those inputs to integers. Then we use the math.max() function to find the maximum of the two numbers the user entered. We can use "import math as MA" to replace the library name with MA. This is helpful if the length library name is long. Then, when we call the built-in function, we can use MA instead of math like this: "biggest_number = MA.max(num1, num2)." In other words, we can use the import math as MA statement to give the math module the short name MA (or whatever). This allows us to access the functions and tools of the math module with the shorter prefix MA. As you can see from the above example, the built-in function saves time and efforts.

9.4.1   Built-In Functions We Know

There are many basic and commonly used built-in functions that we know and use frequently. They provide essential functionality that allows us to interact with users, manipulate data types, display information, and control program flow. Here are a few examples:

- **print**: The print function is used to display information on the screen. It allows us to print text, numbers, or variables to the console or terminal. We can pass multiple arguments to the print function, and it will display them separated by spaces.
- **input**: The input function is used to get input from the user. It prompts the user to enter some text or data, and once the user provides the input, it is returned as a string. It is often used to create interactive programs that require user interaction.
- **str**: The str function is used to convert values to strings. It takes any value or variable and converts it to a string representation.

- **int**: The int function is used to convert values to integers. It takes a string or a floating-point number and converts it into an integer. This function is useful when we want to perform mathematical operations or compare numbers.
- **float**: This function is used to convert values to floating-point numbers. It takes a string or an integer and converts it to a floating-point number. This function is useful when we want to perform mathematical operations or compare numbers.
- **range**: The range function is used to generate a sequence of numbers. It takes one, two, or three arguments: start, stop, and step. By default, range starts at zero and increments by one, but we can change these values. The range function is often used in loops to iterate over a range of numbers.
- **List functions**: Here are some commonly used built-in list functions in Python, along with brief descriptions:
  - len(list): Returns the length (number of items) of a list
  - list.append(item): Appends an item to the end of the list
  - list.remove(item): Removes the first occurrence of the given item from the list
  - list.insert(index, item): Inserts an item at a given index in the list
  - list.clear(): Removes all items from the list, leaving it empty

9.4.2   Some Examples of Built-In Functions

9.4.2.1 Built-In Math Functions

The built-in math functions help us easily perform various mathematical operations in our code. Here are some important built-in functions explained in a simple way:

- **abs(x)**: This function returns the absolute value of a number. For example, the absolute value of –5 is 5, and the absolute value of 10 is 10.
- **round(x)**: When we want to round a number to the nearest integer, we can use this function. It helps us remove the decimal part and gives us the closest whole number. For example, if we round 3.7, we get 4. If we round 9.2, we get 9.
- **max(x, y)**: This function compares two numbers and tells us which one is the maximum. It is like a competition between the numbers to see who is the winner. For example, if we have 5 and 9, the max function tells us that 9 is the maximum number.
- **min(x, y)**: Similar to the max function, this function compares two numbers and tells us which one is smaller. It helps us find the smallest number in a pair. For example, if we have 3 and 7, the min function will tell us that 3 is the smaller number.

9.4.2.2 Built-In Functions with Lists

There are many built-in functions that can help us work with lists. We mentioned some of them above, but there are surely many more. Here are some examples of built-in functions:

- **sum(list)**: This function sums all the numbers in a list. For example, if we have a list of numbers like [5, 10, 15, 20], the sum() function would tell us that the total is 50.
- **max(list)**: This function finds the greatest number in a list. For example, if we have a list of numbers like [7, 3, 12, 9], the max() function would tell us that the maximum number is 12.
- **min(list)**: This function finds the smallest number in a list. For example, if we have a list of numbers like [7, 3, 12, 9], the min() function would tell us the minimum number is 3.
- **sorted(list)**: This function sorts the items in a list, from smallest to largest or from A to Z. For example, if we have a list of numbers like [12, 5, 9, 2], the sorted(list) function would sort them like [2, 5, 9, 12]. If we had a list of words like ["zebra," "apple," "monkey," "banana"], the sorted() function would sort them alphabetically: ["apple," "banana," "monkey," "zebra"].
- **count(item)**: This function tells us how many times an item appears in a list. For example, if we have a list of fruits like ["apple," "banana," "apple," "orange," "apple"], and we use count('apple'), it would tell us that there are three apples in the list.

Note: These are built-in Python functions that can be used directly without any imports.

9.5   Exercises

● Exercise 1: Check the variable scope – 1

The following code has two functions and the main function. Trace the code and the scope of the variable to know what the output of this program is:

```python
# Global variable
favorite_color = "blue"

def change_color():
    # Local variable inside the function
    favorite_color = "green"
    print("Inside change_color(), the favorite color is:", favorite_color)

def reset_color():
    favorite_color = "red"
    print("Inside reset_color(), the favorite color is:", favorite_color)

# main program
print("In the main program, the initial favorite color is:", favorite_color)
change_color()
print("In the main program, the favorite color is still:", favorite_color)
reset_color()
print("In the main program, the favorite color is now:", favorite_color)
```

● **Exercise 2: Check the variable scope – 2**

The following code has three functions and the main function. Trace the code and the scope of the variable to see what the output of this program is:

```
1   def update_score(total_score, score_to_add):
2       total_score += score_to_add
3       print("Total score updated to:", total_score)
4       return total_score, check_high_score(total_score)
5
6   def check_high_score(total_score):
7       high_score = total_score
8       if total_score > high_score:
9           high_score = total_score
10          print("New high score:", high_score)
11      return high_score
12
13  def play_game():
14      score = 10
15      total_score, high_score = update_score(0, score)
16      print("Score from play_game():", score)
17      return total_score, high_score
18
19
20  # main program
21  total_score=0
22  high_score=0
23
24  print("Initial total score: 0")
25  print("Initial high score: 0")
26
27  total_score, high_score = play_game()
28
29  print("Final total score:", total_score)
30  print("Final high score:", high_score)
```

● **Exercise 3: Function calls another function – 1**

The following code shows how one function calls another function. Trace the code and try to predict what the output of this program will be:

```
1   def get_ingredients():
2       print("Let's make a sandwich!")
3       bread = input("What kind of bread would you like? ")
4       filling = input("What filling would you like? ")
5       return bread, filling
6
7   def assemble_sandwich():
8       bread_type, sandwich_filling = get_ingredients()
9       print("Okay, let's assemble your sandwich:")
```

```
10    print("First, we'll take two slices of", bread_type, "bread.")
11    print("Then, we'll add the", sandwich_filling, "filling.")
12    print("And... voila! Your sandwich is ready to eat.")
13
14  # main program
15  assemble_sandwich()
```

● Exercise 4: Function calls another function – 2

The following code shows how one function calls another function. Trace the code and try to predict what the output of this program will be:

```
1   def get_book_info():
2     title = input("What is the title of the book? ")
3     author = input("Who is the author of the book? ")
4     return title, author
5
6   def get_book_rating():
7     rating = int(input("What rating would you give the book (1−5)? "))
8     return rating
9
10  def display_book_info(book_title, book_author, book_rating):
11    print("Title:", book_title)
12    print("Author:", book_author)
13    print("Rating:", book_rating, "out of 5 stars")
14
15  # main program
16  book_title, book_author = get_book_info()
17  book_rating = get_book_rating()
18  display_book_info(book_title, book_author, book_rating)
```

● Exercise 5: Function calls another function – 3

The following code shows how one function calls another function. Trace the code and try to predict what the output of this program will be:

```
1   def get_name():
2     name = input("What is your name? ")
3     return name
4
5   def get_age():
6     age = int(input("What is your age? "))
7     return age
8
9   def get_favorite_color():
10    color = input("What is your favorite color? ")
11    return color
12
13  def display_info(person_name, person_age, person_color):
```

```
14   print("Hello,", person_name)
15   print("You are", person_age, "years old.")
16   print("Your favorite color is", person_color + ".")
17
18   def get_person_info():
19       name = get_name()
20       age = get_age()
21       color = get_favorite_color()
22       return name, age, color
23
24   # main program
25   person_name, person_age, person_color = get_person_info()
26   display_info(person_name, person_age, person_color)
```

● Exercise 6: Recursive Fibonacci

The Fibonacci sequence is a series of numbers where each number is the sum of the previous two, starting with 0 and 1. The sequence goes like this: 0, 1, 1, 2, 3, 5, 8, 13, 21, 34, and so on.

Your task is to write a recursive function that calculates the number n^{th} in the Fibonacci sequence. Here is an example of the output of the program:

> Enter a number: 5
> The Fibonacci of 5 is 3

● Exercise 7: Find max

Write a program that uses one function to find the maximum of two numbers and another function to find the maximum of three numbers. Compare the length and performance of your functions with the built-in max function.

Here is an example of the output of the program:

> Enter the first number: 20
> Enter the second number: 5
> Enter the third number: 16
> The maximum number is 20

● Exercise 8: Calculate the factorial of a number

Write a program that uses a function to calculate the factorial of a number using a loop and another function that calls itself. Compare the length and the performance of your functions with the math.factorial() built-in function.

Here is an example of the output of the program:

Enter a number: 5
The factorial of 5 is 120

● Exercise 9: Calculate the power of a number

Write a program that uses a function to calculate the power of a number using a loop and another function that calls itself. Compare the length and the performance of your functions with the pow() built-in function.

Here is an example of the output of the program:

Enter the base number: 2
Enter the exponent number: 3
The result of 2 raised to the power of 3 is 8

● Exercise 10: Calculate the sum of numbers in a range

Write a program that uses a function to calculate the sum of numbers in a specific range. Compare the length and the performance of your functions with the sum(range(start, end + 1)) built-in function.

Here is an example of the output of the program:

Enter the first number: 2
Enter the end number: 10
The sum of numbers from 2 to 10 is 54

9.6   Glossary

Term	Definition
abs(x)	This function returns the absolute value of a number. It takes a single argument x, which can be an integer or a floating-point number and returns the absolute value of that number.
round(x)	This function returns the nearest integer to the given number x. If x is exactly halfway between two integers, it rounds to the nearest even integer.
max(x, y)	This function returns the maximum of two or more arguments. It can be used with numbers, strings, or other comparable objects.
min(x, y)	This function returns the minimum of two or more arguments. It can be used with numbers, strings, or other comparable objects.
sum(list)	This function calculates the total of all elements in a list of numbers. It returns the sum as a single value.
max(list)	This function returns the largest item in a list or the maximum of two or more arguments. It works with numbers, strings, and other comparable objects.
min(list)	This function returns the smallest item in a list or the minimum of two or more arguments. It works with numbers, strings, and other comparable objects.
sorted(list)	This function arranges the elements of a list in ascending order.
list.count(item)	A function of Python lists that returns the number of times a specified element appears in the list.

9.7   Our Next Adventure in Programming

In this chapter, Kai has learned how to use functions professionally and how to use built-in functions. As a result, Kai is able to write programs that are smaller and easier to understand.

After gathering all this knowledge in the last four chapters, Kai wants to use lists with functions. In addition, Kai wants to use his knowledge of lists and functions to improve the projects presented in Chapter 5. Therefore, in the next chapter, we will explore with Kai the powerful combination of lists and functions and learn how to pass lists as arguments to functions to perform complex operations and transformations on data collections. By working with the combination of lists and functions, we will be able to write more efficient, dynamic, and flexible code to satisfy the goals and tasks described in the checkpoint chapter (Chapter 5).

Checkpoint: Linking Lists and Functions to Strengthen Programming Skills

10

Over the past four chapters, Kai and we have learned about the power of functions and lists and how to use them effectively.

Kai wants to use the knowledge from all the previous chapters to make the code in all the projects he is trying to implement simpler and shorter, which will give him the opportunity to improve these projects and make them more reliable. Therefore, in this checkpoint chapter, we will review the important topics from the previous chapters to ensure a solid understanding of the concepts. We will also learn more about lists and functions and how they relate to each other. We will also explore how lists, functions, and their combinations can help achieve the goals of the projects introduced in Chapter 5. Finally, we will add a new project for further practice.

10.1 Functions with Lists

This section shows how to use the functions to search a list, find the maximum, calculate the sum of the elements in a list, and many other operations on lists. In other words, we will learn how to pass lists as inputs to the functions.

First, we will use a function to find the maximum of an element in a list. The code will look like this:

```python
def find_maximum(lst):
    maximum_value = lst[0]
    for element in lst:
        if element > maximum_value:
            maximum_value = element
    return maximum_value

# Main program
# Example list (main function)
my_list = [5, 2, 8, 3, 1, 6, 9]

```

© Alaa Tharwat 2025
A. Tharwat, *Python Adventures for Young Coders*,
https://doi.org/10.1007/979-8-8688-1067-1_10

```
12   # Find the maximum value in the list
13   maximum_value = find_maximum(my_list)
14   print("The maximum value in the list is: ", maximum_value)
```

In the above program, the "find_maximum" function has an input parameter called "lst." As we can see in the main function, when we call this function, we send a list as an input parameter. Hence, "lst" is a list. Inside the "find_maximum" function, a variable called "maximum_value" will be initialized with the first element of the list (lst). It then iterates over each element in the list and compares it to the current maximum value. If the element is greater than the "maximum_value", it updates "maximum_value" with the new maximum. Finally, it returns the maximum value. The print statement in the last line in the main program will print the maximum value within the list.

Let us think about another function using lists to get more familiar with how lists can be used as input parameters of the functions. In this program, we will calculate the sum of the numbers in a list. The program will look like this:

```
1    def calculate_total(lst):
2        total = 0
3        for number in lst:
4            total += number
5        return total
6
7    # Main program
8    my_list = [5, 2, 8, 3, 1, 6, 9]
9
10   # Calculate the total of the elements in the list
11   total = calculate_total(my_list)
12   print("The total of the elements in the list is:", total)
```

Let us think of another smarter function with lists, like searching within a list to find an item and just printing out whether we can find that item or not. The program will look like this:

```
1    def search_list(lst, target):
2        for element in lst:
3            if element == target:
4                return True
5        return False
6
7    # Main program
8    my_list = [5, 2, 8, 3, 1, 6, 9]
9
10   # Search for an element in the list
11   target = 3
12   found = search_list(my_list, target)
13
14   if found:
15       print("The element", target, " is found in the list.")
16   else:
17       print("The element" target, " is not found in the list.")
```

As can be seen from the code above, the search_list function runs through each element of the input list (lst). It checks whether the element is equal to the target value. If a result is found, it returns True. If the loop is terminated without a match being found, False will be returned.

For more practice with lists and functions, we can try other operations on lists, such as calculating the average of the elements in a list, sorting the elements in a list, reversing a list, and many others (more details in the previous chapter).

10.2 Project A: Math Test

Remember the project we worked on at the beginning of Chapter 5? (See the link to the project's code here: https://github.com/Eng-Alaa/Programming_4_Kids/blob/main/Project_A.py.) We had a lot of fun with it, but we also found some challenges that were a bit tricky. After learning about lists and functions, we want to see how we can make the project shorter, more flexible, and easier to understand.

10.2.1 Flexible Number of Questions

In the code we made before (in this link: https://github.com/Eng-Alaa/Programming_4_Kids/blob/main/Project_A.py), we had a separate "variable" for each question and answer. This worked fine, but it is not very flexible. What do I mean by flexible? Well, it means that it is hard to change or add things easily. For example, if we wanted to add more questions to the game, we would have to create a new "variable" for each new question. This would be a lot of work. Instead, we want to find a way to store all the questions and answers in a way that makes it easier to add or change things. This will make the project more fun and exciting to play or use.

The old code looked like this:

```
1  Q1 = "2x4"
2  A1 = 8
3
4  Q2 = "3x5"
5  A2 = 15
6
7  Q3 = "2X6"
8  A3 = 12
9
10 Q4 = "2X8"
11 A4 = 16
12
13 Q5 = "4X5"
14 A5 = 20
```

Using lists is a really good solution here. With lists, we can easily add new questions and answers whenever we want, without having to create new "variables" each time. Here is how we can do it; first, we make a list for all the questions, and then we make another list for all the answers. That way, if we want to add a new question, we can just "append" it to the list of questions. Similarly, if we want to add a new answer, we can add it to the list of answers. The lists of questions and answers are

```
1  Questions_list=["2x4","3x5","2X6","2X8","4X5"]
2  Answers_list=[8,15,12, 16,20]
```

In the code above, if we wanted to make part of this program to add more questions at runtime, we could easily do this using the append function. For example, if the questions and answers are stored in a file, we can load any number of questions into the list (more details in the next chapter). This makes our project much more flexible and easier to change compared to the way we did it before. It also helps keep the code nice and organized.

10.2.2 Iterate over Lists

From the code (see the link to the project's code here: https://github.com/Eng-Alaa/Programming_4_Kids/blob/main/Project_A.py), since we had no knowledge of lists at that time, we used many lines of code to ask the user each question and get the answer, then check it and increase the score if the user answered correctly. The old code is shown below:

```
1  print(Q1, " = ")
2  answer = int(input(""))
3
4  if answer == A1:
5    score1 +=1
6
7  print(Q2, " = ")
8  answer = int(input(""))
```

The code above is just for asking one question, but what if we want to ask ten questions? By using a for loop to iterate over the list, the code will be much shorter, as follows:

```
1  for i in range(0,len(Questions_list)):
2    answer = int(input(Questions_list[i]+ " = "))
3
4    if answer == Answers_list[i]:
5      score1 +=1
```

As we can see in the code above, instead of writing code for each question, the loop iterates over all the elements in the list, regardless of the length of the list. Therefore, if you check the project after using only lists, you will see that the code length has been reduced from 300 lines to only 57 lines (see the updated code of this project in: the code). This means that using lists saves more effort and makes the program shorter and easier to understand than before.

10.2.3 Select the Questions Randomly

With the old version of the program, the user can memorize the answers to the questions because the questions appear in the same order. Therefore, we should make the questions appear randomly. This could easily be done using the built-in function "random.sample," which is in the "random" class. Hence, the part of the code that asks the user will look like this:

```
number_questions = list(range(0, len(Questions_list)))
# try to generate a random permutation of the indices of the questions in the list
random_permutation = random.sample(number_questions, len(number_questions))

for i in range(0,len(Questions_list)):
    answer = int(input(Questions_list[random_permutation[i]]+ " = "))

    if answer == Answers_list[random_permutation[i]]:
        score1 +=1
```

In the code above, the first line creates a list of indices for the list called "Questions_list". It generates a list of numbers from 0 to the length of the Questions_list − 1. This means, for example, that if we have four questions in the list, "number_questions" will be [0,1,2,3]. Then the second line generates a random permutation[1] of the indices stored in the "number_questions" list. The random.sample() function takes two arguments: the list of elements to sample from (in this case, "number_questions") and the number of elements to sample (in this case, the entire length of the "number_questions" list). The result is a new list random_permutation, which contains the same elements as "number_questions", but in a random order. For example, random_permutation might be [2, 0, 3, 1]. Then the loop iterates through the questions_list. For each question, it retrieves the question from the questions_list using the random_permutation[i] index. This ensures that the questions are presented in random order. Next, the code prompts the user for the answer to the current question. It checks whether the user's answer matches the corresponding answer in the Answers_list (also accessed using the random_permutation[i] index). If the answer is correct, it increments the variable called "score1".

10.2.4 Using Functions for Repetitive Parts

As we can see in the code, there are three levels, and at each level, we iterate over the list of questions and answers and calculate the score. Therefore, these parts of the code are similar, and we can simplify the code by creating a function to calculate and return the score. This function will look like the following:

---

[1] Let us say that we have a list, a permutation is when you take all the elements of that list and arrange them in a different order.

```
1  def calculate_score(Questions_list, Answers_list):
2      score = 0
3      number_questions = list(range(0, len(Questions_list)))
4      # try to generate a random permutation of the indices of the questions in the list
5      random_permutation = random.sample(number_questions, len(number_questions))
6
7      for i in range(0, len(Questions_list)):
8          answer = int(input(Questions_list[random_permutation[i]] + " = "))
9
10         if answer == Answers_list[random_permutation[i]]:
11             score += 1
12
13     return score
```

If we want to evaluate how the user will score on the first level, we can call this function as follows:

```
1  Questions_list_Level1=["2x4","3x5","2X6","2X8","4X5"]
2  Answers_list_Level1=[8,15,12, 16,20]
3
4  score1=calculate_score(Questions_list_Level1, Answers_list_Level1)
```

and we can do the same with other levels.

As you can see, using the function has simplified and shortened the code (the link to the code after using the function and randomizing the questions is here: https://github.com/Eng-Alaa/Programming_4_Kids/blob/main/Project_A_3.py).

10.2.5 Capital and Small Letters

In the main code of this project in Chapter 5, there was a simple problem, because the user's answer could be correct, but maybe it is written in lowercase and the correct answer is written in uppercase. Therefore, the program will find that these two answers are different. To solve this problem, we can use the built-in function ".lower()" to convert the user's answer and the correct answer to lowercase letters.

This modification can only be used if the answers are only strings or characters.

The final code after this will be in this link: https://github.com/Eng-Alaa/Programming_4_Kids/blob/main/Project_A_4.py.

10.2.6 Remaining Challenges

After solving some problems in this project by making it simpler, more flexible, shorter, and making the selection of questions random, there are still some remaining challenges that would be the goals of our next chapters. For example:

- Adding many levels (e.g., three levels), these levels are different in their difficulty. The user can start and reach a certain level and then quit, and the program will save their score and the level they reached.
- Allow many users to use the program. Hence, when user A starts the program, it will load their scores (not the scores of other users).

To handle these two points, we need to know how to save the data while our program is running and after it is finished and also how to reload this data. This will be the goal of the next chapter.

10.3   Project B: The Game of Guessing a Number

The original code of the guessing number game was so simple, but there are many other modifications that can make the game more attractive and challenging. The link of the complete code of this project, done in Chapter 5, is here: https://github.com/Eng-Alaa/Programming_4_Kids/blob/main/Guess_number_1.py.

10.3.1 Randomized Guessing Adventure

To make the game really fun, we will let the computer pick a new random number every time you play. This way, you will have to guess a different number each time – it will not be the same number over and over again. Guessing a random number makes the game more exciting and unpredictable. To do this, we should use the built-in random.randint() function as follows:

```
import random

n = random.randint(1, 100) # Generate a random number between 1 and 100
```

So in the code above, instead of guessing the same number each time, we now guess a new number each time. This makes the game more challenging.

10.3.2 Different Levels of Difficulties

In this number guessing game, we can have different levels of difficulty. Let us try three different levels:

- **Level 1 (easy level):** In the first level, we will give the user some helpful hints to make it easier to guess the secret number. If your guess is lower or higher than the secret number, we will tell you so you can try another number. You have five tries to guess the secret number.
- **Level 2 (medium level):** In the second level, we will not give you any hints. The user will just have to guess the number without knowing if it is higher or lower. But you have seven tries to get the right number.
- **Level 3 (hard level):** The third level is the most difficult. Again, we will not give you any hints. And this time, you only have three attempts to guess the secret number before the game ends.

The different levels let you choose how hard you want the game to be. If you want more help, try level 1. If you want more of a challenge, try level 2 or level 3.

The more tries you have, the easier it is to guess the number, and the fewer tries you have, the harder it gets. See if you can beat all three levels.

The code for the three levels is

```python
import random

n = random.randint(1, 100) # Generate a random number between 1 and 100

# Level 1 (5 trials, hint if guess is higher or lower)
print("Level 1: Guess the number (5 trials, with hints)")
for i in range(0, 5):
    num = int(input("Guess a number: "))
    if num == n:
        print("Wonderful, you got the number!")
        break
    elif num < n:
        print("Your guess is lower than the number. Try again.")
    else:
        print("Your guess is higher than the number. Try again.")
else:
    print(f"You lost. The number was {n}.")

# Level 2 (7 trials, no hints)
print("\nLevel 2: Guess the number (7 trials, no hints)")
n = random.randint(1, 100)
for i in range(0, 7):
    num = int(input("Guess a number: "))
    if num == n:
        print("Wonderful, you got the number!")
        break
    else:
        print("Wrong guess, try again.")
else:
    print(f"You lost. The number was {n}.")

# Level 3 (3 trials, no hints)
print("\nLevel 3: Guess the number (3 trials, no hints)")
n = random.randint(1, 100)
for i in range(0, 3):
    num = int(input("Guess a number: "))
    if num == n:
        print("Wonderful, you got the number!")
        break
    else:
        print("Wrong guess, try again.")
else:
    print(f"You lost. The number was {n}.")
```

10.3.3 Add Some Scores

The idea is to have a scoring system that rewards the player for correctly guessing the number while also penalizing them for each incorrect guess. To calculate the user's score, we have an initial score. This score will decrease when the user guesses incorrectly and increase when the user guesses the secret number correctly. Let me explain the suggested scoring system in more detail. This is how it works:

- **Initial score:** The player's score is initialized to 20 points at the start of the game (check the code below).
- **Penalty for incorrect guesses:** For each incorrect guess, the player's score is reduced by four points. This means that the more mistakes the player makes, the lower their final score will be.
- **Reward for correct guesses:** If the player guesses the secret number correctly, his score is increased based on the difficulty of the level:
  - **Level 1 (easy):** If the player correctly guesses the number in level 1, his score is increased by 50 points.
  - **Level 2 (medium):** If the player correctly guesses the number in level 2, his score is increased by 100 points.
  - **Level 3 (hard):** If the player correctly guesses the number in level 3, his score will increase by 150 points.

The idea behind this scoring system is to encourage the player to try his best and be rewarded for their efforts while also adding a sense of challenge and consequence for making mistakes. Here is how the scoring system would work in practice:

- If the player guesses the number correctly on the first attempt in level 1, their final score is 20 (initial score) + 50 (reward for guessing correctly) = 70 points.
- If the player has 70 points, and they guess incorrectly three times in level 2 before guessing the number correctly, their final score is 70 (initial score) − (3 * 4) (penalty for guessing incorrectly) + 100 (reward for guessing correctly) = 158 points.
- If the player has 158 points, and they guess incorrectly two times in level 3 before guessing the number correctly, their final score is 158 − (2 * 4) (penalty for guessing incorrectly) + 150 (reward for guessing correctly) = 300 points.

The modified program for calculating the score at each level is as follows:

```
1  import random
2
3  # Initialize the score
4  score = 20
5
6  # Level 1 (5 trials, hint if guess is higher or lower)
7  print("Level 1: Guess the number (5 trials, with hints)")
8  n = random.randint(1, 100)
```

```
 9  for i in range(0, 5):
10    num = int(input("Guess a number: "))
11    if num == n:
12      print("Wonderful, you got the number!")
13      score += 50
14      break
15    elif num < n:
16      print("Your guess is lower than the number. Try again.")
17    else:
18      print("Your guess is higher than the number. Try again.")
19    score -= 4
20  else:
21    print(f"You lost. The number was {n}.")
22
23  print(f"Your score for Level 1: {score}")
24
25  # Level 2 (7 trials, no hints)
26  print("\nLevel 2: Guess the number (7 trials, no hints)")
27  n = random.randint(1, 100)
28  for i in range(0, 7):
29    num = int(input("Guess a number: "))
30    if num == n:
31      print("Wonderful, you got the number!")
32      score += 100
33      break
34    else:
35      print("Wrong guess, try again.")
36    score -= 4
37  else:
38    print(f"You lost. The number was {n}.")
39
40  print(f"Your score for Level 2: {score}")
41
42  # Level 3 (3 trials, no hints)
43  print("\nLevel 3: Guess the number (3 trials, no hints)")
44  n = random.randint(1, 100)
45  for i in range(0, 3):
46    num = int(input("Guess a number: "))
47    if num == n:
48      print("Wonderful, you got the number!")
49      score += 150
50      break
51    else:
52      print("Wrong guess, try again.")
53    score -= 4
54  else:
55    print(f"You lost. The number was {n}.")
56
57  print(f"Your score for Level 3: {score}")
```

The modified code for this project after adding all new functions is at this link: https://github.com/Eng-Alaa/Programming_4_Kids/blob/main/Guess_number2.py.

10.3.4 Using Functions to Remove Repetitive Parts

I think the code has a lot of repetitive parts. This is because the three levels work almost the same way. Therefore, we can use the function to have all three levels, and we can add more levels if we want. The modified version of this code will be

```python
import random

def guess_the_number(level):
    # Initialize the score
    score = 20

    # Determine the number of trials and the reward based on the level
    if level == 1:
        print("Level 1: Guess the number (5 trials, with hints)")
        num_trials = 5
        reward = 50
    elif level == 2:
        print("Level 2: Guess the number (7 trials, no hints)")
        num_trials = 7
        reward = 100
    elif level == 3:
        print("Level 3: Guess the number (3 trials, no hints)")
        num_trials = 3
        reward = 150
    else:
        print("Invalid level. Please choose 1, 2, or 3.")
        return

    # Generate the random number
    n = random.randint(1, 100)

    # Start the game
    for i in range(num_trials):
        num = int(input("Guess a number: "))
        if num == n:
            print("Wonderful, you got the number!")
            score += reward
            break
        elif level == 1:
            if num < n:
                print("Your guess is lower than the number. Try again.")
            else:
                print("Your guess is higher than the number. Try again.")
        else:
            print("Wrong guess, try again.")
        score -= 4
    else:
        print(f"You lost. The number was {n}.")

    print(f"Your score for Level {level}: {score}")

# Call the function for each level
```

```
48  guess_the_number(1)
49  guess_the_number(2)
50  guess_the_number(3)
```

It looks like using a function increases the number of lines by three. Yes, you are right, but the code is now more organized. Also, if we want to add more levels with different number of trials and rewards, this may add a few lines to the code. Therefore, we can say that using functions makes the program flexible and easy to update.

The final modified code for this project after using a function is at this link: https://github.com/Eng-Alaa/Programming_4_Kids/blob/main/Guess_number3.py.

10.3.5 Remaining Challenges

We should think about how to improve this program or project by allowing many users to use it. Therefore, when user A starts the program, it will load score details (not other users' details). To do this, we need to know how to save the data while our program is running and after it is finished and also how to reload this data. This is the goal of the next chapter.

10.4   Project C: Question Bank

Remember the project "Question Bank" we worked on at the beginning of Chapter 5? (See the link to the project's code here: https://github.com/Eng-Alaa/Programming_4_Kids/blob/main/Project_C.py.) We had a lot of fun with it, but we also found some challenges that were a bit tricky. First, since this project is similar to project A, we can use the same concepts we introduced in project A. Also, we can use the list and functions to make the code simpler and shorter. Further, in the next subsections, we can think about improving this project by handling some of these challenges.

10.4.1 Number of Trials

In our project, we aim to give the user two or more chances to answer a question. So, if the first answer is wrong, the program asks the user the same question again. In other words, each question has two tries. We want to use the for loop to make this part shorter. The code for providing only one chance for each question is as follows:

```
1   if Qs1==A1:
2       print("Correct answer")
3       Score=Score+1
4   elif Qs1!=A1:
5       print("Uncorrect answer, try again")
6       Qs1=input("Who is the leader of Germany in World War 2 : ")
7       if Qs1==A1:
```

```
 8              print("Correct answer")
 9              Score=Score+1
10          if Qs1!=A1:
11              print("Uncorrect answer")
```

Assuming that all the questions and answers are stored in the lists "Questions_list" and "Answers_list", we can use a for loop to iterate through each question, prompt the user for an answer, and check if it matches the corresponding answer. The code below allows the user two attempts for each question.

```
 1  Questions_list=["2+2","3*8","4*4","8+9"]
 2  Answers_list=["4","24","16","17"]
 3  User_answers=[]
 4  Score=0
 5  for i in range(len(Questions_list)): # for each question
 6    Attempts=2
 7    for j in range(0,Attempts):
 8      Answer = input(Questions_list[i])
 9      User_answers.insert(j,Answer)
10      if Answer == Answers_list[i]:
11        print("Correct answer")
12        Score += 1
13        break
14      elif Answer != Answers_list[i]:
15        print("Uncorrect answer, try again")
```

In the code above, we can increase the number of trials by increasing the number of attempts. We can make the above code into a function because this code will be repeated for all topics. The function will look like this:

```
 1  def get_user_answers(Questions_list_H, Answers_list_H):
 2    User_answers_H=[]
 3    Score=0
 4    for i in range(len(Questions_list_H)): # for each question
 5      Attempts = 2
 6      for j in range(0, Attempts):
 7        Answer = input(Questions_list_H[i])
 8        User_answers_H.insert(i, Answer)
 9        if Answer == Answers_list_H[i]:
10          print("Correct answer")
11          Score += 1
12          break
13        elif Answer != Answers_list_H[i]:
14          print("Incorrect answer, try again")
15          Attempts -= 1
16    return User_answers_H, Score
```

In the main program, for each topic, the above function is called, and we send the questions and answers as two lists. Inside the function, the goal is to ask the user these questions, calculate the score, and return the score and the user's answers for display.

In the code above, the outer for loop is used to iterate over the lists of questions and answers. Within this for, we only give the user two attempts, and this could easily be changed by changing the "Attempts" variable. The inner for loop is used to ask the user as many times as the number of attempts.

Now, after using the for loop to count the number of attempts, we can flexibly change the number of attempts, which could control the difficulty of the topic. Hence, if the user has ten attempts, then they will have a good chance to find the solution compared to the case when there is only one attempt.

10.4.2 The Display Function

We can also make another loop to print each question, the user's answer, and the correct answer. The code is as follows:

```
for i in range(0,len(Questions_list_H)):
    print(Questions_list_H[i])
    print("Your answer is: ", User_answers_H[i])
    print("Correct Answer is: ", Answers_list_H[i])
```

To make it easier, let us put the above code into a function called "display_solutions," because this code will be repeated for each topic. The function will be

```
def display_solutions(Questions_list, User_answers, Answers_list):
    print("The Solutions Of The Exam")
    for i in range(0, len(Questions_list)):
        print(Questions_list[i])
        print("Your answer is: ", User_answers[i])
        print("Correct Answer is: ", Answers_list[i])
```

As we can see from the code above, this function does not return anything, it just prints the questions, the user's answers, and the correct answers. We can use this function throughout the program for all topics.

10.4.3 Remaining Challenges

In this project, after solving some problems in this chapter by making it simpler, more flexible, shorter, and making the selection of questions random (as we did in section "Select the Questions Randomly"), there are still some remaining challenges that would be the goals of our next chapters. For example:

- Allows many users to use the program. Hence, when user A starts the program, it will load the score details of that user (not the details of other users).
- Lists the names of the five best scores using this program.

Again, to solve the above two challenges, we need to know how to save the data while our program is running and after it is finished and also how to reload this data. This will be the goal of the next chapter.

10.5   Project D: The Phone List Project

The purpose of this program is to create a phone list that can be used to add, remove, and update details of persons in the phone list. First, we can add the name, address, first phone number, and second phone number for a person. We can also search for a person in this list by entering the name, address, first phone number, or second phone number. We can also remove a person and update some details. Try to design this project from scratch and try to make the code simple and easy to understand by using lists and functions.

10.5.0.1 Add a New Person

In the phone list project, we should first learn how to add a new person to the phone list. The code will simply be

```python
# Initialize the phone list
phone_list = []

def add_person():
    """Function to add a new person to the phone list"""
    name = input("Enter the name: ")
    address = input("Enter the address: ")
    phone1 = input("Enter the first phone number: ")
    phone2 = input("Enter the second phone number: ")
    person = [name, address, phone1, phone2]
    phone_list.append(person)
    print("Person added successfully!")
```

The code above is very simple, just ask the user for the details of the new person, then add them to the list. We used a function to make the code easy to understand.

10.5.0.2 Update a Person's Details

In order to update or change the details of a person in the phone list project, we should first search for this person. If we find this person in the list of people in the phone list, then we should change their data; otherwise, we should inform the user that this person is not found in the list. The person's details are changed by asking the user for the new details and then updating the person's details. The code is simply as follows:

```python
def update_person():
    """Function to update the details of a person in the phone list"""
    search_term = input("Enter the name, address, phone1, or phone2 to search for the person:
        ")
    found_person = None
    for person in phone_list:
        if (
            search_term.lower() in person[0].lower()
            or search_term.lower() in person[1].lower()
            or search_term in person[2]
            or search_term in person[3]
        ):
```

```
12        found_person = person
13        break
14    if found_person:
15      print("Found person:", found_person)
16      new_name = input("Enter the new name (leave blank to keep the same): ")
17      new_address = input("Enter the new address (leave blank to keep the same): ")
18      new_phone1 = input("Enter the new first phone number (leave blank to keep the same): ")
19      new_phone2 = input("Enter the new second phone number (leave blank to keep the
          same): ")
20      if new_name:
21        found_person[0] = new_name
22      if new_address:
23        found_person[1] = new_address
24      if new_phone1:
25        found_person[2] = new_phone1
26      if new_phone2:
27        found_person[3] = new_phone2
28      print("Person updated successfully!")
29    else:
30      print("Person not found.")
```

In the code above, we first ask the user to enter a search term, which can be the person's name, address, or one of their phone numbers. The function then iterates through the phone_list, which is a list of lists, where each inner list represents one person's information. The structure of the inner list is as follows

- person[0]: Name
- person[1]: Address
- person[2]: First phone number
- person[3]: Second phone number

For each person in the list, the function checks if the search term (in lowercase) is present in the person's name, address, or phone numbers. If a match is found, the found_person variable is set to the list of matching persons containing that person's details. Once a person is found, the function prints the person's details and prompts the user to enter new values for the person's name, address, and phone numbers. If the user leaves a field blank, the corresponding value in the person's dictionary is not updated. After the user enters the new values, the function updates the person's details with the new information. If no person is found, the function prints a message indicating that the person was not found.

10.5.1 Delete a Person

To delete a person from the list of persons in your phone list, we should first search for this person. If we find this person in the list of persons in the phone list, then we delete it; otherwise, we should inform the user that this person is not found in the list. The code will be as follows:

```
1  def delete_person():
2      """Function to delete a person from the phone list"""
3      search_term = input("Enter the name, address, phone1, or phone2 to search for the person:
       ")
4      found_person = None
5      for person in phone_list:
6          if (
7              search_term.lower() in person[0].lower()
8              or search_term.lower() in person[1].lower()
9              or search_term in person[2]
10             or search_term in person[3]
11         ):
12             found_person = person
13             break
14     if found_person:
15         phone_list.remove(found_person)
16         print("Person deleted successfully!")
17     else:
18         print("Person not found.")
```

The only difference between the above code and the code for updating a person's details (last section) is that in the above code, the code searches for a person and then removes this person if we found them; otherwise, it prints "person not found."

10.5.2 Search for a Person

Searching for a person from the list of persons in your phone list was already a part of the update and delete code, and the code will simply be

```
1  def search_person():
2      """Function to search for a person in the phone list"""
3      search_term = input("Enter the name, address, phone1, or phone2 to search for the person:
       ")
4      found_persons = []
5      for person in phone_list:
6          if (
7              search_term.lower() in person[0].lower()
8              or search_term.lower() in person[1].lower()
9              or search_term in person[2]
10             or search_term in person[3]
11         ):
12             found_persons.append(person)
13     if found_persons:
14         print("Found persons:")
15         for person in found_persons:
16             print(person)
17     else:
18         print("No person found.")
```

10.5.3 Display All Persons in the Phone List

To show all persons' details of your phone list, the code is simply as follows:

```python
def display_all_persons():
    """Function to display all the persons in the phone list"""
    if not phone_list:
        print("The phone list is empty.")
    else:
        print("All persons in the phone list:")
        for person in phone_list:
            print("Name:", person[0])
            print("Address:", person[1])
            print("Phone1:", person[2])
            print("Phone2:", person[3])
            print("---")
```

The above function displays the details of all the people in the phone list.

The complete code of this project (phone list) is here.

10.5.4 Remaining Challenges

We should think about how to improve this program or project by saving all the details in a file and loading it when we start our program.

10.6   Our Next Adventure in Programming

In this chapter, which serves as a transition point, Kai has tried to use everything he learned in the last four chapters to improve the code in the projects we introduced in Chapter 5. He has already succeeded in making the code very simple, easy, and short, besides solving some challenges in these projects that make the projects work more realistically.

Kai found that an important common point between all the remaining challenges in all the projects was the urgent need to use files to help him store, update, and retrieve data as needed. Therefore, in the next chapter, we will learn with Kai how to create files, store data, and update or delete data in the files. Furthermore, we will learn with Kai how to use this new file handling knowledge to address the challenges in all the projects we are trying to implement.

Saving and Retrieving Data: File Handling Essentials

11

In the last chapters, Kai and we learned the basics of programming, including the use of lists and functions, and how to combine these concepts to create flexible and understandable projects.

Kai has found that a common challenge in all projects is the need to work with files. Using files will allow him to store, update, and retrieve data as needed, which is a critical skill for building robust and practical applications. Therefore, our adventure in this chapter is to discover the power of working with files in Python. We will learn with Kai how to store our important data, retrieve it, and even update or delete it using special Python file commands.

11.1 Introducing Python Files

Files are special places on our computers where we can store all kinds of information – our stories, drawings, school projects, and much more. In programming, files are used to store and access data that we need over and over again. Without files, all the information we work with in our Python programs would be lost as soon as the program is finished. Files allow us to store our data permanently so that we can retrieve it whenever we need it.

There are different types of files, such as text files, image files, spreadsheet files, and all sorts of other file formats. By using files, we can

- Save our work and access it later. This is like saving the questions and answers in projects A and C, saving the users and their scores in project B, or saving the phone list information in program D.
- Organize our data into different categories. This is like creating a file for each user or student in projects A and C to get reports and information on how they are doing and what their progress is.

© Alaa Tharwat 2025
A. Tharwat, *Python Adventures for Young Coders*,
https://doi.org/10.1007/979-8-8688-1067-1_11

- Share our data with others. For example, after we have a student's file, we can email it to their teacher or parents.
- Keep our information safe and secure.

We can work with many different file types, such as text files (.txt)[1] to store written documents and other text-based data. We can also use data files (.csv, .xlsx)[2] to organize information, such as spreadsheets.[3]

The difference between storing data in .txt (text) files and .csv (comma-separated values) files is mainly in the formatting and organization of the information. Text files are the most basic type of file for storing text-based data. They simply contain a sequence of characters, such as words, sentences, and paragraphs. The data is stored in a simple, unstructured format. Therefore, text files are useful for storing things like notes, stories, code, and other free-form text. ".csv" files, on the other hand, are a type of tabular data format that organizes information into rows and columns, similar to a spreadsheet. Each row represents a new record or data entry, and the values in each row are separated by commas (or another delimiter such as a semicolon). In addition, ".csv" files are great for storing structured data such as lists, databases, and data tables. Since most of our projects will need to store data in a specific structure (e.g., store questions and answers, where each question and answer are in the same row), we will focus on working with CSV files in this chapter.

This chapter also introduces data frames, a tool for working with ".csv" files. This tool can take all the information from the ".csv" file and organize it into a table. Then it can help you perform many operations and processes with this information, such as sorting it, filtering it, and even adding new information. We will try to explain the classic way of handling files and also how to use data frames to show how simple this tool is and how it can make your work easier.

11.2   Creating Files and Saving Your Data

11.2.1 Create a File

The first step in working with ".csv" (comma-separated values) files in Python is to use the open() function. This function allows us to create a new ".csv" file or open an existing one. Here is how it works:

---

[1] Think of a text file as a digital piece of paper. It is a simple file that can store words, sentences, and paragraphs – just like you would write in a notebook. Computers can easily read and write these files.

[2] CSV stands for "comma-separated values." Imagine a table where each row is written on a new line and the columns are separated by commas. It is a way to store lists or simple tables of information that computers can understand.

[3] A spreadsheet is like a big table on your computer. It is used to organize and work with lots of information, especially numbers. You can do math, create charts, and sort data easily. The .xlsx file is a type of spreadsheet file used by Microsoft Excel.

```
1  import csv
2  file = open("filename.csv", "w", newline='')
```

In this example, we will create a new ".csv" file named "filename.csv." The "w" tells Python that we want to write new information to the file. The newline=" argument ensures that there are no extra blank lines between rows. We can also open ".csv" files to read or append data. Just change the "w" to "r" for reading or "a" for appending (more details in the next sections). As we can see, we need to import csv; this will allow us to use some built-in functions that handle and work with ".csv" files.

11.2.2 Writing into a File

Once we have created a file using the open() function, we can start writing our information into it using the csv.writer() function. This allows us to add rows of data, which can contain text, numbers, or any other data we want to store. For example, if we want to write a table of favorite books into our file called "FirstTest.csv," the code will look like this:

```
1   import csv
2
3   file = open("FirstTest.csv", "w", newline='')
4   writer = csv.writer(file)
5   writer.writerow(["Book Title", "Author"])
6   writer.writerow(["Harry Potter and the Sorcerer's Stone", "J.K. Rowling"])
7   writer.writerow(["To Kill a Mockingbird", "Harper Lee"])
8   writer.writerow(["Pride and Prejudice", "Jane Austen"])
9   writer.writerow(["The Great Gatsby", "F. Scott Fitzgerald"])
10  file.close()
```

In the code above, the csv.writer() function creates a writer object that allows us to easily add rows of data to the ".csv" file using the writerow() method. After we are done writing to a file, it is really important that we close it using the ".close()" method. This ensures that all of our data is saved correctly and that the file is ready to be reopened later.

By following these three steps – opening the file, writing to it, and then closing it – we can create and save our own custom files in Python. This is the basis for all sorts of exciting file-based projects.

11.2.3 Writing a List to a File

Now let us try to store the contents of lists, which is important for many of our projects. The previous code will be slightly modified as follows:

```
1   import csv
2
3   # Define the list of questions
4   question_list = [
5       ["Question"],
6       ["What is the capital of France?"],
7       ["What is the capital of Egypt?"],
8       ["What is the largest planet in our solar system?"],
9       ["What is the currency used in Japan?", "Yen"]
10  ]
11
12  # Open the CSV file for writing
13  with open("question_list.csv", "w", newline="") as file:
14      writer = csv.writer(file)
15
16      # Write each row of the list to the CSV file
17      for row in question_list:
18          writer.writerow(row)
```

In this updated program or code, we have created a header for the column of questions and called it "Question." This is because, as we will see later, we can have many columns. Therefore, the column name or header will inform us about the information stored in that column. Next, in the code above, we have defined the question_list. Then we have opened a new ".csv" file called "question_list.csv" for writing. Inside the with block, we create a csv.writer object and use its writerow() function to write each row of the question_list to the CSV file.

In the above code, the "with" statement starts a block of code, and it is used to manage the life cycle of the file we are opening. Moreover, the statement "as file" assigns the opened file to a variable called file. This variable can then be used inside the with block to perform operations on the file. The advantage of using the with statement is that it automatically takes care of closing the file when we are done with it. This is important because when you open a file, you need to make sure you close it when you are finished to free up the computer resources (e.g., the memory) used by the file. Therefore, by using the "with" statement, you do not have to worry about manually closing the file using file.close() at the end of your code. The with statement will automatically close the file for you when the code inside the "with" block is finished executing.

After running this code, you should find a new file called "question_list.csv" in the same directory as your Python script. If you open it, you will see the questions you saved, formatted in a table-like structure.

Let us use the data frame to write a list to a ".csv" file. The code will simply be

```
import csv
import pandas as pd
# Define the list of questions
question_list = [
    ["Question"],
    ["What is the capital of France?"],
    ["What is the capital of Egypt?"],
    ["What is the largest planet in our solar system?"],
    ["What is the currency used in Japan?", "Yen"]
]

# Create the DataFrame
question_df = pd.DataFrame(question_list)

# Save the DataFrame to a CSV file
question_df.to_csv("question_list.csv", index=False, header=False)
```

In the code above, as you can see, we create a pandas[4] data frame called question_df from the question_list data we already have. We then use the to_csv() method to write the data frame to the question_list.csv file. The index=False parameter tells Pandas not to include the row index as a separate column in the ".csv" file. Also, the header=False parameter tells Pandas not to include the column names as the first row in the ".csv" file.

If we have two lists, for example, one for the questions and another for the answers, the program will simply update as follows:

```
import csv

# Define the lists of questions and answers
questions_list = [
    "What is the capital of France?",
    "What is the capital of Egypt?",
    "What is the largest planet in our solar system?",
    "What is the currency used in Japan?"
]

answers_list = [
    "Paris",
    "Cairo",
    "Jupiter",
    "Yen"
]
```

---

[4] There are many data frames, but the most popular is the "Panda" data frame. To install pandas, follow this link: https://pandas.pydata.org/docs/getting_started/install.html.

```
18  # Open the CSV file for writing
19  with open("question_list.csv", "w", newline="") as file:
20      writer = csv.writer(file)
21
22      # Write each row to the CSV file
23      for i in range(len(questions_list)):
24          writer.writerow([questions_list[i], answers_list[i]])
```

In this modified version, we saved the two lists to the ".csv" file. To do this, we used a for loop to iterate over the questions_list and answers_list simultaneously. For each iteration, we write a row to the ".csv" file containing the question and the corresponding answer.

Now we can store all the information we need in files. For example, we can store the scores of each user in projects A, B, and C. Also, we can store the details of persons in project D.

Let us also try to use the data frame to store the two lists in the above program. The code simply will be

```
1   import csv
2   import pandas as pd
3
4   # Define the lists of questions and answers
5   questions_list = [
6       "What is the capital of France?",
7       "What is the capital of Egypt?",
8       "What is the largest planet in our solar system?",
9       "What is the currency used in Japan?"
10  ]
11
12  answers_list = [
13      "Paris",
14      "Cairo",
15      "Jupiter",
16      "Yen"
17  ]
18
19  # Create the DataFrame
20  question_df = pd.DataFrame({
21      "Question": questions_list,
22      "Answer": answers_list
23  })
24
25  # Write the DataFrame to a CSV file
26  question_df.to_csv("question_list.csv", index=False)
```

As we can see in the code above, the data frame makes our code simpler and shorter. After defining the questions_list and answers_list as before, we created a pandas data frame question_df using the pd.DataFrame() function. This data frame has two columns: "Question" and "Answer," corresponding to the two lists. We use the to_csv() function to write the data frame to the file "question_list.csv."

11.2.4 Reading File Contents

To read the contents of a file, to do some processing on it, or to display it, we must first open the file using the open() function. The open() function takes two arguments: the file path and the mode. For reading, the mode should be "r" (read mode). For example:

```
file = open("file.csv", "r")
```

Once the ".csv" file is opened, we can use the csv.reader() function to read the contents. The csv.reader() function returns an iterator that returns each row of the ".csv" file as a list. For example, to read the contents of a file called "data.csv," the code would be

```
import csv

with open("data.csv", "r") as file:
    reader = csv.reader(file)
    for row in reader:
        print(row)
```

In the code above, we have again used the "with" statement as the beginning of a block of code that manages the life cycle of the file we are opening. After reading each row with the csv.reader() function, we can display the contents of the file line by line.

11.2.4.1 Reading into Lists

Let us reload the contents of the file "question_list.csv" that we saved in the previous section. The following code loads the data from the file and saves it in two lists:

```
# Read the CSV file and load the questions and answers into lists
questions_list = []
answers_list = []

with open("question_list.csv", "r") as file:
    reader = csv.reader(file)
    for row in reader:
        questions_list.append(row[0])
        answers_list.append(row[1])
```

In the code above, we created two empty lists: questions_list and answers_list. We then opened the ".csv" file in read-only mode using the "with" statement and the csv.reader() function to read the contents. For each row in the ".csv" file, we append the first element (the question) to questions_list and the second element (the answer) to answers_list. After reading the entire file, we can now work with the questions_list and answers_list as needed.

Now we can store hundreds of questions and answers in the ".csv" file in projects A and C, and then at the beginning of our program, we can load them and randomly select from them to ask the user or student. Further, we can also add the students' scores and some details of the players in program C. Furthermore, in project D (phone list) we can add all the information of all persons and restore them when we need to display them. The question now is how to modify or update these files. The answer will be given in the next section.

11.2.4.2 Reading into Data Frames

Let us reload the contents of the same file "question_list.csv" but into a data frame. This could be done like this:

```
1  import pandas as pd
2
3  # Read the CSV file into a Pandas data frame
4  df = pd.read_csv("question_list.csv")
5
6  # The data frame will have two columns: 'Question' and 'Answer'
7  print(df)
```

The code above shows how the data frame reads the contents of the file in one line. The data frame will have two columns, "Question" and "Answer," which correspond to the two columns in the ".csv" file. Then we can access the data from the data frame and perform any other operations. For example, let us extract the questions and answers from the data frame and store them in two separate lists as follows:

```
1  # Get the list of questions
2  questions_list = df['Question'].tolist()
3
4  # Get the list of answers
5  answers_list = df['Answer'].tolist()
```

11.3   Updating Existing Files

We can update the data in a .csv file by appending new data to it. To do this, we should open the file in "append" mode ("a") and use the csv.writer() function as follows:

```
1  open("data.csv", "a", newline="")
```

For example, to append a row of data consisting of three columns – name, age, city – the code would be

```
1  # Open the CSV file in append mode
2  with open("data.csv", "a", newline="") as file:
3      writer = csv.writer(file)
4      # Write a new row to the CSV file
5      writer.writerow(["New Name", 30, "New City"])
```

Therefore, the only difference between appending new data to an existing file and writing the data to a new or existing file is that when appending new data or in append mode, any new data written to the file is added to the end of the existing content. Thus, the main data remains in the file and the new data is added at the end.

In the write mode, the entire contents of the file are replaced with the new data you write. Let us try to write the above code, but using data frame, the code will be

```
# Assuming you have an existing DataFrame called 'df'
# Add a new row to the DataFrame
df = df.append({'Name': 'New Name', 'Age': 30, 'City': 'New City'}, ignore_index=True)

# Write the DataFrame to the CSV file in append mode
df.to_csv('data.csv', mode='a', header=False, index=False)
```

In the code above, assuming we have an existing Pandas data frame named df, we use the append() method to add a new row to the data frame. Once the new row is added to the data frame, we use the to_csv() method to write the updated data frame to the data.csv file. Again, the mode='a' parameter tells Pandas to append the data to the existing file instead of overwriting it.

Let us try to add a question to the ".csv" file we created earlier. The code will look like this:

```
# Open the CSV file in append mode
with open("question_list.csv", "a", newline="") as file:
    writer = csv.writer(file)
    # Write a new row to the CSV file
    writer.writerow(["What is the capital of France?", "Paris"])
```

Again, in the above code, if we change the append mode ("a") to write mode ("w"), the contents of the file will be replaced with the new data. Now, using data frame the above code will be

```
question_df = question_df.append({'Question': 'What is the capital of France?', 'Answer': 'Paris'
    }, ignore_index=True)
question_df.to_csv('question_list.csv', mode='a', header=False, index=False)
```

The question is, what if we want to search for a piece of data in the file and modify it? Here, we can first read the entire ".csv" file into a list of lists (e.g., list of names list, list of ages, and list of cities). Then we modify the data by changing the age in the second row, second column as follows:

```
import csv

with open("data.csv", "w", newline="") as file:
    writer = csv.writer(file)
    writer.writerow(["Name", "Age", "City"]) # Write the header
    # Add some initial data
    writer.writerow(["Alice", "30", "New York"])
    writer.writerow(["Bob", "25", "Los Angeles"])
    writer.writerow(["Charlie", "35", "Chicago"])

# Read the entire contents into a list
with open("data.csv", "r") as file:
    reader = csv.reader(file)
    data = list(reader) # Read the entire contents into a list
```

```
16  # Check if the CSV has headers and store them
17  headers = data[0] if data else []
18  data = data[1:]  # Exclude the header row for processing
19
20  # Ask the user for the age to modify
21  age_to_modify = int(input("Enter the age you want to modify: "))
22
23  # Search for the row with the specified age
24  row_to_modify = None
25  for i, row in enumerate(data):
26      if len(row) >= 2 and int(row[1]) == age_to_modify:
27          row_to_modify = i
28          break
29
30  if row_to_modify is None:
31      print(f"No row found with age {age_to_modify}. Exiting...")
32      exit()
33
34  # Prompt the user for the new value
35  new_value = input(f"Enter the new value for row {row_to_modify + 1}, column 2 (Age): ")
36
37  # Update the data
38  data[row_to_modify][1] = new_value
39
40  # Open the CSV file in write mode to overwrite the contents
41  with open("data.csv", "w", newline="") as file:
42      writer = csv.writer(file)
43      writer.writerow(headers)  # Write the header back to the file
44      writer.writerows(data)  # Write the updated data back to the file
45
46  print("Data updated successfully.")
```

As we can see, we first read the data and then ask the user for the age they want to update. Then the code searches for it; if this age is already in the data, we ask the user for the new age value and update it; otherwise, we exit and stop the code. Next, we open the file in write mode and use the csv.writer().writerows() function to write the updated data back to the file.

If we try to write the above code using data frames, the code will be

```
1   # Read the CSV file into a DataFrame
2   df = pd.read_csv("data.csv")
3
4   # Ask the user for the age to modify
5   age_to_modify = int(input("Enter the age you want to modify: "))
6
7   # Search for the row with the specified age
8   row_to_modify = df[df["Age"] == age_to_modify].index[0]
9
10  if row_to_modify is None:
11      print(f"No row found with age {age_to_modify}. Exiting...")
12      exit()
13
14  # Prompt the user for the new value
```

```
15  new_value = input(f"Enter the new value for row {row_to_modify+1}, column 2: ")
16
17  # Update the data
18  df.at[row_to_modify, "Age"] = new_value
19
20  # Write the updated DataFrame back to the CSV file
21  df.to_csv("data.csv", index=False)
```

From the above code, it is clear that the reading process in data frames is much simpler than in the above code, but the surprise is the search facility that data frames offer. As we can see, in just one line we can get the index of the row we want to update. Then, we simply update it and write the data in the data frame to the file. This update also works if we want to delete some data from the file.

11.4 Deleting Files

With the ".csv" file, we can use the os.remove() function to remove the file as follows:

```
1  import os
2
3  # Delete the file
4  os.remove("my_data.csv")
```

The above code uses the os.remove() function to delete the file named "my_data.csv." The os module (short for "operating system") provides this function to help you delete files.

11.5 Project D: The Phone List Project

We want to continue the project we started in Chapter 10. In the old version of the project, we managed to add, update, and delete people from our phone list (the code is here). As you remember, we always lost our data right after we finished our program. This is because we did not use files. Let us use what we have learned in this chapter about working with files to improve our program and make it more reliable and professional by adding the option of saving the data in ".csv" files.

11.5.1 Add a New Person

In the last version, we already managed to allow the user of our program to add a new person to their phone list program. The code was as follows:

```python
phone_list = []

def add_person():
    """Function to add a new person to the phone list"""
    name = input("Enter the name: ")
    address = input("Enter the address: ")
    phone1 = input("Enter the first phone number: ")
    phone2 = input("Enter the second phone number: ")

    # Store person's information in a list
    person = [name, address, phone1, phone2]  # Use a list instead of a dictionary
    phone_list.append(person)
    print("Person added successfully!")
```

Using a data frame, we can now modify the above code to save the data in the ".csv" file, as follows:

```python
if not os.path.isfile('phone_list.csv'):
    phone_df = pd.DataFrame(phone_list)
    phone_df.to_csv('phone_list.csv', index=False)
    print("Person added successfully!")
    # If the file exists, append the new data to it
else:
    phone_df = pd.DataFrame(phone_list)
    phone_df.to_csv('phone_list.csv', mode='a', header=False, index=False)
    print("Person added successfully!")
```

In the code above, we first check if the file phone_list.csv exists using os.path.isfile('phone_list.csv'). If the file does not exist, we create a new data frame and write it to the file. If the file already exists, we append the new data to the file using the mode='a' and header=False parameters in the to_csv() method.

11.5.2 Update a Person

In the last version, we used the following code to update a person's data in our phone list:

```python
def update_person():
    """Function to update the details of a person in the phone list"""
    search_term = input("Enter the name, address, phone1, or phone2 to search for the person: ")
    found_person = None
    for person in phone_list:
        if (
            search_term.lower() in person["name"].lower()
```

```
8        or search_term.lower() in person["address"].lower()
9        or search_term in person["phone1"]
10       or search_term in person["phone2"]
11   ):
12       found_person = person
13       break
14   if found_person:
15       print("Found person:", found_person)
16       new_name = input("Enter the new name (leave blank to keep the same): ")
17       new_address = input("Enter the new address (leave blank to keep the same): ")
18       new_phone1 = input("Enter the new first phone number (leave blank to keep the same): ")
19       new_phone2 = input("Enter the new second phone number (leave blank to keep the
         same): ")
20       if new_name:
21           found_person["name"] = new_name
22       if new_address:
23           found_person["address"] = new_address
24       if new_phone1:
25           found_person["phone1"] = new_phone1
26       if new_phone2:
27           found_person["phone2"] = new_phone2
28       print("Person updated successfully!")
29   else:
30       print("Person not found.")
31
```

To save the updated data into the ".csv" file of the phone list, using a data frame, we should just add this simple code:

```
1   # Create or update the DataFrame
2   phone_df = pd.DataFrame(phone_list)
3   phone_df.to_csv('phone_list.csv', index=False)
```

11.5.3 Delete a Person

The latest version uses the following code to update a person from the phone list:

```
1   def update_person():
2       """Function to update the details of a person in the phone list and save to CSV"""
3       search_term = input("Enter the name, address, phone1, or phone2 to search for the person:
          ")
4       phone_df = pd.DataFrame(phone_list)
5       found_person = phone_df[(phone_df['name'].str.contains(search_term, case=False)) |
6                   (phone_df['address'].str.contains(search_term, case=False)) |
7                   (phone_df['phone1'] == search_term) |
8                   (phone_df['phone2'] == search_term)]
9
10      if not found_person.empty:
11          print("Found person:", found_person.to_dict('records')[0])
12          new_name = input("Enter the new name (leave blank to keep the same): ")
13          new_address = input("Enter the new address (leave blank to keep the same): ")
```

```
14    new_phone1 = input("Enter the new first phone number (leave blank to keep the same): ")
15    new_phone2 = input("Enter the new second phone number (leave blank to keep the
         same): ")
16
17    # Update the found person's information
18    if new_name:
19       found_person['name'] = new_name
20    if new_address:
21       found_person['address'] = new_address
22    if new_phone1:
23       found_person['phone1'] = new_phone1
24    if new_phone2:
25       found_person['phone2'] = new_phone2
26
27    # Use a for loop to iterate through each row in found_person
28   for index in range(len(found_person)):
29    phone = found_person.iloc[index]['phone']  # Get the phone number from the current
         row
30    phone_list.append(phone)  # Append the phone number to phone_list
31
32    # Update the DataFrame and write to CSV
33    phone_df = pd.DataFrame(phone_list)
34    phone_df.to_csv('phone_list.csv', index=False)
35
36    print("Person updated successfully and saved to phone_list.csv!")
37   else:
38    print("Person not found.")
39
```

In the function above, we use the data frame to search for the person based on the data that the user entered and stored in the variable called search_term. When the person is found, we print the details and prompt the user for the new information. This new data (new_name, new_address, new_phone1, and new_phone2) that the program receives from the user will update the information of the person we found. Then the updated data will be saved to the data frame, and the data frame will be saved to the ".csv" file.

We want to update the above version of the code and give the ability of our program to delete some data from the ".csv" file that stores the whole data. The code will be as follows:

```
1   def delete_person():
2     """Function to delete a person from the phone list"""
3     search_term = input("Enter the name, address, phone1, or phone2 to search for the person:
         ")
4     found_person = None
5     for person in phone_list:
6       if (
7         search_term.lower() in person["name"].lower()
8         or search_term.lower() in person["address"].lower()
9         or search_term in person["phone1"]
10        or search_term in person["phone2"]
11      ):
```

```
12      found_person = person
13      break
14   if found_person:
15      phone_list.remove(found_person)
16      print("Person deleted successfully!")
17   else:
18      print("Person not found.")
19
```

11.5.4 Search for a Person

To search for a person in the phone list, the old version of the code was

```
1   def search_person():
2      """Function to search for a person in the phone list"""
3      search_term = input("Enter a name, address, or phone number to find: ")
4
5      found_persons = []  # List to store found persons
6
7      for index, person in phone_list.iterrows():  # Go through each person
8         # Check if the search term matches any information
9         if (search_term.lower() in person['name'].lower() or
10           search_term.lower() in person['address'].lower() or
11           search_term in person['phone1'] or
12           search_term in person['phone2']):
13           found_persons.append(person)  # Add to found list
14
15      # Show results
16      if found_persons:
17         print("Found persons:")
18         for person in found_persons:
19            print(person)
20      else:
21         print("No person found.")
```

In the above code, this line "for index, person in phone_list.iterrows()" helps you look at each person in the phone_list one by one, where "phone_list.iterrows():" is a special way to go through each row in the phone_list. Each row represents a person's information (like their name, address, and phone number). The part of the code "for index, person in ..." means that you are creating two things for each row: an **index**, a number that tells you which row you're looking at (like the first row is 0, the second is 1, etc.), and a **person**, all the information about that person from that row.

The updated version simply uses the data frame to search for a person in the phone list. The modified version is

```
1  def search_person():
2    """Function to search for a person in the phone list"""
3    search_term = input("Enter the name, address, phone1, or phone2 to search for the person:
       ")
4    phone_df = pd.DataFrame(phone_list)
5    found_persons = phone_df[(phone_df['name'].str.contains(search_term, case=False)) |
6               (phone_df['address'].str.contains(search_term, case=False)) |
7               (phone_df['phone1'] == search_term) |
8               (phone_df['phone2'] == search_term)]
9
10   if not found_persons.empty:
11     print("Found persons:")
12     print(found_persons.to_string(index=False))
13   else:
14     print("No person found.")
15
```

Much of the above code has already been explained in the previous section. However, the above code searches for a person using the data frame; if the person is found, the program prints their data; otherwise, it prints the message "No person found."

11.5.5 Display the Data of All Persons

To display all stored data for printing, for example, the data frame could also be used as follows:

```
1  def display_all_persons():
2    """Function to display all the persons in the phone list"""
3    phone_list = pd.read_csv('phone_list.csv').to_dict('records')
4    phone_df = pd.DataFrame(phone_list)
5    if phone_df.empty:
6      print("The phone list is empty.")
7    else:
8      print("All persons in the phone list:")
9      print(phone_df.to_string(index=False))
10
```

The code of the modified version of this project (phone list) that was done in Chapter 10 is here.

11.6   Project A: Math Test

The remaining goals we want to achieve in this project could be done using files.

11.6.1 Reading Questions and Answers from Files

One of the goals is to make available the questions and answers that are already in a file, and we just load them and pick some of them randomly and ask the user. This code is done as follows:

```
Questions_list_Level1 = []
Answers_list_Level1 = []

with open("question_list_Level1.csv", "r") as file:
    reader = csv.reader(file)
    for row in reader:
        Questions_list_Level1.append(row[0])
        Answers_list_Level1.append(row[1])
```

Since we have three levels in our program, we will perform these steps three times. To save time and lines of code, we can make the step of reading questions and answers as a function and call it from the main program. This function will be

```
def load_questions_and_answers(file_name):
    Questions_list_Level1 = []
    Answers_list_Level1 = []

    with open(file_name, "r") as file:
        reader = csv.reader(file)
        next(reader)  # Skip the header row
        for row in reader:
            Questions_list_Level1.append(row[0])
            Answers_list_Level1.append(row[1])

    return Questions_list_Level1, Answers_list_Level1
```

Now, to add many levels, we just need to add new questions that have different levels of difficulty.

Since we are doing the same steps for each level, we will do it using the for loop. Hence, the code will simply be as follows:

```
No_levels=3
No_questions=5
for i in range(0,No_levels):
    print("Let's start at the level: ", i+1)
    File_name="question_list_Level" + str(i+1) + ".csv"
    Questions_list_Level, Answers_list_Level=load_questions_and_answers(File_name)
    score=calculate_score(Questions_list_Level, Answers_list_Level)
    print(f"\nTest {i} Results:")
    print("You answered " + str(score) + " out of", No_questions, "questions correctly.")
```

```
10    Total_score+=score
11    if score/No_questions<0.5: # fail
12        # To do: save the total score and the max. level and quit
13        break
```

In the above code, we use the for loop to make a loop for each level. The first challenge in this code was the filename; how to make it flexible to change? First, the filenames are "question_list_Level1.csv," "question_list_Level2.csv," and "question_list_Level3.csv." Thus, only a number in the filename is the part that is changed; this number is simply the value of i+1. Therefore, we can make the filename flexible and then call this file and get the questions and answers using the load_questions_and_answers function. Then we can call the calculate_score function to ask the user and calculate the score and return it. If the user answered more than 50% correctly, they can go to the next level; otherwise, the program will quit.

11.6.2 Registration and Login for Users

In this project and also the others, we may want to have each user register with a username and password. This is important to give the user something like an account. Hence, the user can log in with their username and password, and the program can store some information related to the user and what they are doing with our program. For example, what is the highest score of a user in project A, and what is their last maximum level? Therefore, this user can start their test from this level. This registration and login of users is an important step in many projects, maybe all of ours.

To do this task, we can do the following:

- Let us first create a ".csv" file in the folder of our program; this file will store all the user details; let us call it "users_data.csv."
- Then, at the beginning of our program, we should load all the users in a list; call it users. The code of this step is as follows:

```
1    # User registration and login
2    users = []
3    if os.path.exists("users_data.csv"):
4        with open("users_data.csv", "r") as file:
5            reader = csv.reader(file)
6            for row in reader:
7                users.append([row[0], row[1]])
```

In the code above, we have only used this statement "os.path.exists ("users_data.csv")" to check if the file has already been created and if it exists. If the file exists, the code reads all the rows in the file and adds them to the list, which is called users.

- In a loop, the program repeatedly asks the user to choose between two options: registering or logging in, as follows:

```
1  while True:
2      print("Welcome to the math exam!")
3      print("1. Register")
4      print("2. Login")
5      choice = input("Enter your choice (1 or 2): ")
```

1. If the user is new, they can register with a new username and password. This is very simple, as we mentioned before, just append a line to the end of the file.

```
1      username = input("Enter a username: ")
2      password = input("Enter a password: ")
3      with open("users_data.csv", "a", newline="") as file:
4          writer = csv.writer(file)
5          writer.writerow([username, password])
6      print("Registration successful!")
7      users.append([username, password])
8      break
```

The above code simply asks the user for their username and password, appends that line to the file, and then uses the break statement at the end to exit this infinite loop (loop forever).

2. If the user is already registered, they can log in with their username and password. If the user enters their username and password, they can access and use the program; otherwise, they cannot use our program. The code for this part is

```
1  login_username = input("Enter your username: ")
2  login_password = input("Enter your password: ")
3  Found=False
4  for user in users:
5      if user[0] == login_username and user[1] == login_password:
6          Found=True
7          break
8      else:
9          continue
10
11     if Found==True:
12         print("Welcome")
13     else:
14         print("Wrong password or username")
15         break
```

The above code also prompts the user to enter their username and password and uses the for loop to search if the username and password exist and are correct. If our program finds the user's username and password in the list of users, the boolean variable "Found" is changed to true, which means that the username and password are correct; then the code uses break to end this for loop. If the username and/or password are incorrect, the Found variable remains false. At the end of this part, we can print "Welcome" to the user if they enter correct login details; otherwise, the code will print "Wrong password or username."

3. The third choice, if the user enters numbers other than the normal choices 1 and 2, the program will print "Invalid choice. Please try again." and then prompts the user to reenter the right choice until a normal choice is obtained.

Finally, as we mentioned before, since this piece of code could be used with different projects, we want to make it in a function. This function will be

```python
def user_registration_and_login():
    Login_Register=0
    Current_User=[]
    users = []
    if os.path.exists("users_data.csv"):
        with open("users_data.csv", "r") as file:
            reader = csv.reader(file)
            for row in reader:
                users.append([row[0], row[1]])

    Found = False
    while True:
        print("Welcome to the math exam!")
        print("1. Register")
        print("2. Login")
        choice = input("Enter your choice (1 or 2): ")

        if choice == "1":
            Login_Register=0
            username = input("Enter a username: ")
            password = input("Enter a password: ")
            with open("users_data.csv", "a", newline="") as file:
                writer = csv.writer(file)
                writer.writerow([username, password])
            print("Registration successful!")
            users.append([username, password])
            Current_User=[username, password]
            break
        elif choice == "2":
            Login_Register=1
            login_username = input("Enter your username: ")
            login_password = input("Enter your password: ")
            Found = False
            for user in users:
                if user[0] == login_username and user[1] == login_password:
```

```
36          Found = True
37          Current_User=[login_username,login_password]
38          break
39        else:
40          continue
41      break
42    else:
43      print("Invalid choice. Please try again.")
44      user_registration_and_login()
45      break
46
47  return Login_Register, Found, Current_User
```

As we can see in the above code, this function returns the variable "Login_Register"; this tells us if the user wants to register as a new user or log in to an existing account. Also, the function returns "Found"; if the user is trying to log in, this tells us if their login details are correct. If they are wrong, the user will need to exit. Furthermore, the function returns the variable called "Current_User" that has the name and password of the user to use their details during the execution of the program. Now we can easily copy this function to other projects.

11.7   Project B: The Game of Guessing a Number

We should think about how to improve this program or project by allowing many users to use the program. So when user A starts the program, it will load their scores (not the scores of other users). We can also use the registration step we did before.

11.8   Project C: Question Bank

Remember the project we worked on earlier in Chapter 5? We found a few things that were a bit tricky, and now we are going to use the lists and functions to achieve some of the goals we mentioned before. First, since this project is similar to project A, we can use the same concepts that we introduced with project A. Hence, now we can read the questions and answers directly from files. Further, we can use the files to save also scores and other details about the users.

11.9 Glossary

Term	Definition
open("filename.csv", "w", newline=")	The open() function is used to open a file for reading, writing, or appending. In this example, the file "filename.csv" is opened in write mode ("w"), and the newline=" parameter is used to ensure that no extra blank lines are added between rows when writing data to the file.
file.close()	A method used to close a file that has been opened with the open() function. It is important to close files after you are done working with them to free up system resources and ensure all data is properly saved.
writer = csv.writer(file)	A line of code that creates a ".csv" writer object. This object is used to write data to a ".csv" file that has been opened. The "csv.writer()" function is part of Python's CSV module and makes it easier to properly format data for ".csv" files.
reader = csv.reader(file)	A line of code that creates a ".csv" reader object. This object is used to read data from a ".csv" file that has been opened. The "csv.reader()" function is part of Python's CSV module and helps to properly interpret and extract data from ".csv" files.
import csv	A Python statement that brings in the CSV module. This module provides special tools and functions for working with ".csv" (comma-separated values) files, making it easier to read from and write to these types of files in your programs.
import pandas as pd	A Python statement that imports the pandas library and gives it a short nickname "pd." Pandas is a powerful tool for working with structured data, like tables and spreadsheets. It provides many functions to analyze, clean, and manipulate data easily.
q_df = pd.DataFrame(q_list)	A pandas command that converts a list called q_list into a data frame called "q_df."
questions_list = df['Question'].tolist()	A line of code that takes a column named "Question" from a pandas DataFrame "df" and turns it into a Python list called "questions_list." This is useful when you want to work with the data from one column as a simple list of items.
import os	A Python statement that brings in the "os" (operating system) module. This module provides a way for your Python program to interact with your computer's operating system (e.g., Windows), allowing you to do things like work with files and folders or get information about the computer environment.
os.remove("my_data.csv")	A command in Python that is used to delete the file called "my_data.csv."

11.10 Our Next Adventure in Programming

In this chapter, Kai has learned how to use files to meet and handle some of the challenges he has found in the projects he is trying to implement, most of which were introduced in Chapter 10. He has already managed to make the projects more real by using files to store and retrieve data as needed.

Kai realizes that he needs to create something interesting, and he dreams of making a simple game that could add some entertainment and a fun environment. He decides that his new project will be to implement his first game. It is really interesting not only to play games but also to create them. Together with Kai, in the next chapter, we will learn about some built-in functions that allow us to work with graphics and actions, and then we will use this knowledge to create our own simple game.

From Projects to Play: Designing and Implementing a Fun Game

12

In the last chapter, Kai and we learned how to use files to improve all the projects we are trying to implement. This new feature allows us to store, update, and retrieve data as needed.

Kai wants to create something interesting and fun, so he decides that his new project will be to implement his first simple game. He believes that not only playing games but also creating them can be an exciting and rewarding experience. Together with Kai, in this chapter we will learn about some built-in Python functions that allow us to work with graphics, and then we will apply this knowledge to create our own simple game.

12.1 Creating Our Game

12.1.1 Creating Background

The first step in designing our game is to create a background. In this simple game, we want a black background to serve as a place to display our game elements. To create this background, the code is as follows:

```python
import pygame

# Initialize Pygame
pygame.init()

# Set the window size
window_width = 800
window_height = 600
window = pygame.display.set_mode((window_width, window_height))

# Set the window title
pygame.display.set_caption("Simple Game")

```

© Alaa Tharwat 2025
A. Tharwat, *Python Adventures for Young Coders*,
https://doi.org/10.1007/979-8-8688-1067-1_12

```
14  # Set the background color to black
15  background_color = (0, 0, 0)
16
17  # Game loop
18  running = True
19  while running:
20    # Handle events
21    for event in pygame.event.get():
22      if event.type == pygame.QUIT:
23        running = False
24
25    # Fill the background with black color
26    window.fill(background_color)
27
28    # Update the display
29    pygame.display.update()
30
31  # Quit Pygame
32  pygame.quit()
```

In the code above, we use the Pygame library[1] to create the black background. First, we initialize the Pygame library by calling pygame.init(). Then we set the window size to 800 pixels wide and 600 pixels high using pygame.display.set_mode(). Thus, we can change these dimensions to make our game have a large or small area. The window caption is set to "Simple game" using pygame.display.set_caption(). Then we define the background color as a group of RGB (red, green, blue) values, where each value ranges from 0 to 255. In this case, we set the background color to black (0, 0, 0). If we want to change the background to red color, the color will be (255, 0, 0).

In the game loop, we handle events (in this case, the user closing the window) and also fill the window with the black background color using window.fill(background_color). An event is something that happens in a game or program that the computer can react to. It is like a signal that tells the program to do something. Here are some examples of events:

- **Key press**: When you press a key on the keyboard, like the spacebar to jump. For example, when the user presses the spacebar, an object might jump or shoot a bullet.
- **Mouse click**: When you click the mouse to shoot or select something. The right and left clicks could also be different events.
- **Touch**: When you tap the screen on a tablet or phone.
- **Time**: When a certain amount of time has passed, like a timer running out.

Finally, in the above code, we update the display to reflect the changes using pygame.display.update(). Next, we quit Pygame with pygame.quit().

---

[1] To install Pygame, follow this link: https://www.pygame.org/wiki/GettingStarted.

This simple background setup provides a solid foundation for building our game and adding more elements to it.

12.1.2 Creating a Shape

The next step in our game is to design an object, for example, a rectangle, in a certain position with a certain color. Here is the code for this new object:

```
1  # Set the color for the rectangle
2  rectangle_color = (255, 255, 255)
3
4  # Set the dimensions for the rectangle
5  rectangle_width = 100
6  rectangle_height = 50
7  rectangle_x = 100
8  rectangle_y = 275
```

In the code above, we have a simple white rectangle on a black background. We also set rectangle_width to 100 and rectangle_height to 50. We also set rectangle_x and rectangle_y to position the rectangle on the screen. Inside the game loop, we draw the rectangle with pygame.draw.rect() as follows:

```
1  pygame.draw.rect(window, rectangle_color, (rectangle_x, rectangle_y, rectangle_width,
       rectangle_height))
```

The above line of code draws this rectangle with the above details on the game window. To move the rectangle to the bottom of the window, the code will be as follows:

```
1  rectangle_x = window_width // 2 − rectangle_width // 2
2  rectangle_y = window_height − rectangle_height
```

The first line above, for example, calculates the x-coordinate of the position of the rectangle. Let us try to understand how to calculate it. The window_width is the width of the game window, which we have set to 800 pixels, and the rectangle_width is the width of the rectangle we want to draw. In the above line, we divide both window_width and rectangle_width by 2 to find the center of the window and the center of the rectangle, respectively. By subtracting the half-width of the rectangle from the half-width of the window, we get the x-coordinate of the left side of the rectangle, which will be positioned horizontally close to the center of the window. Similarly, the second line above calculates the y-coordinate of the rectangle's position. window_height is the height of the game window, which we have set to 600 pixels, and rectangle_height is the height of the rectangle we want to draw. By subtracting the height of the rectangle from the height of the window, we get the y-coordinate of the upper-left corner of the rectangle, which will be at the bottom of the window.

Figure 12-1 shows how the dimensions and positions of an object or shape are displayed. The image shows the width and length of the rectangle. It also shows

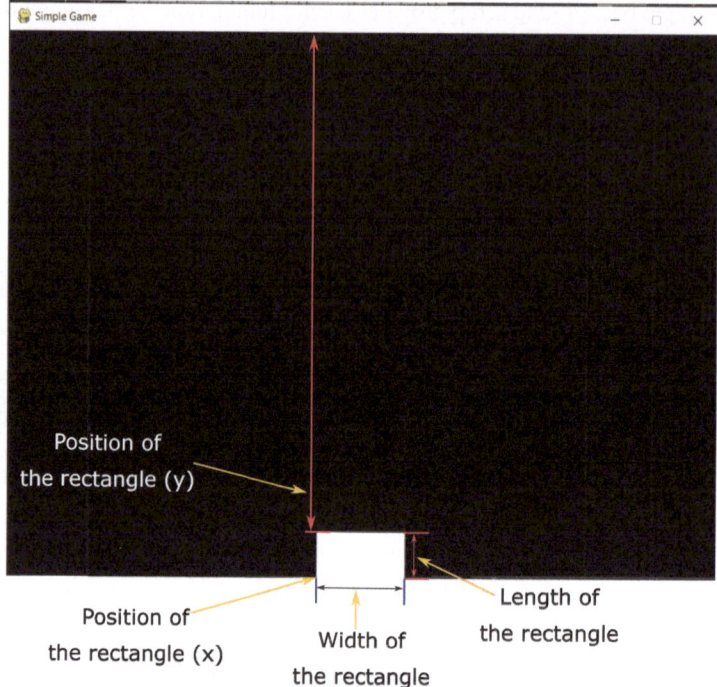

Figure 12-1. Visualization of the dimensions and the positions of an object (rectangle) appears in the window of our game

what the positions (x and y values) represent. As shown, increasing rectangle_x moves the object to the right. Also, increasing rectangle_y moves the object down.

We can also draw different shapes. For example, to draw a triangle, the code simply will be

```
1  # Define triangle points
2  point1 = (400, 100)  # Top vertex
3  point2 = (300, 400)  # Bottom left vertex
4  point3 = (500, 400)  # Bottom right vertex
5  triangle_points = [point1, point2, point3]
```

After defining the triangle points' list as in the above code, we can draw the triangle as follows:

```
1  triangle_color = (255, 255, 255)
2  pygame.draw.polygon(window, triangle_color, triangle_points)
```

To draw a circle, we need to define the center and the radius of the circle as follows:

```
1 # Define circle parameters
2 circle_center = (400, 300) # Center of the circle
3 circle_radius = 100      # Radius of the circle
```

After that, we can draw the circle as follows:

```
1 circle_color= (255, 255, 255)
2 pygame.draw.circle(window, circle_color, circle_center, circle_radius)
```

12.1.3 Moving the Rectangle

In this part of the game, we want the rectangle to move left and right, but we do not want it to go outside the edges of the game window. This means that we need to be able to capture the user's actions, such as pressing the left or right arrow keys on the keyboard, and then move the rectangle in that direction. This way, the user can control the movement of the rectangle by using the arrow keys, and the rectangle will stay inside the game window. The following code is doing this step:

```
1  rectangle_speed=5
2  # Handle key presses
3  keys = pygame.key.get_pressed()
4  if keys[pygame.K_LEFT]:
5      rectangle_x -= rectangle_speed
6      if keys[pygame.K_RIGHT]:
7          rectangle_x += rectangle_speed
8
9      # Ensure the rectangle stays within the window boundaries
10     rectangle_x = max(0, min(window_width – rectangle_width, rectangle_x))
11
12     # Draw the rectangle
13     pygame.draw.rect(window, rectangle_color, (rectangle_x, rectangle_y, rectangle_width,
             rectangle_height))
```

Let us explain the above code:

- "keys = pygame.key.get_pressed()": This line checks which keys the user is currently pressing on their keyboard.
- "if keys[pygame.K_LEFT]:": This checks if the user is pressing the left arrow key. If so, then we want to move the rectangle to the left, as follows: "rectangle_x -= rectangle_speed." This means that we subtract the rectangle_speed value from the rectangle_x position. This makes the rectangle move to the left. Hence, this speed value controls the speed of the movement of the rectangle; if the speed value is high, the movement will be fast and may not be controllable.
- "if keys[pygame.K_RIGHT]:": This checks if the user is pressing the right arrow key; if so, then we want to move the rectangle to the right as follows: rectangle_x += rectangle_speed.

- "rectangle_x = max(0, min(window_width - rectangle_width, rectangle_x))": This line makes sure that the rectangle stays within the game window boundaries. It checks if the rectangle_x position is less than zero (going off the left side) and, if so, sets it to zero. It also checks if the rectangle_x position plus the rectangle_width is greater than the window_width (going off the right side) and, if so, sets it to the maximum allowed value. This ensures the rectangle never goes outside the game window.
- "pygame.draw.rect(window, rectangle_color, (rectangle_x, rectangle_y, rectangle_width, rectangle_height))": This line actually draws the rectangle on the game window.

12.1.4 Creating Other Rectangles (Targets)

In our game, we want to add some special shapes called "targets" for the player to try and hit. These targets will be like small rectangles. The player's rectangle (main object), which we will call the "shooter," will try to hit these target rectangles. Each target rectangle will have a random number inside it, and that number is the score you get for hitting that target. When the shooter's rectangle hits a target rectangle, that target will disappear from the game, and the score inside it will be added to the player's total score. The goal is to hit as many targets as possible to get a high score. Once the player hits a certain number of targets, they will move on to the next level, where there will be even more targets to hit. It is like a game of catch, but instead of catching a ball, the shooter is trying to hit the targets to score points. The more targets you hit, the higher your score will be. The following code tries to make this step:

```
1  # Set the colors and scores for the top rectangles
2  rectangle_colors = [(255, 0, 0), (0, 255, 0), (0, 0, 255), (255, 255, 0), (255, 0, 255),(0, 255, 255),
       (128, 128, 128), (255, 128, 0), (128, 0, 128), (0, 128, 128)]
3  # Set the scores for the top rectangles
4  rectangle_scores = []
5  for _ in range(10):
6    rectangle_scores.append(str(random.randint(0, 100)))
7
8  # Set the dimensions for the rectangles
9  rectangle_width = (window_width − 90) // 10
10 rectangle_height = 30
11 rectangle_spacing = 10
```

Let us explain the above code:

- "rectangle_colors = [(255, 0, 0), (0, 255, 0), (0, 0, 255), ...]:": This line creates a list of ten RGB color values used to set the colors of the rectangles. Each RGB color value represents a different color, such as red, green, blue, yellow, and so on.

- The next for loop tries to generate a list of 10 random integer scores between 0 and 100 and converts each score to a string. These scores will be used to display some value or information associated with each rectangle.
- "rectangle_width = (window_width - 90) // 10:": This line calculates the width of each rectangle. The variable window_width represents the total width of the display area. The calculation (window_width - 90) // 10 divides the available width (minus 90 pixels) by 10 to get the width of each rectangle, ensuring that they are evenly spaced.
- "rectangle_height = 30:": This line sets the height of each rectangle to 30 pixels.
- "rectangle_spacing = 10:": This line sets the spacing between each rectangle to 10 pixels.

The above code describes the features and properties of the rectangles (or targets) but did not add them yet. To add them to the game, we need the following code:

```
# Draw the top rectangles
for i in range(len(rectangle_colors)):
    x = i * (rectangle_width + rectangle_spacing) + rectangle_spacing
    y = rectangle_spacing
    pygame.draw.rect(window, rectangle_colors[i], (x, y, rectangle_width, rectangle_height))
    font = pygame.font.Font(None, 24)
    text = font.render(rectangle_scores[i], True, (255, 255, 255))
    text_rect = text.get_rect(center=(x + rectangle_width // 2, y + rectangle_height // 2))
    window.blit(text, text_rect)
```

The above code begins with a for loop that iterates over the indices of the rectangle_colors list. The loop runs ten times because the rectangle_colors list has ten elements. The line "x = i * (rectangle_width + rectangle_spacing) + rectangle_spacing:" calculates the x-coordinate for the current rectangle in the loop. The formula i * (rectangle_width + rectangle_spacing) + rectangle_spacing calculates the positions of each rectangle with a constant distance between them. The variable i represents the current index, and it is multiplied by the sum of rectangle_width and rectangle_spacing to determine the x-coordinate. So, if i=0, this will be the calculated x for the first rectangle. The rectangle_spacing is then added to the result to allow some space between the rectangles. The line "y = rectangle_spacing:" sets the y-coordinate for the current rectangle to rectangle_spacing, which positions the rectangles at the top of the game window. These rectangles will then be drawn into the game. The last three lines are for setting the font and the text, which includes the scores we get when we hit that rectangle. Finally, this line "window.blit(text, text_rect):" draws the text (the score that will be inside the rectangle) on the window surface, using the calculated text_rect position.

12.1.5 Creating Shots or Bullets

In this section of the game, we set up the properties and behavior of the "shots" or "bullets" that will be used in the game or application. These shots represent the bullets that are fired from the main object, and they are an important gameplay mechanic that allows the player to interact with and affect the game world. To do this, let us first describe the form of the shots, which will be as follows:

```
1  # Set the shot properties
2  shot_radius = 5
3  shot_speed = 10
4  shot_x = rectangle_x + rectangle_width // 2
5  shot_y = rectangle_y
6  shot_active = False
```

In the above code, the shots will be in circles. The code sets the radius of the shot or bullet to five units; the radius determines the size or diameter of the shot when it is drawn on the screen. A larger radius will make the shot appear bigger, while a smaller radius will make it appear smaller. Next, we set the speed of the shot or bullet to ten units per update or frame. The speed determines how fast the shot will move across the game world. A higher speed will make the shot travel faster, while a lower speed will make it move slower. shot_x and shot_y calculate the initial x-coordinate and y-coordinate of the shot. For example, the shot takes the x-coordinate of the "main rectangle" (the player's object) and adds half the width of the main rectangle. This positions the shot at the center of the main rectangle (the shooter or the player), which is a common starting point for shots or bullets. Similarly, the y-coordinates will be adjusted to the y-coordinate of the main rectangle. The line "shot_active = False:" sets the shot_active boolean variable to False. This indicates that the shot is not currently in use or being fired. When the player triggers a shot (make an action or event), this variable will be set to True to activate the shot and allow it to be moved and checked for collisions.

The question now is when this shot will create and appear. We plan to create it when the user presses a space button. Then, the shot will appear as follows:

```
1  if event.type == pygame.QUIT:
2      running = False
3  elif event.type == pygame.KEYDOWN and event.key == pygame.K_SPACE:
4      shot_x = main_rectangle_x + main_rectangle_width // 2
5      shot_y = main_rectangle_y
6      shot_active = True
```

As we can see in the above code, if the user presses the space button, the shot positions will be initialized and then appear.

Finally, how to move the shot vertically from the shooter and going up? Moving objects means changing their positions and redrawing them again. The following code tries to do this task:

```
# Move the shot
if shot_active:
    shot_y -= shot_speed
    if shot_y < 0:
        shot_active = False

# Draw the shot
if shot_active:
    pygame.draw.circle(window, (255, 0, 0), (int(shot_x), int(shot_y)), shot_radius)
```

In the above code, if the variable shot_active is true (the shot has been created and is currently in use), then this line "shot_y -= shot_speed" decreases the shot_y value by the shot_speed value. This makes the shot move upward on the screen. There is another check, "if shot_y < 0"; this checks if the shot_y value has become less than zero; this means the shot has gone off the top of the screen. If the shot has gone off the top of the screen, the shot_active variable will be set to False. This indicates that the shot is no longer in use and can be reused or removed from the game.

Finally, if our shot hits one of those rectangles (targets), a few things will happen:

- The rectangle that you hit will disappear and go away.
- Your score in the game will go up by the number that was inside that rectangle.

For example, if you hit a rectangle with the number 50 inside it, your score will increase by 50 points. The more rectangles you hit with your shot, the more points you will get. The below code is just making all of that happen. It checks to see if your shot hits one of the rectangles at the top, then makes the rectangle disappear and adds the points to your score.

```
player_score = 0
# Check for collisions between the shot and the top rectangles
for i in range(len(rectangle_colors)):
    if rectangle_active[i]:
        x = i * (rectangle_width + rectangle_spacing) + rectangle_spacing
        y = rectangle_spacing
        rect = pygame.Rect(x, y, rectangle_width, rectangle_height)
        if shot_active and rect.collidepoint(shot_x, shot_y):
            # Remove the rectangle and update the player's score
            rectangle_active[i] = False
            player_score += int(rectangle_scores[i])
            shot_active = False
            break
```

The top code checks for collisions between the shot and all the top rectangles. As we can see, in the for loop, the code gets the x and y positions for each rectangle. Then we get a special "rectangle" object that the code can use to check for collisions. The collision happens when our shot is active (being used) and when the shot's position is inside the current rectangle. If this happens (the shot has hit the rectangle), this part makes the rectangle disappear by setting it to "not active." Next, it adds the points that were inside the rectangle to your overall score in the game, and finally it makes your shot disappear since it now hit a rectangle. The "break" statement at the end stops the code from checking the other rectangles, since it has already found a collision.

In this game, the player can play for a set time of 30 seconds. During this time, the player collects points by hitting targets. The game ends when the player has finished all the targets or when the 30 seconds are up.

Figure 12-2 shows the game we created. At the start, the score is zero, and the player has 29 seconds (still at the beginning of the game) left to play. After hitting two rectangles, the player's score goes up, as shown in Figure 12-3. The player has destroyed two rectangles, and there are still eight left to hit. The player needs to destroy all the rectangles before the time runs out, which is now 22 seconds.

The code of this game is available at this link: https://github.com/Eng-Alaa/Programming_4_Kids/blob/main/Game_1.py.

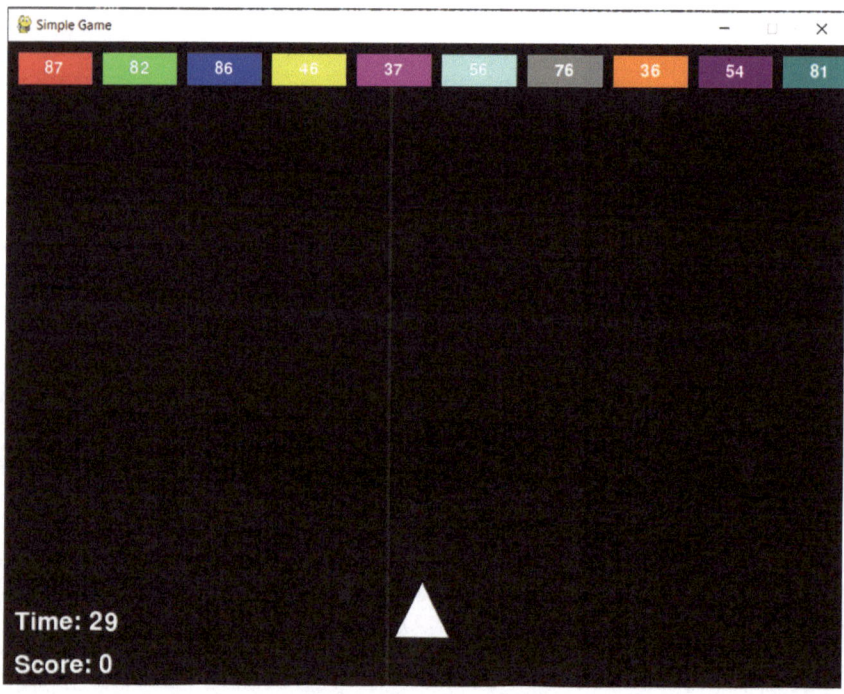

Figure 12-2. Visualization of the game we created

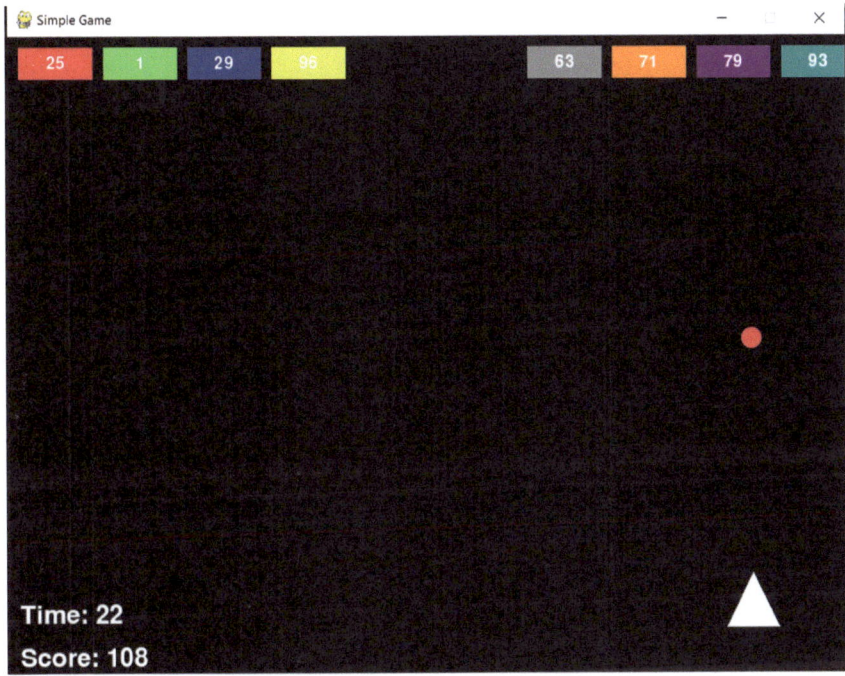

Figure 12-3. Visualization of the game we created in the running mode

12.2   Our Next Adventure in Programming

In this chapter, Kai learned how to design and create his own video game from scratch. He got to choose all the details – how easy or hard it would be, possibility to add different levels, and what the game would look like. Kai used his coding skills to write the computer code that makes the game work. He programmed the movements, the scoring, and the simple graphics. This gave him complete control over his game. Creating his own game made Kai feel very proud. All the hard work paid off, and he ended up with a game that was perfect for him. Kai now knows that he has the skills to design and create the simple games he wants in the future.

In the next chapter, Kai and we will briefly learn about some other really cool things we can do with programming. These new topics are related to the coding skills we have already learned. These new areas will allow us to take our coding skills even further. Then we will be able to expand our knowledge and discover all the amazing things we can do with programming.

Toward Exploring Future Programming Directions

13

In all previous chapters, Kai has guided us through the process of learning the basics of programming. Kai is surprised at how his skills have grown, allowing him to control the robot to perform all sorts of tasks – from simple things like printing messages to more complex projects like creating games and working with files.

Now Kai is curious about what other directions he can explore to further improve his skills and do even more amazing things with programming. This chapter will introduce Kai and us to some exciting topics that are closely related to the programming skills we have developed. These new areas will allow us to expand our knowledge and take our coding skills to the next level.

13.1   What Is Next?

As Kai looks around at all the books and resources available, he is excited to see that there are several key areas he can delve into to further enhance his programming skills. The four main directions he is identifying are

- **Object-oriented programming (OOP)**: Kai has learned the basics of programming, but now he wants to explore a paradigm that allows him to create more complex and organized code. OOP introduces concepts like classes, objects, and inheritance that will help him build bigger and more sophisticated programs.
- **Data structure**: Kai realizes that the ability to store, manage, and manipulate data efficiently is critical to many real-world applications. Exploring different data structures, such as arrays, linked lists, and trees, will give him powerful tools to tackle more complex problems.
- **Introduction to algorithms**: Kai knows that programming is not just about writing code but also about finding efficient ways to solve problems. Learning about common algorithms and algorithmic thinking will enable him to optimize his code and tackle increasingly challenging tasks.

© Alaa Tharwat 2025

A. Tharwat, *Python Adventures for Young Coders*,

https://doi.org/10.1007/979-8-8688-1067-1_13

- **Problem-solving**: Underlying all of these topics is the vital skill of problem-solving. Kai wants to develop strategies and techniques that will help him break down complex problems, analyze them, and come up with effective solutions.

More details about each topic are provided in the following sections.

13.2 Object-Oriented Programming (OOP)

13.2.1 From Functions to Objects

Do you remember functions in Chapters 8 and 9? This tool allows us to write code in a more organized and modular way. By breaking down our code into smaller and reusable pieces called functions, we can make our programs more manageable, easier to understand, and easier to maintain. Additionally, using functions, we can group related code together, give it a descriptive name, and call it whenever we need it. This helps us avoid repeating the same code over and over again, which can make our programs cleaner and less error-prone.

Building on the use of functions, object-oriented programming (OOP) is a natural extension that can make writing code even easier and simpler. In OOP, we organize our code around objects, which are like self-contained units that have their own properties and behaviors. With OOP, we can create classes, which are like templates for objects. Each class can have its own functions, called methods, that define the behavior of objects created from that class. For example, suppose we want to create an object that represents a dog. We can create a "Dog" class that contains information about the dog's name, age, and breed. We can also add functions, called methods, that describe what the dog can do, such as bark, sit, or fetch. Once we have the Dog class, we can use it to create as many Dog objects as we want, each with its own name, age, and breed. And each dog object will have its own special abilities, such as barking or sitting, that we have defined in the class. Thus, in general, OOP allows us to create objects that can encapsulate both data and functionality, making our code more modular, reusable, and easier to understand.

13.2.2 Creating Classes

In OOP, we start by creating something called a "class." A class is like a blueprint or template for an object. It defines the properties (information) and methods (actions or functions) that the object will have. Let us create a class for an object called "Dog." We can give the Dog class properties like name, breed, and age. We can also give it methods like "bark()" and "fetch()."

Here is an example of how we can create a Dog class in code:

```python
class Dog:
    def __init__(self, name, breed, age):
        self.name = name
        self.breed = breed
        self.age = age
```

The above code begins by defining a class called "Dog." In Python, we use the "class" keyword to create a new class. The function "def __init__(self, name, breed, age)" is a special method or function called the __init__ method, which is the constructor[1] for the Dog class. This method is automatically called whenever we create a new Dog object. The "self.name = name" line inside the __init__ method is assigning the name parameter to the name attribute of the Dog object. The self keyword refers to the current Dog object being created. Similarly, we assign the breed and age parameters to the breed and age attributes of the Dog object.

When we create a new Dog object, we will need to provide the name, breed, and age values, and the __init__ method will automatically set those values as attributes of the Dog object. For example, if we want to create a new Dog object, we can do it like this:

```python
my_dog = Dog("Buddy", "Golden Retriever", 5)
```

Now, the my_dog object will have the following attributes:

- my_dog.name = "Buddy"
- my_dog.breed = "Golden Retriever"
- my_dog.age = 5

We can also add functions (methods) to the Dog class to define the behaviors and actions of the dogs. Let us expand on the Dog class example to include some additional methods.

```python
class Dog:
    def __init__(self, name, breed, age):
        self.name = name
        self.breed = breed
        self.age = age

    def bark(self):
        print(f"{self.name} says: Woof!")

    def fetch(self, item):
        print(f"{self.name} fetched the {item}!")

    def sit(self):
```

---

[1] In OOP, a constructor is like a special method or function that helps create a new object. When you want to create a new object, you must follow the instructions in the constructor.

```
14      print(f"{self.name} is sitting down.")
15
16   def roll_over(self):
17      print(f"{self.name} rolled over!")
```

In this updated Dog class, we have added several methods:

- bark(): When called, this method displays a message that the dog is barking.
- fetch(item): This method takes an item parameter and prints a message saying that the dog has fetched this item.
- sit(): This method prints a message saying that the dog is sitting.
- roll_over(): This method prints a message saying that the dog has rolled over.

Now, let us see how we can use these methods with a Dog object:

```
1  my_dog = Dog("Buddy", "Golden Retriever", 5)
2  my_dog.bark()  # Buddy says: Woof!
3  my_dog.fetch("ball")  # Buddy fetched the ball!
4  my_dog.sit()  # Buddy is sitting down.
5  my_dog.roll_over()  # Buddy rolled over!
```

By adding these methods to the Dog class, we provide a way for our code to interact with and control the behavior of the Dog objects. This makes the class more useful and flexible, since we can now call these methods on any Dog object to make it perform different actions.

The benefits of adding these methods to the class include

- **Encapsulation**: The behaviors of the dog are neatly encapsulated within the Dog class, making the code more organized and easier to maintain.
- **Reusability**: Any Dog object can now call these methods, promoting code reuse and consistency.
- **Abstraction**: The implementation details of these methods are hidden from the user, who can simply call the methods without worrying about the underlying logic.
- **Extensibility**: If we need to add more behaviors to the dog, we can easily extend the Dog class by adding more methods.

Overall, adding these methods to the Dog class makes the class more powerful and useful and demonstrates the benefits of using object-oriented programming in creating organized, reusable, and extensible code.

Inheritance is another powerful feature of object-oriented programming that can be very useful when working with classes. Inheritance allows you to create a new class based on an existing class, inheriting its properties and methods. Let us say we want to create a specialized type of dog called a GuardDog that inherits from the base Dog class. The GuardDog class might have some additional properties and methods specific to guard dogs. This could be achieved using inheritance. However, there are many other powerful features in OOP that can help in organizing the code and make it reusable and extensible.

13.3 Data Structure

Do you remember when we learned about lists in Chapters 6 and 7? Those lists are awesome containers that can hold many different things. Well, guess what? Lists are actually part of something even cooler called "data structures."

Data structures are like special ways of organizing and storing information in our programs. Lists are just one kind of data structure, but there are many others. Think of data structures as different kinds of toy boxes. You might have a toy chest for big toys, a shelf for books, and small boxes for Lego pieces. In programming, we use different data structures to store different types of information in the best possible way.

Why is the topic of data structures important? This is because

- **They help us keep things tidy**: Just like how different toy containers help keep your room organized, data structures help keep our information organized in programs.
- **They make our programs run faster**: Imagine if all your toys were in one big box – it would take forever to find anything. Data structures help our programs find and use information quickly.
- **They let us solve big problems**: With the right data structure, we can handle lots of information and do complex things easily.

Some examples of data structures besides lists are

- **Dictionaries**: Dictionaries are like a special kind of book, where you can store information in a very organized way. Just like a regular dictionary helps you find the meaning of a word, a computer dictionary, or a "dictionary data structure," helps you find information quickly. We can use it to store all kinds of information, like the names and ages of your friends, the prices of items in a store, or the capital cities of different countries.
- **Stacks**: Imagine a stack of plates in a restaurant. You can only take a plate from the top of the stack or add a new plate to the top. Stacks work the same way in computers. They are a way of storing information where you can only access the item on top. It is like a stack of books – you can only take the one on top or add a new one to the top.
- **Queues**: Queues are like the lines of people waiting to get on a ride at an entertainment park. The first person in line is the first to get on the ride. Queues in computers work the same way – the first piece of information to go in the queue is the first to come out. It's a very organized way of storing information, just like waiting in line at the entertainment park.

Exploring the world of data structures will help us learn about these different types of data structures and when to use each one. Just as you choose the right container for your toys, we choose the right data structure for our information in programming. This helps us write better, faster, and more awesome programs.

13.4   Introduction to Algorithms

Do you remember when we learned how to sort a list in Exercise 7 in Chapter 7? That was actually your first step into the world of algorithms. An algorithm is like a recipe or a set of instructions that tells a computer how to solve a problem or complete a task.

Let us think about sorting a list of numbers. There are many different algorithms we can use to do this, just like there are many ways to clean up a messy room. Some ways are quicker, some use less energy, and some work better for different kinds of messes. Let us look at three different sorting algorithms:

- **Bubble sort**: Imagine you have a line of kids, and you want to sort them by height. Bubble sort works like this:
  - Start at the beginning of the line.
  - Compare the first two kids. If they are in the wrong order, swap them.
  - Move to the next pair and do the same.
  - Keep doing this until you reach the end of the line. Start over from the beginning until no more swaps are needed.
- **Insertion sort**: Think of how you might sort a hand of playing cards.
  - Start with the first card as your sorted portion.
  - Take the next card and insert it into the sorted portion (this is why the algorithm is called insertion sorting).
  - Repeat this for each card until all are sorted.
- **Merge sort**: This is a divide and conquer method. It is a bit more complicated, but very efficient:
  - Split the list in half.
  - Keep splitting each half until you have many tiny lists of one or two items.
  - Sort these tiny or small lists.
  - Merge the sorted tiny lists back together, keeping them in order.

Hence, the bubble sort is simple, but it can take a long time especially for big lists. The insertion sort works well for small lists or when the list is already partially sorted. The merge sort is usually faster for big lists, but it needs more computer memory. For example, if we had 1000 numbers to sort, bubble sort might take about 1,000,000 steps, insertion sort might take around 250,000 steps, and merge sort would only need about 10,000 steps. This is why choosing the right algorithm is so important. As your lists get bigger, the difference in speed becomes huge.

Therefore, just like choosing the right tool makes a job easier, picking the right algorithm can make your program work much faster, especially when dealing with lots of information. Algorithms help you figure out the best way to sort things, find information, or solve puzzles in your code. By learning different algorithms, you become a better problem-solver and can create programs that work more efficiently. This enables us to tackle all sorts of coding challenges and make your programs run smoothly and quickly.

13.5 Problem-Solving

Imagine you are a superhero and your superpower is solving problems with code. This is what programming problem-solving is all about. It is like going on exciting adventures where you face challenges and figure out how to overcome them using the most appropriate algorithm or method.

One of the first challenges you might face is creating a simple guessing game, as we did in one of our projects. In this game, the computer thinks of a secret number, and you have to guess what it is. To make the game more fun, you could add features like hints or different difficulty levels. By problem-solving, you can figure out how to create these exciting new features.

Problem-solving is also helpful when you want to make your programs work faster. For example, if you have a long list of numbers that you need to sort these numbers, problem-solving can help you find a quick way to sort these numbers. Another way problem-solving can help is when you want to solve a problem using the least amount of resources, like the minimum number of variables or memory. This can make your programs more efficient and take up less space on the computer.

Being a programmer is like being a superhero, and problem-solving is your superpower. Whenever you face a challenge, you can use your problem-solving skills to find the best way to overcome it. It is one of the most exciting parts of being a programmer.

Solutions of Chapter 1

● **Exercise 1: Line of stars (horizontal)**

Write a program that prints a horizontal line of stars using the print statement.
The program should print

> ********************

The solution or the code is as follows:

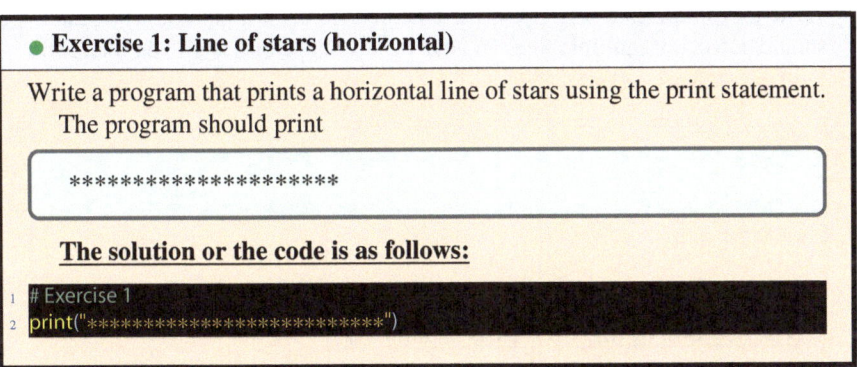

```
1  # Exercise 1
2  print("************************")
```

● **Exercise 2: Line of stars (vertical)**

Write a program that prints a vertical line of stars using the print statement.
The program should print

```
*
*
*
*
*
```

The solution or the code is as follows:

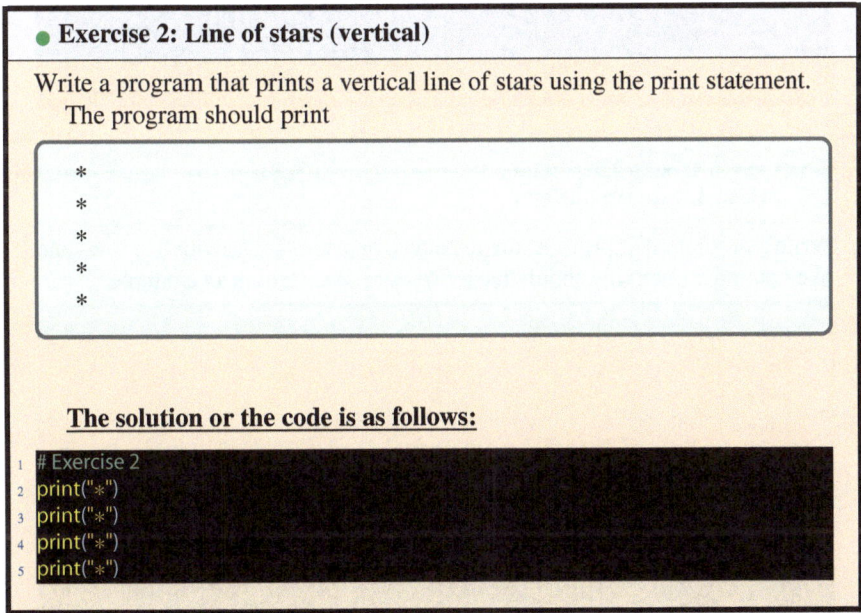

```
1  # Exercise 2
2  print("*")
3  print("*")
4  print("*")
5  print("*")
```

© Alaa Tharwat 2025
A. Tharwat, *Python Adventures for Young Coders*,
https://doi.org/10.1007/979-8-8688-1067-1

```
6  print("*")
7  print("*")
```

or

```
1  print("*\n*\n*\n*\n*\n*")
```

This "\n" means new line, so the above code prints "*" and then goes to a new line and then "*" and so on.

● Exercise 3: Print a pattern

Write a program that uses the print statement to print a pattern. The pattern should consist of multiple lines and can be any shape or design you like. Here is an example of a simple pattern:

```
*
**
***
****
*****
```

The solution of this exercise is as follows:

```
1  # Exercise 3
2  print("*")
3  print("**")
4  print("***")
5  print("****")
6  print("*****")
7  print("******")
```

● Exercise 4: Square pattern

Write a program that prints a square pattern of asterisks (*) with five rows and five columns. Each row should have five asterisks. Here is an example:

```
*****
*****
*****
*****
*****
```

The solution of this exercise is as follows:

```
1  # Exercise 4
2  print("*****")
```

```
3  print("****")
4  print("****")
5  print("****")
6  print("****")
```

● Exercise 5: Number pattern

Write a program that uses the print statement to print a pattern of numbers from 1 to 5. Each line should display the numbers in ascending order. Here is the output:

```
1
1 2
1 2 3
1 2 3 4
1 2 3 4 5
```

The solution of this exercise is as follows:

```
1  # Exercise 5
2  print("1")
3  print("1 2")
4  print("1 2 3")
5  print("1 2 3 4")
6  print("1 2 3 4 5")
```

● Exercise 6: Diamond pattern

Write a program that prints a seven-line diamond pattern using asterisks (*). The middle line should have seven asterisks, and each line above and below should have two less asterisk than the previous line. Here is the output:

```
   *
  ***
 *****
*******
 *****
  ***
   *
```

The code of this exercise is as follows:

```
1  # Exercise 6
2  print("*  ")
3  print("*** ")
```

```
4  print("*****")
5  print("*******")
6  print("*****")
7  print("*** ")
8  print("* ")
```

• Exercise 7: Find the mistake

What is the mistake(s) in the following program and what is the output of this program?

```
1  Score = input("Enter your Score: )
2  print("Your score is " + score)
```

The solution of this exercise is as follows:

In this program, there is a mistake in the line Score = input("Enter your Score:). The closing double quotation mark is missing. It should be Score = input("Enter your Score: ").

In the second line, print("Your score is " + score), there is a mistake in the variable name. The variable defined is Score (capital s), but it is used as score (small s). Python is case-sensitive, so Score and score are considered as two different variables. To fix this, you should change score to Score in the print statement.

Assuming these mistakes are corrected, the output of the corrected program will be

Enter your Score: 85
Your score is 85

• Exercise 8: Find the mistake

What is the mistake(s) in the following program and what is the output of this program?

```
1  name = input("Enter your name: ")
2  print("Hello, nice to meet you, " + name
```

The solution of this exercise is as follows:

In this program, there is a mistake in the line print("Hello, nice to meet you, " + name. The closing parenthesis is missing. It should be print("Hello, nice to meet you, " + name).

Assuming this mistake is corrected, the output of the corrected program will be

Enter your name: John
Hello, nice to meet you, John

● Exercise 9: Find the mistake

What is the mistake(s) in the following program and what is the output of this program?

```
1  favorite_color = INPUT("Enter your favorite color:")
2  PRINT("Your favorite color is" + favorite_color)
```

The solution of this exercise is as follows:

In this program, there is a mistake in the first line, because "INPUT" should be "input." Also, in the second line, "PRINT" should be "print." Assuming this mistake is corrected, the output of the corrected program will depend on the user input. For example, if the user enters "blue" as the favorite color, the output will be

Enter your favorite color: blue
Your favorite color is blue

● Exercise 10: Welcome message

Ask the user to enter their name, age, nationality, and gender and then print all these details. For example, if the name is Alaa, the age is 43, the nationality is Egyptian, and the gender is male, print Welcome Alaa, you are an Egyptian male and 43 years old.

The expected output of this program is

Enter your name: Alaa
Enter your age: 43
Enter your nationality: Egyptian
Enter your gender: male
Welcome Alaa, you are an Egyptian male and you are 43 years old.

The solution of this exercise is as follows:

```
1  # Exercise 10
2  name = input("Enter your name: ")
3  age = input("Enter your age: ")
4  nationality = input("Enter your nationality: ")
5  gender = input("Enter your gender: ")
6  print("Welcome " + name + " you are " + nationality + " " +
7  gender+ " and you are " + age + " years old.")
```

● **Exercise 11: Favorite things**

Ask the user to enter their favorite color, animal, and food. Then, print a message that combines these details. For example, if the favorite color is red, the favorite animal is a lion, and the favorite food is pizza, the program should print

What is your favorite color? red
What is your favorite animal?: lion
What is your favorite food? pizza
Your favorite color is red, your favorite animal is a lion, and your favorite food is pizza.

The code of this exercise is as follows:

```
1  # Exercise 11
2  fav_color = input("What is your favorite color? ")
3  fav_animal = input("What is your favorite animal? ")
4  fav_food = input("What is your favorite food? ")
5
6  print("Your favorite color is ", fav_color, "your favorite animal is ", fav_animal, "and your
        favorite food is ", fav_food)
```

● **Exercise 12: Enter three numbers**

Ask the user to enter three numbers and then print the three numbers.
   The expected output of this program is

First number: 5
Second number: 8
Third number: 10
The first number is 5 and the second number is 8 and the third number is 10

The solution of this exercise is as follows:

```
1  # Exercise 12
2  first_number = input("First number: ")
3  second_number = input("Second number: ")
4  third_number = input("Third number: ")
5
6  print("The first number is " + first_number + " and the second number is"
7  + second_number + "and the third number is" + third_number)
```

Solutions of Chapter 2

● Exercise 1: Valid or invalid variable name

In the following variable names, which ones are valid and which ones are not? Explain why.

```
1  alpha_beta = "gamma"
2  23_variable = 5
3  student_score = 85
4  my variable = 10
5  _private_data = 100
6  super@hero = "Batman"
7  myVariable = "hello"
8  color123 = "blue"
```

The solution is as follows:

- alpha_beta = "gamma": **Valid**. This is a valid variable name as it follows the standard naming conventions for Python variables, which allow for a combination of lowercase letters, uppercase letters, digits, and underscores.
- 23_variable = 5: **Invalid**. Variable names in Python cannot start with a digit, as this would be interpreted as a numeric literal.
- student_score = 85: **Valid**. This is a valid variable name as it follows the standard naming conventions.
- my variable = 10: **Invalid**. Variable names in Python cannot contain spaces. The correct way to write this would be my_variable = 10.
- _private_data = 100: **Valid**. Variable names in Python can start with a single underscore, which is often used to indicate that the variable is intended for internal use (i.e., it's a "private" variable).

© Alaa Tharwat 2025
A. Tharwat, *Python Adventures for Young Coders*,
https://doi.org/10.1007/979-8-8688-1067-1

- super@hero = "Batman": Invalid. Variable names in Python cannot contain special characters like @.
- myVariable = "hello": **Valid**.
- color123 = "blue": **Valid**.

● **Exercise 2: Age in months**

Ask the user to enter their age and print this age in months (the year has 12 months). For example, if the user is 14 years old, print $14 \times 12 = 168$ months.
The expected output of this program is

> Enter your age in years: 20
> Your age in months is 240.

The solution will be as follows:

```
1  # Exercise 2
2  age_years = int(input("Enter your age in years: "))
3  age_months = age_years * 12
4  print("Your age in months is", age_months)
```

● **Exercise 3: Seconds to minutes**

Ask the user for a number of seconds and print out the time value in minutes. You know that one minute corresponds to 60 seconds.
The expected output of this program is

> Enter a number of seconds: 180
> 180 seconds is equal to 3 minutes.

The solution is as follows:

```
1  # Exercise 3
2  seconds = int(input("Enter a number of seconds: "))
3  minutes = seconds // 60
4
5  print(seconds, "seconds is equal to", minutes, "minutes.")
```

In this solution, we used // instead of /; what is the difference?

- x/3: This performs floating-point division, which returns a floating-point number. The result will include the decimal part of the division, even if the result is a whole number. For example, 10/3 will return 3.3333333333333335.
- x//3: This performs integer division, which returns an integer result. The decimal part of the division is discarded, and the result is rounded down to the nearest integer. For example, 10//3 will return 3.

● Exercise 4: Circle area

Write a program that asks the user to enter the radius of a circle. The program should calculate and print the area of the circle. The area of the circle with radius r is $A = \pi r^2$, where $\pi = \frac{22}{7} = 3.14$.

The expected output of this program is

> Enter the radius of the circle: 5
> The area of the circle is 78.53975 square units.

The solution or the code is as follows:

```
1  # Exercise 4
2  # Prompt the user to enter the radius of the circle
3  radius = float(input("Enter the radius of the circle: "))
4
5  # Calculate the area of the circle
6  area = (22/7) * (radius ** 2) # pi=22/7
7
8  # Print the area of the circle
9  print("The area of the circle is", area, "square units.")
```

● Exercise 5: Speed converter

Write a program that asks the user to enter a speed in kilometers per hour (km/h). The program should convert the speed to miles per hour (mph) and print the result. Assume that 1 mile is equal to 1.60934 kilometers.

The expected output of this program is

> Enter the speed in kilometres per hour: 60
> The speed in miles per hour is 37.28227153424 mph.

The solution is as follows:

```
1  # Exercise 5
2  # Prompt the user to enter the speed in kilometers per hour
3  speed_kmph = float(input("Enter the speed in kilometres per hour: "))
4
5  # Convert the speed from kilometers per hour to miles per hour
6  speed_mph = speed_kmph / 1.60934
7
8  # Print the speed in miles per hour
9  print("The speed in miles per hour is", speed_mph, "mph.")
```

• Exercise 6: Temperature converter

Write a program that asks the user to enter a temperature in Celsius. The program should convert the temperature to Fahrenheit and print the result. Note: $F = (C \times \frac{9}{5}) + 32$.

The output:

> Enter the temperature in Celsius: 25
> The temperature in Fahrenheit is 77.0 degrees.

The solution or the code is as follows:

```
1  # Exercise 6
2  celsius = float(input("Enter the temperature in Celsius: "))
3  fahrenheit = (celsius * 9/5) + 32
4  print("The temperature in Fahrenheit is", fahrenheit, "degrees.")
```

• Exercise 7: Calorie calculator

Our user is on a diet to lose some weight. Tell them that an apple has 49 calories, a banana has 95 calories, and an orange has 37 calories. Ask the user to enter the number of apples, bananas, and oranges they eat and calculate the number of calories consumed.

The expected output of this program is

> Enter the number of apples you ate: 2
> Enter the number of bananas you ate: 1
> Enter the number of oranges you ate: 3
> You consumed a total of 304 calories.

The solution or the code is as follows:

```
1  # Exercise 7
2  # Calorie values per fruit
3  calories_per_apple = 49
4  calories_per_banana = 95
5  calories_per_orange = 37
6
7  # Prompt the user to enter the number of fruits eaten
8  apples = int(input("Enter the number of apples you ate: "))
9  bananas = int(input("Enter the number of bananas you ate: "))
10 oranges = int(input("Enter the number of oranges you ate: "))
11
12 # Calculate the total number of calories consumed
13 total_calories = (apples * calories_per_apple) + (bananas * calories_per_banana) + (
       oranges * calories_per_orange)
14
15 # Print the total number of calories consumed
16 print("You consumed a total of", total_calories, "calories.")
```

Solutions of Chapter 3

● **Exercise 1: Indentation output**

What is the expected output of this program? [**Suggestion**: Read the indentation part first.]

```
1  temperature = 32
2
3  if temperature < 32:
4      print("It's freezing outside!")
5      print("Wear a warm coat.")
6  elif temperature < 65:
7      print("It's chilly today.")
8      print("You might need a jacket.")
9  else:
10     print("It's a nice day!")
11     print("Enjoy the weather!")
12
13 print("Have a great day!")
```

The solution is as follows: The indentation level defines which block of code belongs to which control structure (e.g., if, elif, else). In the code above, the initial value of temperature is set to 32. The first if statement checks to see if the temperature is less than 32. Since temperature is 32, this condition is not met, and the block of code below the if statement is not executed. The next elif statement checks whether the temperature is less than 65. Since 32 is less than 65, the condition is true and the block of code under the elif statement is executed.

The output is

```
It's chilly today.
You might need a jacket.
Have a great day!
```

© Alaa Tharwat 2025
A. Tharwat, *Python Adventures for Young Coders*,
https://doi.org/10.1007/979-8-8688-1067-1

● **Exercise 2: Indentation output**

What is the expected output of this program? [**Suggestion**: Read the indentation part first.]

```
1  day = "Monday"
2  temperature = 72
3  rain_chance = 30
4
5  if day == "Monday":
6    print("It's the start of the week!")
7    if temperature < 50:
8      print("It's a bit chilly today.")
9      if rain_chance > 50:
10        print("Better bring an umbrella!")
11      else:
12        print("It should be a dry day.")
13    elif temperature < 70:
14      print("The temperature is pleasant.")
15    else:
16      print("It's a warm day today.")
17      if rain_chance > 20:
18        print("There's a chance of rain later.")
19      else:
20        print("It will be a sunny day.")
21  elif day == "Friday":
22    print("The weekend is almost here!")
23    if temperature < 60:
24      print("It's a bit cool for the end of the week.")
25    else:
26      print("The weather is great for the weekend.")
27  else:
28    print("It's a regular day.")
29    if rain_chance > 0:
30      print("There's a chance of rain today.")
31    else:
32      print("It should be a dry day.")
33
34  print("Have a wonderful day!")
```

The solution is as follows: Initial values are set for day, temperature, and rain_chance. The first if statement checks whether day is Monday. Since the condition is true, the block of code below this if statement is executed. The output will be "It's the start of the week!" Then there is a nested if statement that checks if the temperature is less than 50. Since the temperature is 72, this condition is not met, and the block of code under this if statement is skipped. The next elif statement checks whether the temperature is less than 70. Since 72 is not less than 70, this condition is not met, and the block of code under this elif statement is skipped. The final else block is executed because the previous conditions were not met. The output will be "It's a warm day today."

The nested if statement on line 17 checks whether rain_chance is greater than 20. Since 30 is greater than 20, this condition is met, and the block of code below this if statement is executed. Therefore, the output will be "There is a chance of rain later."

Since the first if condition for "Monday" has been met, the remaining elif and else blocks are skipped. The final print statement is executed, which prints "Have a wonderful day!"

The expected output of the program is

It's the start of the week!
It's a warm day today.
There's a chance of rain later.
Have a wonderful day!

● Exercise 3: else if to elif

Rewrite the following program, and instead of using "else if," use "elif":

```python
# Original code with if–else
day = input("Enter the day of the week: ")

if day == "monday":
    print("It's the start of the work week.")
else:
    if day == "tuesday":
        print("It's the second day of the week.")
    else:
        if day == "wednesday":
            print("It's the middle of the week.")
        else:
            if day == "thursday":
                print("The weekend is almost here!")
            else:
                if day == "friday":
                    print("It's the end of the work week!")
                else:
                    if day == "saturday":
                        print("It's the weekend!")
                    else:
                        if day == "sunday":
                            print("It's the start of the next week.")
                        else:
                            print("That's not a valid day of the week.")
```

The solution or code is as follows:

```
1  # Exercise 3
2  # Original code with if—else
3  day = input("Enter the day of the week: ")
4
5  if day == "monday":
6     print("It's the start of the work week.")
7  elif day == "tuesday":
8     print("It's the second day of the week.")
9  elif day == "wednesday":
10    print("It's the middle of the week.")
11 elif day == "thursday":
12    print("The weekend is almost here!")
13 elif day == "friday":
14    print("It's the end of the work week!")
15 elif day == "saturday":
16    print("It's the weekend!")
17 elif day == "sunday":
18    print("It's the start of the next week.")
19 else:
20    print("That's not a valid day of the week.")
```

● Exercise 4: elif to else if

Rewrite the following program, and instead of using "elif," use "else if."

```
1  # Original code with elif
2  fruit = input("Enter a fruit: ")
3
4  if fruit == "apple":
5     print("An apple a day keeps the doctor away.")
6  elif fruit == "banana":
7     print("Bananas are a great source of potassium.")
8  elif fruit == "orange":
9     print("Oranges are high in vitamin C.")
10 elif fruit == "strawberry":
11    print("Strawberries are sweet and juicy.")
12 else:
13    print("I don't have any information about that fruit.")
```

The solution or code is as follows:

```
1  # Exercise 4
2  fruit = input("Enter a fruit: ")
3  if fruit == "apple":
4     print("An apple a day keeps the doctor away.")
5  else:
6     if fruit == "banana":
7        print("Bananas are a great source of potassium.")
8     else:
```

```
9      if fruit == "orange":
10        print("Oranges are high in vitamin C.")
11     else:
12        if fruit == "strawberry":
13          print("Strawberries are sweet and juicy.")
14        else:
15          print("I don't have any information about that fruit.")
```

● Exercise 5: Child or adult

Write a program that asks the user to enter their age. If their age is greater than or equal to 18, print "You are an adult." Otherwise, print "You are a child."

The output of this code should be

```
Enter your age: 40
You are an adult.
```

or

```
Enter your age: 10
You are a child.
```

The solution or code is as follows:

```
1  # Exercise 5
2  # Ask the user to enter their age and convert it to an integer
3  age = int(input("Enter your age: "))
4
5  if age >= 18:
6    print("You are an adult.")
7  else:
8    print("You are a child.")
```

● Exercise 6: Child, teenager, or adult

Write a program that asks the user to enter an age and determines whether the person is a child, teenager, or adult.

The output of this code should be

```
Enter your age: : 6
You are a child.
```

or

> Enter your age: : 50
> You are an adult.

The solution or code is as follows:

```python
# Exercise 6
# Ask the user to enter their age
age = int(input("Please enter your age: "))

# Check the age range
if age < 13:
    print("You are a child.")
elif 13 <= age < 20:
    print("You are a teenager.")
else:
    print("You are an adult.")
```

● Exercise 7: Favorite fruit

Write a program that asks the user to enter their favorite fruit. If the fruit is "apple," print "Apples are delicious!" If the fruit is "banana," print "Bananas are a great choice!" For any other fruit, print "That's a nice fruit too!"

The output of this code should be

> Enter your favorite fruit: apple
> Apples are delicious!

The solution or code is as follows:

```python
# Exercise 7
fruit = input("Enter your favorite fruit: ")  # Ask the user to enter their favorite fruit

if fruit == "apple":
    print("Apples are delicious!")
elif fruit == "banana":
    print("Bananas are a great choice!")
else:
    print("That's a nice fruit too!")
```

In the above code or solution, the comparison is case-sensitive. This means that if the user enters "Apple" (with an uppercase "A") instead of "apple," it will not match the condition fruit == "apple", and the output will be "That's a nice fruit too!"

● Exercise 8: Birth month

Write a program that asks the user to enter their birth month (as a number from 1 to 12). If the month is between 1 and 3, print "It is in the first quarter of the year." If the month is between 4 and 6, print "It is in the second quarter of the year." If the month is between 7 and 9, print "It is in the third quarter of the year." If the month is between 10 and 12, print "It is in the fourth quarter of the year."

The output of this code should be

> Enter your birth month (as a number from 1 to 12): 2
> It's in the first quarter of the year.

The solution or code is as follows:

```
1  # Exercise 8
2  # Ask the user to enter their birth month and convert it to an integer
3  month = int(input("Enter your birth month (as a number from 1 to 12): "))
4
5  if month >= 1:
6      if month <= 3:
7          print("It's in the first quarter of the year.")
8
9  if month >= 4:
10     if month <= 6:
11         print("It's in the second quarter of the year.")
12
13 if month >= 7:
14     if month <= 9:
15         print("It's in the third quarter of the year.")
16
17 if month >= 10:
18     if month <= 12:
19         print("It's in the fourth quarter of the year.")
```

You can try this exercise again after you learn more about logical operators in Chapter 5.

● Exercise 9: What school are you in?

Write a program that asks the user to enter their age. If their age is between 5 and 10 (inclusive), print "You are in elementary school." If their age is between 11 and 13 (inclusive), print "You are in middle school." If their age is between 14 and 18, print "You are in high school."

The output of this code should be

> Enter your age: 10
> You are in elementary school.

The solution or code is as follows:

```python
# Exercise 9
age = int(input("Enter your age: ")) # Ask the user to enter their age

if age >= 5:
  if age <= 10:
    print("You are in elementary school.")

if age >= 11:
  if age <= 13:
    print("You are in middle school.")

if age >= 14:
  if age <= 18:
    print("You are in high school.")
```

● Exercise 10: Favorite color

Write a program that asks the user to enter their favorite color. If the color is "red," print "Your favorite color is red." If the color is "blue," print "Your favorite color is blue." For any other color, print "Your favorite color is not red or blue."

The output of this code should be

> Enter your favorite color: blue
> Your favorite color is blue.

The solution or code is as follows:

```python
# Exercise 10
color = input("Enter your favorite color: ") # Ask the user to enter their favorite color

if color == "red":
  print("Your favorite color is red.")
elif color == "blue":
  print("Your favorite color is blue.")
else:
  print("Your favorite color is not red or blue.")
```

● Exercise 11: Multiple of a number

Write a program that asks the user to enter a number. If the number is a multiple of 4, print "The number is a multiple of 4." If the number is a multiple of 2 but not 4, print "The number is a multiple of 2 but not 4." Otherwise, print "The number is neither a multiple of 2 nor 4."

The output of this code should be

Enter a number: 40
The number is a multiple of 4.

The solution or code is as follows:

```python
# Exercise 11
number = int(input("Enter a number: "))  # Ask the user to enter a number

if number % 4 == 0:
    print("The number is a multiple of 4.")
elif number % 2 == 0:
    print("The number is a multiple of 2 but not 4.")
else:
    print("The number is neither a multiple of 2 nor 4.")
```

● Exercise 12: Maximum score calculation

Write a program that asks the user to enter the scores of ten students. The program should then find and print the maximum score among all the students.

Example output:

Enter the score for student 1: 85
Enter the score for student 2: 72
Enter the score for student 3: 94
Enter the score for student 4: 88
Enter the score for student 5: 77
Enter the score for student 6: 90
Enter the score for student 7: 81
Enter the score for student 8: 95
Enter the score for student 9: 79
Enter the score for student 10: 83

The maximum score among all students is: 95

Note that in this example, you have some variables, and you want to find the maximum value, which is not an easy task. Because if we have numbers (e.g., 2, 3, 9, 7), we easily know that the maximum of these four numbers is 9, but we do not know how to find this maximum to explain this method (the way to find the maximum) in steps to the computer in our program. But, as you know, if we have some variables, each with a content, we can write a program to find the maximum of these variables. To do this, we define, for example, four variables V1, V2, V3, and V4 and set the maximum equal to the first variable (Max=V1). Next, we compare V2 to Max; if V2>Max, then Max is equal to V2; otherwise, Max is still equal to V1. Similarly, we compare V3 to Max and then V4 to Max. After that, the maximum variable is Max. Similarly, we can find the minimum value among some variables.

The solution or code is as follows:

```python
# Exercise 12
# Prompt the user to enter the scores for all ten students
score1 = int(input("Enter the score for student 1: "))
score2 = int(input("Enter the score for student 2: "))
score3 = int(input("Enter the score for student 3: "))
score4 = int(input("Enter the score for student 4: "))
score5 = int(input("Enter the score for student 5: "))
score6 = int(input("Enter the score for student 6: "))
score7 = int(input("Enter the score for student 7: "))
score8 = int(input("Enter the score for student 8: "))
score9 = int(input("Enter the score for student 9: "))
score10 = int(input("Enter the score for student 10: "))

# Initialize the maximum score with the first score
max_score = score1

# Compare the remaining scores with the current maximum score
if score2 > max_score:
    max_score = score2
if score3 > max_score:
    max_score = score3
if score4 > max_score:
    max_score = score4
if score5 > max_score:
    max_score = score5
if score6 > max_score:
    max_score = score6
if score7 > max_score:
    max_score = score7
if score8 > max_score:
    max_score = score8
if score9 > max_score:
    max_score = score9
if score10 > max_score:
    max_score = score10

# Print the maximum score
print("\nThe maximum score among all students is:", max_score)
```

● Exercise 13: Passing students

Write a program that asks the user to enter the scores of ten students. The program should then determine and print the number of students who passed the test. Consider a passing score to be 60 or above.

Example output:

> Enter the score for student 1: 85
> Enter the score for student 2: 72
> Enter the score for student 3: 45
> Enter the score for student 4: 88
> Enter the score for student 5: 77
> Enter the score for student 6: 90
> Enter the score for student 7: 52
> Enter the score for student 8: 95
> Enter the score for student 9: 79
> Enter the score for student 10: 83
> The number of students who passed the test: 8

Notice that in this exercise on counting the number of students passing, we should know how to create a counter. This counter is nothing more than a variable initialized to zero. For example, let us say we have a numeric variable called counter that is set to zero. After getting the score of each student, we should check if this score is below or above 60. If the score is greater than or equal to 60, it means that the student has passed, so the counter should be increased by one (counter=counter+1). The same step is done with the other students to get the final number. The number of students who have passed is stored in the variable counter.

The solution or code is as follows:

```
1  # Exercise 13
2  # Initialize a variable to keep track of the number of students who passed
3  num_passed = 0
4
5  # Prompt the user to enter the scores of ten students
6  score_1 = int(input("Enter the score for student 1: "))
7  score_2 = int(input("Enter the score for student 2: "))
8  score_3 = int(input("Enter the score for student 3: "))
9  score_4 = int(input("Enter the score for student 4: "))
10 score_5 = int(input("Enter the score for student 5: "))
11 score_6 = int(input("Enter the score for student 6: "))
12 score_7 = int(input("Enter the score for student 7: "))
13 score_8 = int(input("Enter the score for student 8: "))
14 score_9 = int(input("Enter the score for student 9: "))
15 score_10 = int(input("Enter the score for student 10: "))
16
17 # Check if each student's score is above or equal to 60
```

```
18  if score_1 >= 60:
19      num_passed = num_passed + 1
20  if score_2 >= 60:
21      num_passed = num_passed + 1
22  if score_3 >= 60:
23      num_passed = num_passed + 1
24  if score_4 >= 60:
25      num_passed = num_passed + 1
26  if score_5 >= 60:
27      num_passed = num_passed + 1
28  if score_6 >= 60:
29      num_passed = num_passed + 1
30  if score_7 >= 60:
31      num_passed = num_passed + 1
32  if score_8 >= 60:
33      num_passed = num_passed + 1
34  if score_9 >= 60:
35      num_passed = num_passed + 1
36  if score_10 >= 60:
37      num_passed = num_passed + 1
38
39  # Print the number of students who passed the test
40  print("The number of students who passed the test:", num_passed)
```

● Exercise 14: Area calculator

Write a program that allows the user to calculate the area of different shapes (triangle, circle, square, rectangle). The program should provide a menu of options for the user to select the shape and then ask for the necessary inputs to calculate the area. Note that

- **Triangle**: The area of a triangle can be calculated using the formula $Area = 0.5 * base * height$.
- **Circle**: The area of a circle can be calculated using the formula $Area = \pi * radius^2$.
- **Square**: The area of a square can be calculated using the formula $Area = side^2$.
- **Rectangle**: The area of a rectangle can be calculated using the formula $Area = length * width$.

Example output:

— Area Calculator —
1. Triangle
2. Circle
3. Square
4. Rectangle
5. Quit

Enter your choice: 1
Enter the base of the triangle: 5
Enter the height of the triangle: 8
The area of the triangle is: 20.0

The solution or code is as follows:

```python
# Exercise 14
# Display the menu options
print("——— Area Calculator ———")
print("1. Triangle")
print("2. Circle")
print("3. Square")
print("4. Rectangle")
print("5. Quit")

# Get the user's choice
choice = input("Enter your choice: ")

# Calculate the area based on the user's choice
if choice == "1":
    base = float(input("Enter the base of the triangle: "))
    height = float(input("Enter the height of the triangle: "))
    area = 0.5 * base * height
    print("The area of the triangle is:", area)
elif choice == "2":
    radius = float(input("Enter the radius of the circle: "))
    area = 3.14159 * radius ** 2
    print("The area of the circle is:", area)
elif choice == "3":
    side = float(input("Enter the side length of the square: "))
    area = side ** 2
    print("The area of the square is:", area)
elif choice == "4":
    length = float(input("Enter the length of the rectangle: "))
    width = float(input("Enter the width of the rectangle: "))
    area = length * width
    print("The area of the rectangle is:", area)
elif choice == "5":
    print("Goodbye!")
else:
    print("Invalid choice.")
```

● **Exercise 15: Average score calculation**

Write a program that asks the user to enter the scores of ten students. The program should then calculate and print the average score of all the students. Note: The average is the sum of all values or variables divided by the number of values. For example, the average of the four values 2, 4, 5, 9 is $\frac{2+4+5+9}{4} = 5$.

The expected output of this program will be as follows:

Enter the score of student 1: 85
Enter the score of student 2: 90
Enter the score of student 3: 78
Enter the score of student 4: 92
Enter the score of student 5: 87
Enter the score of student 6: 80
Enter the score of student 7: 95
Enter the score of student 8: 89
Enter the score of student 9: 83
Enter the score of student 10: 91
The average score of all the students is: 87.0

The solution or code is as follows:

```
1  # Exercise 15
2  # Ask the user to enter the scores of ten students
3  score1 = float(input("Enter the score of student 1: "))
4  score2 = float(input("Enter the score of student 2: "))
5  score3 = float(input("Enter the score of student 3: "))
6  score4 = float(input("Enter the score of student 4: "))
7  score5 = float(input("Enter the score of student 5: "))
8  score6 = float(input("Enter the score of student 6: "))
9  score7 = float(input("Enter the score of student 7: "))
10 score8 = float(input("Enter the score of student 8: "))
11 score9 = float(input("Enter the score of student 9: "))
12 score10 = float(input("Enter the score of student 10: "))
13
14 # Calculate the average score
15 total = score1 + score2 + score3 + score4 + score5 + score6 + score7 + score8 + score9
        + score10
16 average = total / 10
17
18 # Print the average score
19 print("The average score of all the students is:", average)
```

● Exercise 16: Weather display

Write a program to read the temperature in Celsius and display a suitable message according to the temperature state below:

- Temp < 0, then Freezing weather
- Temp 0–10, then Very Cold weather
- Temp 10–20, then Cold weather
- Temp 20–30, then Normal in Temp
- Temp 30–40, then It's Hot
- Temp ≥ 40, then It's Very Hot

The expected output will be as follows:

Enter the temperature : 42
It's very hot.

The solution will be as follows:

```
1  # Exercise 16
2  temperature = float(input("Enter the temperature: "))
3
4  if temperature < 0:
5    print("Freezing weather")
6  else:
7    if temperature < 10:
8      print("Very Cold weather")
9    else:
10     if temperature < 20:
11       print("Cold weather")
12     else:
13       if temperature < 30:
14         print("Normal in Temp")
15       else:
16         if temperature < 40:
17           print("Its Hot")
18         else:
19           print("Its Very Hot")
```

Or using elif, the solution will be

```
1  # Exercise 16
2  temperature = float(input("Enter the temperature: "))
3
4  if temperature < 0:
5    print("Freezing weather")
6  elif temperature < 10:
7    print("Very Cold weather")
8  elif temperature < 20:
```

```
9    print("Cold weather")
10 elif temperature < 30:
11    print("Normal in Temp")
12 elif temperature < 40:
13    print("Its Hot")
14 else:
15    print("Its Very Hot")
```

● Exercise 17: Print the day name

Write a program to read any day number in integer and display the day name in word format.

The expected output will be as follows:

> Enter the number : 4
> Thursday

The solution or code is as follows:

```
1  # Exercise 17
2  day_number = int(input("Enter the number: "))
3
4  if day_number == 1:
5    print("Monday")
6  elif day_number == 2:
7    print("Tuesday")
8  elif day_number == 3:
9    print("Wednesday")
10 elif day_number == 4:
11    print("Thursday")
12 elif day_number == 5:
13    print("Friday")
14 elif day_number == 6:
15    print("Saturday")
16 elif day_number == 7:
17    print("Sunday")
18 else:
19    print("Invalid day number. Please enter a number between 1 and 7.")
```

Write another version of this program to read any month number and display the month name as a word.

The solution for this will be as follows:

```
1  # Ask the user to enter a month number
2  month_number = int(input("Enter a month number (1-12): "))
3
4  # Determine the month name based on the number
5  if month_number == 1:
```

```python
 6      month_name = "January"
 7  elif month_number == 2:
 8      month_name = "February"
 9  elif month_number == 3:
10      month_name = "March"
11  elif month_number == 4:
12      month_name = "April"
13  elif month_number == 5:
14      month_name = "May"
15  elif month_number == 6:
16      month_name = "June"
17  elif month_number == 7:
18      month_name = "July"
19  elif month_number == 8:
20      month_name = "August"
21  elif month_number == 9:
22      month_name = "September"
23  elif month_number == 10:
24      month_name = "October"
25  elif month_number == 11:
26      month_name = "November"
27  elif month_number == 12:
28      month_name = "December"
29  else:
30      month_name = "Invalid month number"
31
32  # Display the month name
33  print("The month is:", month_name)
```

Solutions of Chapter 4

● **Exercise 1: Print output**

What is the expected output of this program?

```
for i in range(1, 4):
    for j in range(1, 4):
        print(i, j)
```

The solution is as follows:

```
1 1
1 2
1 3
2 1
2 2
2 3
3 1
3 2
3 3
```

● **Exercise 2: Print output**

What is the expected output of this program?

```
for i in range(1, 4):
    for j in range(1, i):
        print(i, "*", j, "=", i*j)
```

© Alaa Tharwat 2025
A. Tharwat, *Python Adventures for Young Coders*,
https://doi.org/10.1007/979-8-8688-1067-1

The solution is as follows:

```
2 * 1 = 2
3 * 1 = 3
3 * 2 = 6
```

● **Exercise 3: Print output**

What is the expected output of this program?

```
1  for i in range(1, 100):
2    if (i%3)==0:
3      print(i)
```

The solution is as follows:

```
3
6
9
:
99
```

Exercise 4: Print numbers

Write a program that uses the for loop to iterate over the numbers from 1 to 10 (inclusive) and prints each number on a new line. The output will be:

```
1
2
3
4
5
6
7
8
9
10
```

The solution is as follows:

The solution using a for loop is

```
1  for num in range(1, 11):
2      # Print the number
3      print(num)
```

Without using any loop:

```
1   print(1)
2   print(2)
3   print(3)
4   print(4)
5   print(5)
6   print(6)
7   print(7)
8   print(8)
9   print(9)
10  print(10)
```

● Exercise 5: Print a pattern

Write a program to display a pattern such as a right-angled triangle with a number.

Example of the output:

```
1
12
123
1234
```

Note: You can use "print(j, end="")" to print the number without a line break after it.

The solution is as follows:

```
1  for i in range(1, 5):
2      for j in range(1, i+1):
3          print(j, end="")
4      print()
```

● **Exercise 6: Print a pattern**

Write a program to make a pattern like a right-angled triangle with a number that repeats a number in a row.
Example of the output:

```
1
22
333
4444
```

The solution is as follows:

```
1  for i in range(1, 5):
2      for j in range(i):
3          print(i, end="")
4      print()
```

● **Exercise 7: Sum of series**

Write a program to display the sum of the series [9 + 99 + 999 + 9999 ...].
Example of the output:

```
Input the number or terms :5
Expected Output :
9 90 900 9000 90000
The sum of the series = 99999
```

The solution is as follows:

```
1   num_terms = int(input("Input the number of terms: "))
2
3   total_sum = 0
4
5   for i in range(num_terms):
6       term = 9 * (10 ** i)
7       print(term, end=" ")
8       total_sum = total_sum + term
9
10  print("\nThe sum of the series =", total_sum)
```

● Exercise 8: Print numbers in descending order

Write a program that uses a for loop to iterate over the numbers from 10 to 1 (inclusive) in descending order and prints each number on a new line.
   The output will be:

```
10
9
8
7
6
5
4
3
2
1
```

The solution is as follows:

```python
# Use a for loop to iterate over the numbers from 10 to 1 in descending order
for num in range(10, 0, -1):
    # Print the number
    print(num)
```

or

```python
# Use a for loop to iterate over the numbers from 10 to 1 in descending order
for num in range(0, 10):
    # Print the number
    print(10 - num)
```

● Exercise 9: Print text

Write a program that uses the for loop to print a word (e.g., "Hello") for ten times.
   Example output:

```
Hello
Hello
Hello
Hello
⋮
Hello
```

The solution is as follows:

```
1  for i in range(10):
2      print("Hello")
```

● **Exercise 10: Print numbers in a sequence**

Write a program that uses the for loop to print a sequence of numbers 2, 4, 6, 8, ... or 3, 6, 9; also, try to print 100, 98, 96, 94, ..., 0.

Example of the output:

```
2
4
6
8
⋮
```

The solution is as follows:

```
1  for i in range(2, 21, 2):
2      print(i)
```

● **Exercise 11: Sum of numbers**

Write a program that takes a positive integer as input and uses the for loop to calculate the sum of all numbers from 1 to that integer. The program should print the sum.

Example of the output:

```
For input 5
Sum: 15
```

The solution is as follows:

```
1   # Take input for the number
2   num = int(input("Enter a positive integer: "))
3
4   # Initialize the sum variable
5   sum_numbers = 0
6
7   # Calculate the sum using a for loop
8   for i in range(1, num+1):
9       sum_numbers = sum_numbers + i
10
11  # Print the sum
12  print("Sum:", sum_numbers)
```

• Exercise 12: Square a number

Write a program that uses a for loop to iterate over the numbers from 1 to 5 (inclusive). For each number, calculate and print its square.

Example of the output:

```
1
4
9
16
25
```

The solution is as follows:

```
# Use a for loop to iterate over the numbers from 1 to 5
for num in range(1, 6):
    # Calculate the square
    square = num ** 2

    # Print the square
    print(square)
```

• Exercise 13: Factorial

Write a program that takes a positive integer as input and calculates its factorial using the for loop. The factorial of a number n is the product of all positive integers from 1 to n.

Example of the output:

```
For input: 5
Factorial of 5 is 120
```

The solution is as follows:

```
num = int(input("Enter a positive integer: "))
factorial = 1

for i in range(1, num + 1):
    factorial = factorial * i

print("Factorial of", num, "is", factorial)
```

● Exercise 14: Sum of even numbers

Write a program that takes as input two integers representing the starting and ending numbers of a range. The program should use a for loop to iterate over the numbers in the range (inclusive) and compute the sum of all even numbers in the range. Assume that the starting number is always less than or equal to the ending number.

Example of the output:

Starting number: 1
End number: 10
Sum of even numbers: 30

The solution is as follows:

```python
start = int(input("Enter the starting number: "))
end = int(input("Enter the ending number: "))
sum_even = 0

for num in range(start, end + 1):
    if num % 2 == 0:
        sum_even = sum_even + num

print("Sum of even numbers:", sum_even)
```

● Exercise 15: Password entry

Write a program that asks the user to enter a password and continues to ask for the password until the correct password is entered. Once the correct password is entered, the program should display a success message and exit.

Example of the output:

Enter the password: 12345
Incorrect password. Please try again.
Enter the password: password123
Incorrect password. Please try again.
Enter the password: 1234
Success! You have entered the correct password.

The solution is as follows:

```python
# Define the correct password
correct_password = "1234"

# Set the maximum number of trials
max_trials = 5
```

```
6
7  # Prompt the user for the password
8  for trial in range(max_trials):
9    password = input("Enter the password: ")
10
11   # Check if the password is correct
12   if password == correct_password:
13     print("Success! You have entered the correct password.")
14     break
15   else:
16     print("Incorrect password. Please try again.")
17
18   # Check if the maximum number of trials has been reached
19   if trial == max_trials - 1:
20     print("Maximum number of trials reached. Access denied.")
```

Solutions of Chapter 5

> ● **Exercise 1: Print the output**
>
> Write the output of this program:
>
> ```python
> 1  # Integer to other types
> 2  i = 42
> 3  print("Integer i =", i)
> 4  print("Integer to float:", float(i))
> 5  print("Integer to string:", str(i))
> 6
> 7  # Float to other types
> 8  f = 3.14
> 9  print("\nFloat f =", f)
> 10 print("Float to integer:", int(f))
> 11 print("Float to string:", str(f))
> 12
> 13 # String to other types
> 14 s1 = "12"
> 15 s2 = "3.45"
> 16 s3 = "hello"
> 17 print("\nStrings:")
> 18 print("s1 =", s1)
> 19 print("s2 =", s2)
> 20 print("s3 =", s3)
> 21 print("String to integer:", int(s1))
> 22 print("String to float:", float(s2))
> 23 # print("String to float:", float(s3)) # ValueError: could not convert string to float: 'hello'
> ```
>
> Note that with the code "print("String to integer:", int(s3))", an error will occur when trying to convert the string "hello" to an integer, because the int() function in Python can only convert strings that represent valid integer numbers. Similarly, with "print("String to float:", float(s3))" there will be an

© Alaa Tharwat 2025
A. Tharwat, *Python Adventures for Young Coders*,
https://doi.org/10.1007/979-8-8688-1067-1

error because the string "hello" cannot be converted to a valid floating-point number.

The solution is as follows:

```
Integer i = 42
Integer to float: 42.0
Integer to string: 42

Float f = 3.14
Float to integer: 3
Float to string: 3.14

Strings:
s1 = 12
s2 = 3.45
s3 = hello
String to integer: 12
String to float: 3.45
```

● **Exercise 2: Print the output**

Write the output of this program:

```
1   small_basket_size = 10
2   medium_basket_size = 15
3   large_basket_size = 20
4
5   small_basket = 0
6   medium_basket = 0
7   large_basket = 0
8
9   while True:
10      produce_size = int(input("Enter the size of the produce (1−20): "))
11
12      if produce_size >= 1 and produce_size <= 10:
13          small_basket += 1
14          print("Small basket now has", {small_basket}, " items.")
15          if small_basket == small_basket_size:
16              print("The small basket is full!")
17              small_basket = 0
18      elif produce_size >= 11 and produce_size <= 15:
19          medium_basket += 1
20          print("Medium basket now has", {medium_basket}, " items.")
21          if medium_basket == medium_basket_size:
22              print("The medium basket is full!")
23              medium_basket = 0
```

```
24   elif produce_size >= 16 and produce_size <= 20:
25      large_basket += 1
26      print("Large basket now has", {large_basket}, " items.")
27      if large_basket == large_basket_size:
28         print("The large basket is full!")
29         large_basket = 0
30   else:
31      print("Invalid produce size. Please enter a number between 1 and 20.")
```

The output is as follows:

> Enter the size of the produce (1-20): 5
> Small basket now has 1 items.
> Enter the size of the produce (1-20): 12
> Medium basket now has 1 items.
> Enter the size of the produce (1-20): 18
> Large basket now has 1 items.
> Enter the size of the produce (1-20): 10
> Small basket now has 2 items.
> Enter the size of the produce (1-20): 16
> Large basket now has 2 items.
> Enter the size of the produce (1-20): 21
> Invalid produce size. Please enter a number between 1 and 20.

In the above program, the user enters produce sizes, and the program places them in the appropriate baskets. When a basket becomes full, the program prints a message indicating that the basket is full and resets the count for that basket. The program continues to run until the user interrupts it (e.g., by pressing Ctrl+C).

● Exercise 3: Print the output

Write the output of this program:

```
1   total_cost = 0
2   item_count = 0
3
4   while item_count < 5:
5      item_price = float(input("Enter the price of item " + str(item_count + 1) + ": "))
6      total_cost += item_price
7      item_count += 1
8
9      if item_count == 5:
10        print("The total cost of the purchase is: ",total_cost)
11        break
12     else:
13        print("The current total cost is:", total_cost)
```

The output will be as follows:

Enter the price of item 1: 10.50
The current total cost is: 10.5 Enter the price of item 2: 15.75
The current total cost is: 26.25 Enter the price of item 3: 7.99
The current total cost is: 34.24 Enter the price of item 4: 12.25
The current total cost is: 46.49 Enter the price of item 5: 18.75
The total cost of the purchase is: 65.24

What will be the output if we replace break with continue?
The answer is that instead of stopping after the fifth item, the program will continue to prompt the user for input indefinitely. Try it yourself.

● **Exercise 4: Print the output**

Write the output of the two programs below:

```
for i in range(10):
    if i == 5:
        print("Breaking the loop at i =", i)
        break
    print("Iteration", i)
```

The output will be as follows:

Iteration 0
Iteration 1
Iteration 2
Iteration 3
Iteration 4
Breaking the loop at i = 5

```
for i in range(10):
    if i == 5:
        print("Skipping iteration at i =", i)
        continue
    print("Iteration", i)
```

The output will be as follows:

Iteration 0
Iteration 1
Iteration 2
Iteration 3
Iteration 4
Skipping iteration at i = 5
Iteration 6
Iteration 7
Iteration 8
Iteration 9

● Exercise 5: Print the output

Write the output of this program:

```python
# Initialize some variables
a = 10
b = 5
c = 20

print("Initial values:")
print("a =", a)
print("b =", b)
print("c =", c)

# Compound assignment operators
a += 3  # a = a + 3
b -= 2  # b = b - 2
c *= 4  # c = c * 4
print("\nAfter compound assignment:")
print("a =", a)
print("b =", b)
print("c =", c)

# Chained assignments
x = y = z = 15
print("\nChained assignment:")
print("x =", x)
print("y =", y)
print("z =", z)

# Augmented assignments with various operators
x += 2   # x = x + 2
y -= 3   # y = y - 3
z *= 4   # z = z * 4
c /= 2   # c = c / 2
```

```
32  print("\nAugmented assignments:")
33  print("x =", x)
34  print("y =", y)
35  print("z =", z)
36  print("c =", c)
```

The output will be as follows:

Initial values:
a = 10
b = 5
c = 20

After compound assignment:
a = 13
b = 3
c = 80

Chained assignment:
x = 15
y = 15
z = 15

Augmented assignments:
x = 17
y = 12
z = 60
c = 40.0

● **Exercise 6: Convert for to while**

Write the following program using a while statement instead of using the for loop:

```
1  for i in range(1, 4):
2      for j in range(1, 4):
3          print(i, j)
```

Note: This is nested for, so you may need nested while.

The program using while is as follows:

```
1  i = 1
2  while i < 4:
3    j = 1
4    while j < 4:
5      print(i, j)
6      j += 1
7    i += 1
```

The output of this program is

```
1 1
1 2
1 3
2 1
2 2
2 3
3 1
3 2
3 3
```

• Exercise 7: Print numbers in descending order

Write a program that uses the while statement to iterate over the numbers from 10 to 1 (inclusive) in descending order and prints each number on a new line (this exercise was in Chapter 4, but using the for loop).

The output will be as follows:

```
10
9
8
7
6
5
4
3
2
1
```

The solution using the while loop will be as follows:

```
# Initialize the starting number
number = 10

# Use a while loop to iterate from 10 to 1
while number >= 1:
    print(number)  # Print the current number
    number -= 1    # Decrease the number by 1
```

Without using any loop:

```
print(10)
print(9)
print(8)
print(7)
print(6)
print(5)
print(4)
print(3)
print(2)
print(1)
```

Solutions of Chapter 6

● **Exercise 1: The output of the program**

Write the output of the following program:

```python
1  # Create a list of numbers
2  numbers = [10, 20, 30, 40, 50, 60, 70, 80, 90, 100]
3
4  print("Original list of numbers:")
5  print(numbers)
6
7  # Remove a specific number
8  num_to_remove = int(input("Enter the number you want to remove: "))
9  if num_to_remove in numbers:
10     numbers.remove(num_to_remove)
11     print(f"{num_to_remove} has been removed from the list.")
12 else:
13     print(f"{num_to_remove} is not in the list.")
14
15 print("\nUpdated list of numbers:")
16 print(numbers)
17
18 # Remove a number at a specific index
19 index_to_remove = int(input("\nEnter the index of the number you want to remove: "))
20 if index_to_remove >= 0 and index_to_remove < len(numbers):
21     removed_num = numbers.pop(index_to_remove)
22     print(f"{removed_num} has been removed from the list.")
23 else:
24     print("Invalid index.")
25
26 print("\nUpdated list of numbers:")
27 print(numbers)
28
29 # Clear the entire list
30 clear_list = input("\nDo you want to clear the entire list of numbers? (y/n) ")
```

```
31  if clear_list == 'y':
32      numbers.clear()
33      print("The list of numbers has been cleared.")
34  else:
35      print("The list of numbers remains unchanged.")
36
37  print("\nThe final list of numbers:")
38  print(numbers)
```

The output will be as follows:

Original list of numbers: [10, 20, 30, 40, 50, 60, 70, 80, 90, 100]
Enter the number you want to remove: 30
30 has been removed from the list.

Updated list of numbers: [10, 20, 40, 50, 60, 70, 80, 90, 100]
Enter the index of the number you want to remove: 4
60 has been removed from the list.

Updated list of numbers:[10, 20, 40, 50, 70, 80, 90, 100]

Do you want to clear the entire list of numbers? (y/n) n
The final list of numbers: [10, 20, 40, 50, 70, 80, 90, 100]

● Exercise 2: Months

Write a program that asks the user to create a list called "Month_list" and asks the user to enter the names of the months and put them into the list.
   Example output:

Let's make a list of the 12 months
Enter the name of month 1: January
Enter the name of month 2: February
Enter the name of month 3: March
Enter the name of month 4: April
Enter the name of month 5: May
Enter the name of month 6: June
Enter the name of month 7: July
Enter the name of month 8: August

Enter the name of month 9: September
Enter the name of month 10: October
Enter the name of month 11: November
Enter the name of month 12: December
Great! Here is the list of months you entered:
['January', 'February', 'March', 'April', 'May', 'June', 'July',
'August', 'September', 'October', 'November', 'December']

The solution will be as follows:

```
1  # Create an empty list to store the months
2  Month_list = []
3
4  print("Let's make a list of the 12 months")
5
6  # Use a loop to prompt the user for each month
7  for i in range(1, 13):
8      month_name = input(f"Enter the name of month {i}: ")
9      Month_list.append(month_name)
10
11 # Print the final list of months
12 print("Great! Here is the list of months you entered:")
13 print(Month_list)
```

● Exercise 3: Favorite colors

Write a program that asks the user to create a list called "Color_list" and enter
their favorite color. The program will first ask how many favorite colors the
user has.

Example output:

How many colors do you want to add? 5
Enter color 1: Blue
Enter color 2: Green
Enter color 3: Red
Enter color 4: Yellow
Enter color 5: Purple
Great! Here is your list of favorite colors: ['Blue', 'Green', 'Red',
'Yellow', 'Purple']

The solution will be as follows:

```
1  # Create an empty list to store the user's favorite colors
2  Color_list = []
3
4  # Ask the user how many colors they want to add
5  num_colors = int(input("How many colors do you want to add? "))
6
7  # Use a loop to prompt the user for each color
8  for i in range(1, num_colors + 1):
9      color = input("Enter color "+ str(i) + ": ")
10     Color_list.append(color)
11
12 # Print the final list of favorite colors
13 print("Great! Here is your list of favorite colors:", Color_list)
```

● **Exercise 4: Remove a fruit**

The following program has a list of fruits as in the code below. Write a program that asks the user which item in the list to remove. If the item is in the list, remove it and print the list; otherwise, print "This fruit is not in the list."

```
1  # Create a list of fruits
2  fruits = ['apple', 'banana', 'cherry', 'date', 'elderberry', 'fig']
```

Example output:

Here is the current list of fruits:
'apple', 'banana', 'cherry', 'date', 'elderberry', 'fig'
Which fruit do you want to remove? date
date has been removed from the list.
Here is the updated list of fruits: ['apple', 'banana', 'cherry', 'elderberry', 'fig']

The solution will be as follows:

```
1  # Create a list of fruits
2  fruits = ['apple', 'banana', 'cherry', 'date', 'elderberry', 'fig']
3
4  print("Here is the current list of fruits:")
5  print(fruits)
6
7  # Ask the user which fruit to remove
8  fruit_to_remove = input("Which fruit do you want to remove? ")
9
```

```
10   # Check if the fruit is in the list
11   if fruit_to_remove in fruits:
12       fruits.remove(fruit_to_remove)
13       print(f"{fruit_to_remove} has been removed from the list.")
14       print("Here is the updated list of fruits:")
15       print(fruits)
16   else:
17       print(f"This fruit ({fruit_to_remove}) is not in the list.")
```

Try to write the same program, but try to remove a fruit at a specific index. Here is the solution of removing an element given its index:

```
1    # Create a list of fruits
2    fruits = ['apple', 'banana', 'cherry', 'date', 'elderberry', 'fig']
3
4    print("Here is the current list of fruits:")
5    print(fruits)
6
7    # Ask the user which index to remove
8    index_to_remove = int(input("Enter the index of the fruit you want to remove (0-{}): ".
         format(len(fruits) - 1)))
9
10   # Check if the index is valid
11   if 0 <= index_to_remove < len(fruits):
12       removed_fruit = fruits[index_to_remove]  # Get the fruit at the specified index
13       fruits.remove(removed_fruit)  # Remove the fruit from the list
14       print(removed_fruit, " has been removed from the list.")
15       print("Here is the updated list of fruits:")
16       print(fruits)
17   else:
18       print("Invalid index (" + str(index_to_remove)+ "). Please enter a number between 0
         and " + str(len(fruits) - 1) + ".")
```

● Exercise 5: Update a fruit

The following program has a list of fruits as in the code below. Write a program that asks the user which item in the list to update. If the item is in the list, update it and print the list; otherwise, print "This fruit is not in the list."

```
1    # Create a list of fruits
2    fruits = ['apple', 'banana', 'cherry', 'date', 'elderberry', 'fig']
```

Example output:

Here is the current list of fruits:
['apple', 'banana', 'cherry', 'date', 'elderberry', 'fig']
Which fruit do you want to update? date
What do you want to update 'date' to? peach
'date' has been updated to 'peach'.

The solution will be as follows:

```python
# Create a list of fruits
fruits = ['apple', 'banana', 'cherry', 'date', 'elderberry', 'fig']

print("Here is the current list of fruits:")
print(fruits)

# Ask the user which fruit to update
update_fruit = input("Which fruit do you want to update? ")

# Check if the fruit is in the list
if update_fruit in fruits:
    new_fruit = input(f"What do you want to update '{update_fruit}' to? ")
    index = fruits.index(update_fruit)
    fruits[index] = new_fruit
    print(f"'{update_fruit}' has been updated to '{new_fruit}'.")
else:
    print(f"'{update_fruit}' is not in the list.")
```

In the above code, the line "index = fruits.index(update_fruit)" is used to get the index of an item in the list. This index is used in the next line "fruits[index] = new_fruit" to update the contents of the list at that index.

Here is another solution:

```python
# Create a list of fruits
fruits = ['apple', 'banana', 'cherry', 'date', 'elderberry', 'fig']

# Print the current list of fruits
print("Here are the fruits in the list:")
print(fruits)

# Ask the user which fruit to update
update_fruit = input("Which fruit do you want to change? ")

# Check if the fruit is in the list
if update_fruit in fruits:
    # Get the new name for the fruit
    new_fruit = input(f"What do you want to change '{update_fruit}' to? ")

    # Update the fruit in the list
    for i in range(len(fruits)):
```

```
18      if fruits[i] == update_fruit:
19          fruits[i] = new_fruit
20          print(f"'{update_fruit}' has been changed to '{new_fruit}'.")
21          break
22  else:
23      print(f"'{update_fruit}' is not in the list.")
```

The above code iterates over the entire list of items to find the item that should be updated and then modifies it with the new value entered by the user.

● **Exercise 6: Sum of numbers**

Write a program that asks the user to enter five numbers and stores them in a list. Then, print the sum of the numbers.

Example output:

```
2
4
6
8
10
The sum of the numbers is: 30
```

The solution will be as follows:

```
1   # Create an empty list to store the numbers
2   numbers = []
3   total=0
4
5   # Ask the user to enter 5 numbers and store them in the list
6   print("Please enter 5 numbers:")
7   for i in range(5):
8       num = int(input(f"Number {i+1}: "))
9       numbers.append(num)
10      total+=num
11
12  # Print the list of numbers
13  print("\nThe numbers you entered are:")
14  print(numbers)
15
16  # Print the sum of the numbers
17  print(f"\nThe sum of the numbers is: {total}")
```

● Exercise 7: Largest and smallest numbers

Write a program that takes a list of five numbers as input and prints the largest and smallest numbers in the list. Example output:

```
2
8
9
1
4
Largest number: 9
Smallest number: 1
```

The solution will be as follows:

```python
# Create an empty list to store the numbers
numbers = []

largest=−float('inf')
smallest=float('inf')
# Ask the user to enter 5 numbers and store them in the list
print("Please enter 5 numbers:")
for i in range(5):
    num = int(input(f"Number {i+1}: "))
    numbers.append(num)

    # Find the largest number in the list
    if num>largest:
        largest=num
    # Find the smallest number in the list
    if num<smallest:
        smallest=num

# Print the list of numbers
print("\nThe numbers you entered are:")
print(numbers)

# Print the largest and smallest numbers
print(f"\nLargest number: {largest}")
print(f"Smallest number: {smallest}")
```

• Exercise 8: Positive and negative numbers

Write a program that asks the user to enter a number of items and separates them into two lists: one for positive numbers and one for negative numbers. To do this:

1. Ask the user to enter the number of numbers they want to input.
2. Create two new lists: one for positive numbers and one for negative numbers.
3. Use a loop to ask the user to enter each number one by one.
4. Iterate over the input list and check each number. If the number is positive, add it to the list of positive numbers. If the number is negative, add it to the negative numbers list.
5. Display the positive numbers list and the negative numbers list.

Example output:

```
Enter the number of items: 5
Enter a number: 10
Enter a number: -5
Enter a number: 7
Enter a number: -3
Enter a number: 8
Positive numbers: [10, 7, 8]
Negative numbers: [−5, −3]
```

The solution will be as follows:

```python
num_items = int(input("Enter the number of items: "))

positive_numbers = []
negative_numbers = []
for i in range(num_items):
    number = int(input("Enter a number: "))
    if number > 0:
        positive_numbers.append(number)
    elif number < 0:
        negative_numbers.append(number)

print("Positive numbers:", positive_numbers)
print("Negative numbers:", negative_numbers)
```

● **Exercise 9: Shopping list organizer**

Write a program that allows the user to create and organize a shopping list. To do this:

1. Start by creating an empty list called shopping_list to store the items.
2. Ask the user if they want to add items to the shopping list. If they answer "yes," proceed to the next step. If they answer "no," skip to step 5.
3. Inside a loop, ask the user to enter a new item to add to the shopping list. Append each item to the shopping_list list.
4. After adding the item, ask the user if they want to add more items. If they answer "yes," go back to step 2. If they answer "no," proceed to step 5.
5. Display the final shopping list to the user.
6. After displaying the final shopping list, ask the user if they want to remove any items. If they answer "yes," ask them to enter the name of the item they want to remove. Remove the item from the shopping_list if it exists.

Example output:

> Would you like to add items to the shopping list? (yes/no): yes
> Enter a new item to add: Apples
> Do you want to add more items? (yes/no): yes
> Enter a new item to add: Bread
> Do you want to add more items? (yes/no): yes
> Enter a new item to add: Milk
> Do you want to add more items? (yes/no): no
> Shopping List:
> - Apples
> - Bread
> - Milk
> Would you like to remove any items from the shopping list? (yes/no):
> yes
> Enter the name of the item to remove: Bread
> Item "Bread" removed from the shopping list.
> Updated Shopping List:
> - Apples
> - Milk

The solution will be as follows:

```
1  # Start by creating an empty list called shopping_list to store the items.
2  shopping_list = []
3
4  # Ask the user if they want to add items to the shopping list.
5  add_items = input("Would you like to add items to the shopping list? (yes/no): ")
```

```
6
7   # If the user answers "yes", proceed to the next step.
8   if add_items == "yes":
9       # Ask the user to enter a new item to add to the shopping list.
10      new_item = input("Enter a new item to add: ")
11      # Append each item to the shopping_list list.
12      shopping_list.append(new_item)
13
14      # Ask the user if they want to add more items.
15      while True:
16          add_more = input("Do you want to add more items? (yes/no): ")
17          if add_more== "yes":
18              new_item = input("Enter a new item to add: ")
19              shopping_list.append(new_item)
20          elif add_more == "no":
21              break
22          else:
23              print("Invalid input. Please enter 'yes' or 'no'.")
24
25  # Display the final shopping list to the user.
26  print("\nShopping List:")
27  for item in shopping_list:
28      print("- " + item)
29
30  # Ask the user if they want to remove any items from the shopping list.
31  remove_items = input("\nWould you like to remove any items from the shopping list? (
        yes/no): ")
32  if remove_items == "yes":
33      item_to_remove = input("Enter the name of the item to remove: ")
34      if item_to_remove in shopping_list:
35          shopping_list.remove(item_to_remove)
36          print(f"Item \"{item_to_remove}\" removed from the shopping list.")
37      else:
38          print("Item not found in the shopping list.")
39
40  # Display the updated shopping list.
41  print("\nUpdated Shopping List:")
42  for item in shopping_list:
43      print("- " + item)
```

● **Exercise 10: Positive number sum**

Write a program that prompts the user to enter a series of positive numbers and stores them in a list. The program should continue to ask for numbers until the user enters a negative number. Afterward, it should calculate and display the sum of all the positive numbers entered. To do this:

- Create an empty list called number_list to store the positive numbers.
- Ask the user to enter a positive number.

- Check whether the number is positive.
  - If the number is positive, append it to number_list.
  - If the number is negative, break (or exit) the loop and proceed to the next step.
- Keep asking the user to enter positive numbers until they enter a negative number.
- Calculate the sum of all the positive numbers in number_list.
- Display the sum to the user.

Example output:

Enter a positive number (or a negative number to quit): 5
Enter a positive number (or a negative number to quit): 3
Enter a positive number (or a negative number to quit): 8
Enter a positive number (or a negative number to quit): -2

Sum of positive numbers: 16

The solution will be as follows:

```
1   # Create an empty list to store positive numbers
2   number_list = []
3   total=0
4   # Continuously ask the user to enter a positive number
5   while True:
6       number = int(input("Enter a positive number (or a negative number to quit): "))
7
8       # Check if the number is positive
9       if number >= 0:
10          # Add the positive number to the list
11          number_list.append(number)
12          # Calculate the sum of the positive numbers
13          total+=number
14      else:
15          break
16
17  # Display the sum to the user
18  print("\nSum of positive numbers:", total)
```

● Exercise 11: Temperature converter

Write a program that prompts the user to enter a series of temperatures in Celsius and stores them in a list. The program should then convert each temperature to Fahrenheit and display both the Celsius and Fahrenheit temperatures side by side. To do this:

- Create an empty list called celsius_temperatures to store the temperatures in Celsius.
- Create a new list called fahrenheit_temperatures that contains the Fahrenheit equivalents of the temperatures in celsius_temperatures. The conversion formula is $Fahrenheit = Celsius * 9/5 + 32$.
- Ask the user to enter a series of temperatures in Celsius, one at a time.
- For each temperature entered by the user, append it to the celsius_temperatures list.
- Convert the celsius_temperatures into fahrenheit_temperatures and add it to the fahrenheit_temperatures list.
- Continue asking the user to enter temperatures until they choose to stop; display the temperatures side by side.

Example output:

```
Enter a temperature in Celsius (or 'q' to quit): 20
Enter a temperature in Celsius (or 'q' to quit): 10
Enter a temperature in Celsius (or 'q' to quit): 30
Enter a temperature in Celsius (or 'q' to quit): q

Temperature Conversion:
Celsius   Fahrenheit
20              68.0
10              50.0
30              86.0
```

The solution will be as follows:

```python
# Create an empty list to store temperatures in Celsius
celsius_temperatures = []

# Continuously ask the user to enter a temperature in Celsius
while True:
    temperature = input("Enter a temperature in Celsius (or 'q' to quit): ")

    # Check if the user wants to quit
    if temperature == 'q':
        break

    # Convert the temperature to a float and add it to the list
    celsius_temperatures.append(float(temperature))

# Create a list to store temperatures in Fahrenheit
fahrenheit_temperatures = []

# Convert each temperature from Celsius to Fahrenheit and store it in the new list
for celsius in celsius_temperatures:
```

```
20    fahrenheit = celsius * 9/5 + 32
21    fahrenheit_temperatures.append(fahrenheit)
22
23  # Display the Celsius and Fahrenheit temperatures side by side
24  print("\nTemperature Conversion:")
25  print("Celsius\t\tFahrenheit")
26  for i in range(len(celsius_temperatures)):
27    celsius = celsius_temperatures[i]
28    fahrenheit = fahrenheit_temperatures[i]
29    print(f"{celsius}\t\t{fahrenheit}")
```

Solutions of Chapter 7

The program below has two lists, one for questions and one for answers. Write a program that asks the user a question from the question list, compares their answer with the correct answer in the answer list, keeps track of the score, and prints the score. [Note: This exercise should help in enhancing projects A and C in the previous chapter.]

```
1  # List of questions and answers
2  questions = [
3    "What is the capital of France?",
4    "What is the largest ocean on Earth?",
5    "Who wrote the novel 'To Kill a Mockingbird'?",
6    "What is the symbol for the chemical element gold?",
7    "What is the tallest mountain in the world?" ]
8
9  answers = ["paris", "pacific","harper lee", "au","mount everest"]
```

The solution is as follows:

```
1  # List of questions and answers
2  questions = [
3    "What is the capital of France?",
4    "What is the largest ocean on Earth?",
5    "Who wrote the novel 'To Kill a Mockingbird'?",
6    "What is the symbol for the chemical element gold?",
7    "What is the tallest mountain in the world?"
8  ]
9
10 answers = ["paris", "pacific", "harper lee", "au", "mount everest"]
11
12 # Initialize the score
13 score = 0
14
```

© Alaa Tharwat 2025
A. Tharwat, *Python Adventures for Young Coders*,
https://doi.org/10.1007/979-8-8688-1067-1

```
15  # Loop through the questions and answers
16  for i, question in enumerate(questions):
17      # Ask the user for their answer
18      user_answer = input(f"{question} ")
19
20      # Check if the user's answer matches the correct answer
21      if user_answer == answers[i]:
22          print("Correct!")
23          score += 1
24      else:
25          print(f"Incorrect. The correct answer is: {answers[i]}")
26
27  # Print the final score
28  print(f"\nYour final score is: {score}/{len(questions)}")
```

● Exercise 2: Unique names

Write a program that prompts the user to enter a list of names and then removes any duplicate names from the list. To do this:

- Ask the user to enter the number of names they want to enter.
- Using a loop, prompt the user to enter each name one by one and store them in a list.
- Remove any duplicate names from the list.
- Display the final list of unique names.

Example output:

> Enter the number of names: 4
> Enter name 1: John
> Enter name 2: John
> Enter name 3: Mary
> Enter name 4: Mary
> Unique names: ['John', 'Mary']

The solution is as follows:

```
1   num_names = int(input("Enter the number of names: "))
2
3   names = []
4
5   for i in range(num_names):
6       name = input(f"Enter name {i+1}: ")
7       names.append(name)
8
9   unique_names = []
10
```

```
11  for name in names:
12    if name not in unique_names:
13      unique_names.append(name)
14
15  print("\nUnique names:", unique_names)
```

● **Exercise 3: Unique number list**

Write a program that allows the user to enter a series of numbers and stores them in a list. The program should store only unique numbers and discard duplicates. To do this:

- Create an empty list called number_list to store the unique numbers.
- Ask the user to enter a series of numbers, one at a time.
- For each number entered by the user, check if it already exists in the number_list.
  - If the number is not in the list, append it to number_list.
  - If the number is already in the list, ignore it and proceed to the next number.
- Continue asking the user to enter numbers until they choose to stop.
- Display the final list of unique numbers to the user.

Example output:

```
Enter a number (or 'q' to quit): 5
Enter a number (or 'q' to quit): 3
Enter a number (or 'q' to quit): 8
Enter a number (or 'q' to quit): 5
Enter a number (or 'q' to quit): 2
Enter a number (or 'q' to quit): q

Unique Number List:
[5, 3, 8, 2]
```

The solution is as follows:

```python
# Create an empty list to store unique numbers
number_list = []

# Continuously ask the user to enter a number until they choose to stop
while True:
    number = input("Enter a number (or 'q' to quit): ")

    # Check if the user wants to quit
    if number == 'q':
        break

    # Convert the input to an integer (assuming valid input)
    number = int(number)

    # Check if the number is already in the list
    if number not in number_list:
        # Add the unique number to the list
        number_list.append(number)

# Display the final list of unique numbers
print("\nUnique Number List:")
print(number_list)
```

● Exercise 4: List merger

Write a program that prompts the user to enter a series of elements and stores them in three separate lists. The program should then merge the three lists into a single list, remove any duplicates, and display the merged list. To do this:

- Create three empty lists called list1, list2, and list3 to store the elements.
- Ask the user to enter elements for each list, one at a time.
- For each element entered by the user, append it to the corresponding list.
- Continue asking the user to enter elements until they choose to stop for each list.
- Create a new list called merged_list by concatenating the three lists together.
- Try to remove any duplicates from merged_list.
- Display the merged list to the user.

Example output:

Enter elements for list 1 (or 'q' to quit): 5
Enter elements for list 1 (or 'q' to quit): 10
Enter elements for list 1 (or 'q' to quit): q

Enter elements for list 2 (or 'q' to quit): 10
Enter elements for list 2 (or 'q' to quit): 15
Enter elements for list 2 (or 'q' to quit): 20
Enter elements for list 2 (or 'q' to quit): q

Enter elements for list 3 (or 'q' to quit): 5
Enter elements for list 3 (or 'q' to quit): 20
Enter elements for list 3 (or 'q' to quit): 25
Enter elements for list 3 (or 'q' to quit): q

Merged List: [5, 10, 15, 20, 25]

The solution is as follows:

```python
# Create three empty lists to store the elements
list1 = []
list2 = []
list3 = []

# Ask the user to enter elements for list 1
while True:
    element = input("Enter elements for list 1 (or 'q' to quit): ")
    if element.lower() == 'q':
        break
    list1.append(element)

# Ask the user to enter elements for list 2
while True:
    element = input("Enter elements for list 2 (or 'q' to quit): ")
    if element.lower() == 'q':
        break
    list2.append(element)

# Ask the user to enter elements for list 3
while True:
    element = input("Enter elements for list 3 (or 'q' to quit): ")
    if element.lower() == 'q':
        break
    list3.append(element)

# Merge the three lists into a single list
merged_list = list1 + list2 + list3
```

```
29
30  # Remove duplicates from the merged list
31  unique_list = []
32  for element in merged_list:
33    if element not in unique_list:
34      unique_list.append(element)
35
36  # Display the merged list without duplicates
37  print("Merged List:", unique_list)
```

● **Exercise 5: Score frequencies**

Write a program that prompts the user to enter a series of scores and stores them in a list. The program should then count the frequencies of each score and display the results. To do this:

- Create an empty list called scores to store the scores.
- Ask the user to enter scores, one at a time. Continue asking the user until they choose to stop.
- Create an empty list called frequency to store the frequencies of each score.
- Iterate over each score in the scores list. Check if the score is already within the list. If it is, increment the corresponding value by one. If it is not, add a new key-value pair with the score as the key and an initial value of one.
- Display the frequencies of each score to the user.

    Here in this exercise, we can explain what is a dictionary in programming. A dictionary is like a real dictionary, where you look up a word and find its meaning. In programming, a dictionary helps us store information in pairs: a key and a value. Key: This is like the word you are looking up. It is unique and helps you find the information you need. Value: This is the information or meaning associated with the key.
    Imagine you have a box of toys. You want to keep track of how many of each toy you have. You could use a dictionary like this:

- Key: The name of the toy (e.g., "Teddy Bear")
- Value: The number of this toy you have (e.g., 3)

So your dictionary might look like this:

```
{
"Teddy Bear": 3,
"Car": 5,
"Doll": 2
}
```

Suppose you want to count the scores of your friends in a game:

- Key: The score (such as 10, 20, or 30)
- Value: How often that score was achieved

If your friends have the following scores – Alice: 10, Bob: 20, Carol: 10, and Dave: 30 – you can create a dictionary to count the scores:

```
{
10: 2, # two friends scored 10
20: 1, # One friend scored 20
30: 1 # One friend scored 30
}
```

This idea about the dictionary might help you find the solution to this exercise, where the key is the score and the value is the number of times that key appears in the list.

Example output:

Enter a score (or 'q' to quit): 85
Enter a score (or 'q' to quit): 90
Enter a score (or 'q' to quit): 85
Enter a score (or 'q' to quit): 80
Enter a score (or 'q' to quit): q

Score Frequencies:
85: 2
90: 1
80: 1

The solution is as follows:

```
# Create an empty list to store the scores
scores = []

# Ask the user to enter scores
while True:
    score = input("Enter a score (or 'q' to quit): ")
    if score.lower() == 'q':
        break
    scores.append(int(score))
```

```
10
11  # Create an empty dictionary to store the frequencies
12  frequency = {}
13
14  # Count the frequencies of each score
15  for score in scores:
16      if score in frequency:
17          frequency[score] += 1
18      else:
19          frequency[score] = 1
20
21  # Display the frequencies of each score
22  print("Score Frequencies:")
23  for score, freq in frequency.items():
24      print(f"{score}: {freq}")
```

● Exercise 6: List reversal

Write a program that prompts the user to enter a list of numbers and then reverses the order of the elements in the list. The program should display the reversed list to the user. To do this:

- Create an empty list called numbers to store the input numbers.
- Ask the user to enter numbers, one at a time. Continue asking the user until they choose to stop.
- Reverse the order of the elements in the numbers list.
- Display the reversed list to the user.

Example output:

```
Enter a number (or 'q' to quit): 5
Enter a number (or 'q' to quit): 10
Enter a number (or 'q' to quit): 15
Enter a number (or 'q' to quit): q

Reversed List: [15, 10, 5]
```

The solution is as follows:

```
1  # Create an empty list to store the numbers
2  numbers = []
3
4  # Ask the user to enter numbers
5  while True:
6      number = input("Enter a number (or 'q' to quit): ")
7      if number.lower() == 'q':
```

```
 8      break
 9    numbers.append(int(number))
10
11  # Reverse the order of the elements in the list
12  start = 0
13  end = len(numbers) − 1
14
15  while start < end:
16      # Swap elements at start and end positions
17      numbers[start], numbers[end] = numbers[end], numbers[start]
18      start += 1
19      end −= 1
20
21  # Display the reversed list
22  print("Reversed List:", numbers)
```

● **Exercise 7: Number sorter**

Write a program that prompts the user to enter a series of numbers and stores them in a list. The program should then sort the numbers in ascending order and display the sorted list. To do this:

- Create an empty list called number_list to store the numbers.
- Ask the user to enter a series of numbers, one at a time.
- For each number entered by the user, append it to the number_list.
- Continue asking the user to enter numbers until they choose to stop.
- Sort the number_list in ascending order. Assign the sorted list to a new variable called sorted_numbers.
- Display the sorted list to the user.

Example output:

Enter a number (or 'q' to quit): 5
Enter a number (or 'q' to quit): 10
Enter a number (or 'q' to quit): 2
Enter a number (or 'q' to quit): 7
Enter a number (or 'q' to quit): q

Sorted Numbers: [2, 5, 7, 10]

The solution is as follows:

```python
# Create an empty list to store the numbers
number_list = []

# Continuously ask the user to enter a number
while True:
    number = input("Enter a number (or 'q' to quit): ")

    # Check if the user wants to quit
    if number.lower() == 'q':
        break

    # Convert the number to an integer and add it to the list
    number_list.append(int(number))

# Sort the numbers in ascending order using the bubble sort algorithm
n = len(number_list)
for i in range(n):
    # Iterate over the unsorted part of the list
    for j in range(0, n-i-1):
        # Check if the current number is greater than the next number
        if number_list[j] > number_list[j+1]:
            # Swap the numbers
            number_list[j], number_list[j+1] = number_list[j+1], number_list[j]

# Display the sorted list to the user
print("Sorted Numbers:", number_list)
```

Solutions of Chapter 8

● **Exercise 1: Print line of stars**

Write a program that uses a function to print a line of stars.
Example output:

```
**********
```

The solution is as follows:

```
1 def print_stars():
2     print("**********")
3
4 # main program
5 print_stars()
```

The solution using the for loop is

```
1 def print_stars():
2     for i in range(10):
3         print("*", end="")
4     print()
5
6 # main program
7 print_stars()
```

● **Exercise 2: Print line of stars**

Modify the program from the first exercise that prints a row of stars. In this exercise, the user passes or sends a number to a function that prints a row of stars with the number entered by the user.

© Alaa Tharwat 2025
A. Tharwat, *Python Adventures for Young Coders*,
https://doi.org/10.1007/979-8-8688-1067-1

Example output:

Enter the number of stars: 10
****

The solution is as follows:

```
def print_stars(num_stars):
    for i in range(num_stars):
        print("*", end="")
    print()

# main program
num_stars = int(input("Enter the number of stars: "))
print_stars(num_stars)
```

Modify this program again by adding arguments to control the character used for the line. Hence, we can print a line of stars ("******") or other characters, for example, "#########."

The solution for the modified program will be

```
def print_line(num_chars, char):
    for i in range(num_chars):
        print(char, end="")
    print()

# main program
num_chars = int(input("Enter the number of characters: "))
char = input("Enter the character to use: ")
print_line(num_chars, char)
```

We can also add another option to this program by giving it the ability to print several lines instead of one line.

The solution after adding the option of printing several lines is

```
def print_lines(num_lines, num_chars, char):
    for _ in range(num_lines):
        for i in range(num_chars):
            print(char, end="")
        print()

# main program
num_lines = int(input("Enter the number of lines: "))
num_chars = int(input("Enter the number of characters per line: "))
char = input("Enter the character to use: ")
print_lines(num_lines, num_chars, char)
```

Example of the output:

Enter the number of lines: 3
Enter the number of characters per line: 5
Enter the character to use: #
#####
#####
#####

● **Exercise 3: Celsius to Fahrenheit**

Write a program that uses a function to convert the temperature from Celsius to Fahrenheit.
Example output:

Enter the temperature in Celsius: 25
The temperature in Fahrenheit is: 77.0

The solution is as follows:

```python
def celsius_to_fahrenheit(celsius):
    """
    Converts a temperature in Celsius to Fahrenheit.

    Args:
      celsius (float): The temperature in Celsius.

    Returns:
      float: The temperature in Fahrenheit.
    """
    fahrenheit = (celsius * 9/5) + 32
    return fahrenheit

# main program
celsius = float(input("Enter the temperature in Celsius: "))
fahrenheit = celsius_to_fahrenheit(celsius)

print("The temperature in Fahrenheit is: ", fahrenheit)
```

● **Exercise 4: Find maximum**

Write a program that uses a function to find the maximum of two numbers.
Example output:

Enter the first number: 7
Enter the second number: 12
The maximum number is: 12

The solution is as follows:

```python
def find_maximum(num1, num2):
    """
    Finds the maximum of two numbers.

    Args:
        num1 (float): The first number.
        num2 (float): The second number.

    Returns:
        float: The maximum of the two numbers.
    """
    if num1 > num2:
        return num1
    else:
        return num2

# main program
num1 = float(input("Enter the first number: "))
num2 = float(input("Enter the second number: "))

max_num = find_maximum(num1, num2)

print("The maximum number is:", max_num)
```

● **Exercise 5: Find average**

Write a program that uses a function to calculate the average of three numbers.
Example output:

Enter the first number: 7
Enter the second number: 12
Enter the third number: 5
The average of the three numbers is: 8

The solution is as follows:

```python
def calculate_average(num1, num2, num3):
    """
    Calculates the average of three numbers.

    Args:
        num1 (float): The first number.
        num2 (float): The second number.
        num3 (float): The third number.

    Returns:
        float: The average of the three numbers.
    """
    average = (num1 + num2 + num3) / 3
    return average

# main program
num1 = float(input("Enter the first number: "))
num2 = float(input("Enter the second number: "))
num3 = float(input("Enter the third number: "))

avg = calculate_average(num1, num2, num3)

print(f"The average of the three numbers is: {avg:.0f}")
```

● **Exercise 6: Even or odd**

Write a program that uses a function to determine whether a number is even or odd. The program should take a number as input from the user and call the function to check whether the number is even or odd. Display an appropriate message indicating whether the number is odd or even.

Example output:

```
Enter a number: 9
The number is odd.
```

The solution is as follows:

```python
def is_even(num):
    """
    Determines whether a number is even or odd.

    Args:
        num (int): The number to be checked.

    Returns:
        bool: True if the number is even, False if the number is odd.
    """
```

```
11    if num % 2 == 0:
12        return True
13    else:
14        return False
15
16 # main program
17 user_input = int(input("Enter a number: "))
18
19 if is_even(user_input):
20    print("The number is even.")
21 else:
22    print("The number is odd.")
```

● Exercise 7: Leap year

Write a program that uses a function to determine whether or not a year is a leap year. The program should take a year as input from the user and call the function to check if it is a leap year. Display an appropriate message indicating whether the year is a leap year or not.

Example output:

Enter a year: 2020
The year is a leap year.

The solution is as follows:

```
1 def is_leap_year(year):
2     """
3     Determines whether a year is a leap year.
4
5     Args:
6         year (int): The year to be checked.
7
8     Returns:
9         bool: True if the year is a leap year, False otherwise.
10    """
11    if year % 4 == 0:
12        if year % 100 == 0:
13            if year % 400 == 0:
14                return True
15            else:
16                return False
17        else:
18            return True
19    else:
20        return False
21
22 # main program
```

```
23  user_input = int(input("Enter a year: "))
24
25  if is_leap_year(user_input):
26      print(f"{user_input} is a leap year.")
27  else:
28      print(f"{user_input} is not a leap year.")
```

● Exercise 8: Multiplication table

Write a program that uses a function to display the multiplication table of a given number. The program should take a number as input from the user and call the function to display the multiplication table up to a certain limit (e.g., up to 10).

Example output:

```
Enter a number: 5
Multiplication Table:
5 × 1 = 5
5 × 2 = 10
5 × 3 = 15
...
5 × 10 = 50
```

The solution is as follows:

```
1  def multiplication_table(num, limit=10):
2      """
3      Displays the multiplication table of a given number up to a certain limit.
4
5      Args:
6          num (int): The number whose multiplication table is to be displayed.
7          limit (int, optional): The maximum number to include in the multiplication table.
                                    Defaults to 10.
8      """
9      print(f"Multiplication Table of {num}:")
10     for i in range(1, limit + 1):
11         print(f"{num} x {i} = {num * i}")
12
13  # main program
14  user_input = int(input("Enter a number: "))
15
16  multiplication_table(user_input)
```

● **Exercise 9: Factorial calculation**

Write a program that uses a function to calculate the factorial of a given number. The program should prompt the user to enter a number and call the function to calculate and display its factorial.

Example output:

Enter a number: 5
The factorial of 5 is 120.

The solution is as follows:

```python
def factorial(n):
    """
    Calculates the factorial of a given number.

    Args:
        n (int): The number whose factorial is to be calculated.

    Returns:
        int: The factorial of the given number.
    """
    if n == 0 or n == 1:
        return 1
    else:
        return n * factorial(n - 1)

# main program
user_input = int(input("Enter a number: "))
result = factorial(user_input)
print(f"The factorial of {user_input} is {result}.")
```

● **Exercise 10: Calorie calculator**

Write a program that uses a function to calculate the calories because our user is on a diet to lose some weight. Tell the user that an apple has 49 calories, a banana has 95 calories, and an orange has 37 calories. Ask the user to enter the number of apples, bananas, and oranges they eat and calculate the number of calories consumed (this exercise is similar to Exercise 7 in Chapter 2).

The expected output of this program is

Enter the number of apples you ate: 2
Enter the number of bananas you ate: 1
Enter the number of oranges you ate: 3
You consumed a total of 304 calories.

The solution is as follows:

```python
def calculate_calories(apples, bananas, oranges):
    """
    Calculates the total calories consumed based on the number of fruits eaten.

    Args:
        apples (int): The number of apples eaten.
        bananas (int): The number of bananas eaten.
        oranges (int): The number of oranges eaten.

    Returns:
        int: The total calories consumed.
    """
    apple_calories = apples * 49
    banana_calories = bananas * 95
    orange_calories = oranges * 37
    total_calories = apple_calories + banana_calories + orange_calories
    return total_calories

# main program
print("An apple has 49 calories, a banana has 95 calories, and an orange has 37 calories.
    ")

apples = int(input("Enter the number of apples you ate: "))
bananas = int(input("Enter the number of bananas you ate: "))
oranges = int(input("Enter the number of oranges you ate: "))

total_calories = calculate_calories(apples, bananas, oranges)
print(f"You consumed a total of {total_calories} calories.")
```

● Exercise 11: Square a number

Write a program to find the square of any number using a function. The expected output of this program is

> Enter a number: 2
> The square of 2 is 4

The solution is as follows:

```python
def square(num):
    """
    Calculates the square of a given number.

    Args:
        num (int or float): The number to be squared.

    Returns:
```

```
9       int or float: The square of the input number.
10      """
11      return num ** 2
12
13  # main program
14  user_input = float(input("Enter a number: "))
15  result = square(user_input)
16  print(f"The square of {user_input} is {result}")
```

● Exercise 12: Swap two numbers

Write a program to swap two numbers using a function. For example, to swap two numbers, if x=2 and y=3, after the swap, the two variables will exchange their contents, so x will be 3 and y will be 2. The expected output of this program is

> Enter the first number: 2
> Enter the second number: 5
> Before swapping: x=2, y=5
> After swapping: x=5 and y=2

The solution is as follows:

```
1  def swap_numbers(a, b):
2      temp = a
3      a = b
4      b = temp
5      return a, b
6
7  # main program
8  # Get input from the user
9  x = int(input("Enter the first number: "))
10 y = int(input("Enter the second number: "))
11
12 print(f"Before swapping: x={x}, y={y}")
13
14 # Call the swap function
15 x, y = swap_numbers(x, y)
16
17 print(f"After swapping: x={x} and y={y}")
```

● Exercise 13: Print numbers in a range

Write a program that uses a function to print all the numbers in a given range.
The expected output of this program is

> Enter the starting number: 1
> Enter the end number: 100
> The numbers are:
> 1
> 2
> 3
> :
> 100

The solution is as follows:

```python
def print_range(start, end):
    for num in range(start, end + 1):
        print(num)

# main program
# Get input from the user
start = int(input("Enter the starting number: "))
end = int(input("Enter the end number: "))

print("The numbers are:")
print_range(start, end)
```

Modify the function to include another parameter to print the numbers in a sequence or with a step, for example, 2, 4, 6, ...

The solution is as follows:

```python
def print_range(start, end, step=1):
    for num in range(start, end + 1, step):
        print(num)

# main program
# Get input from the user
start = int(input("Enter the starting number: "))
end = int(input("Enter the end number: "))
step = int(input("Enter the step (press Enter for default step of 1): ") or "1")

print("The numbers are:")
print_range(start, end, step)
```

● Exercise 14: Seconds to minutes

Write a program that uses a function to convert seconds to minutes. In the program, ask the user for a number of seconds and print the equivalent in minutes. You know that 1 minute equals 60 seconds.

The expected output of this program is as follows:

> Enter a number of seconds: 180
> 180 seconds is equal to 3 minutes.

The solution is as follows:

```python
def seconds_to_minutes(seconds):
    minutes = seconds // 60
    remaining_seconds = seconds % 60
    return minutes, remaining_seconds

# main program
# Get input from the user
seconds = int(input("Enter a number of seconds: "))

# Convert seconds to minutes
minutes, remaining_seconds = seconds_to_minutes(seconds)

# Print the result
if remaining_seconds == 0:
    print(f"{seconds} seconds is equal to {minutes} minutes.")
else:
    print(f"{seconds} seconds is equal to {minutes} minutes and {remaining_seconds} seconds.")
```

Solutions of Chapter 9

● **Exercise 1: Check the variable scope – 1**

The following code has two functions and the main function. Trace the code and the scope of the variable to know what the output of this program is:

```
1  # Global variable
2  favorite_color = "blue"
3
4  def change_color():
5      # Local variable inside the function
6      favorite_color = "green"
7      print("Inside change_color(), the favorite color is:", favorite_color)
8
9  def reset_color():
10     favorite_color = "red"
11     print("Inside reset_color(), the favorite color is:", favorite_color)
12
13 # main program
14 print("In the main program, the initial favorite color is:", favorite_color)
15 change_color()
16 print("In the main program, the favorite color is still:", favorite_color)
17 reset_color()
18 print("In the main program, the favorite color is now:", favorite_color)
```

The solution will be as follows: Let us trace the code and understand the scope of the variables.

- The program starts by defining a global variable favorite_color and assigning it the value "blue."
- The change_color() function is defined next. This function defines a local variable favorite_color and assigns it the value "green." Inside this

© Alaa Tharwat 2025
A. Tharwat, *Python Adventures for Young Coders*,
https://doi.org/10.1007/979-8-8688-1067-1

function, it prints the value of the local favorite_color variable, which is "green."

- The reset_color() function is defined next. This function also defines a local variable favorite_color and assigns it the value "red." Inside this function, it prints the value of the local favorite_color variable, which is "red."
- In the main program
  - The initial value of the global favorite_color is printed, which is "blue."
  - The change_color() function is called, which changes the local favorite_color variable to "green," but does not affect the global favorite_color.
  - The value of the global favorite_color is printed again, which is still "blue."
  - The reset_color() function is called, which changes the local favorite_color variable to "red," but does not affect the global favorite_color.
  - The value of the global favorite_color is printed again, which is still "blue."

The expected output will be

```
In the main program, the initial favorite color is: blue
Inside change_color(), the favorite color is: green
In the main program, the favorite color is still: blue
Inside reset_color(), the favorite color is: red
In the main program, the favorite color is now: blue
```

This means that the global favorite_color variable is not affected by the changes made to the local favorite_color variables inside the change_color() and reset_color() functions. The global favorite_color variable retains its initial value of "blue" throughout the program.

● **Exercise 2: Check the variable scope – 2**

The following code has three functions and the main function. Trace the code and the scope of the variable to see what the output of this program is:

```python
def update_score(total_score, score_to_add):
    total_score += score_to_add
    print("Total score updated to:", total_score)
    return total_score, check_high_score(total_score)

def check_high_score(total_score):
    high_score = total_score
    if total_score > high_score:
        high_score = total_score
```

```
10      print("New high score:", high_score)
11    return high_score
12
13  def play_game():
14    score = 10
15    total_score, high_score = update_score(0, score)
16    print("Score from play_game():", score)
17    return total_score, high_score
18
19
20  # main program
21  total_score=0
22  high_score=0
23
24  print("Initial total score: 0")
25  print("Initial high score: 0")
26
27  total_score, high_score = play_game()
28
29  print("Final total score:", total_score)
30  print("Final high score:", high_score)
```

The solution will be as follows: Let us trace the code and understand the scope of the variables.

- The update_score() function takes two arguments: total_score and score_to_add. It adds the score_to_add to the total_score, prints the updated total_score, and then returns the updated total_score and the high_score (which is obtained by calling the check_high_score() function).
- The check_high_score() function takes one argument: total_score. It initializes a high_score variable to the total_score value, and then checks if the total_score is greater than the high_score. If it is, it updates the high_score and prints the new high_score. Finally, it returns the high_score.
- The play_game() function initializes a score variable to 10 and then calls the update_score() function with the arguments 0 and score. It prints the score value from the play_game() function and then returns the total_score and high_score values.
- In the main program
  - The initial total_score and high_score variables are both set to 0.
  - The initial total_score and high_score are printed.
  - The play_game() function is called, and the returned total_score and high_score values are assigned to the main program's total_score and high_score variables.
  - The final total_score and high_score values are printed.

The output of this program will be

```
Initial total score: 0
Initial high score: 0
Total score updated to: 10
Score from play_game(): 10
Final total score: 10
Final high score: 10
```

Here is the step-by-step execution:

- The play_game() function is called, which initializes the score variable to 10.
- The update_score() function is called with total_score=0 and score_to_add=10. This updates the total_score to 10 and calls the check_high_score() function, which sets the high_score to 10.
- The score value from the play_game() function is printed, which is 10.
- The total_score and high_score values returned from the play_game() function are assigned to the main program's total_score and high_score variables.
- The final total_score and high_score values are printed, which are both 10.

● Exercise 3: Function calls another function – 1

The following code shows how one function calls another function. Trace the code and try to predict what the output of this program will be:

```python
def get_ingredients():
    print("Let's make a sandwich!")
    bread = input("What kind of bread would you like? ")
    filling = input("What filling would you like? ")
    return bread, filling

def assemble_sandwich():
    bread_type, sandwich_filling = get_ingredients()
    print("Okay, let's assemble your sandwich:")
    print("First, we'll take two slices of", bread_type, "bread.")
    print("Then, we'll add the", sandwich_filling, "filling.")
    print("And... voila! Your sandwich is ready to eat.")

# main program
assemble_sandwich()
```

The solution will be as follows: Let us trace the code and predict the output.

- The get_ingredients() function is defined. This function prints a message, prompts the user for the type of bread and filling, and then returns these two values.
- The assemble_sandwich() function is defined. This function calls the get_ingredients() function, which returns the bread type and sandwich filling. It then prints a series of messages assembling the sandwich.
- In the main program, the assemble_sandwich() function is called.

Now, let us predict the output:

- When the assemble_sandwich() function is called, it will call the get_ingredients() function.
- The get_ingredients() function will print the message "Let's make a sandwich!" and then prompt the user for the type of bread and filling.
- The user will enter the desired bread and filling.
- The get_ingredients() function will return the bread and filling to the assemble_sandwich() function.
- The assemble_sandwich() function will then print the messages assembling the sandwich, using the bread and filling provided by the user.

The output of this program will be

```
Let's make a sandwich
What kind of bread would you like? Sourdough
What filling would you like? Turkey
Okay, let's assemble your sandwich:
First, we'll take two slices of Sourdough bread.
Then, we'll add the Turkey filling.
And... voila! Your sandwich is ready to eat.
```

The key points to note are as follows: First, the get_ingredients() function is called by the assemble_sandwich() function to obtain the bread and filling information. Second, the assemble_sandwich() function then uses this information to print the messages assembling the sandwich.

● **Exercise 4: Function calls another function – 2**

The following code shows how one function calls another function. Trace the code and try to predict what the output of this program will be:

```
1  def get_book_info():
2      title = input("What is the title of the book? ")
3      author = input("Who is the author of the book? ")
4      return title, author
5
6  def get_book_rating():
7      rating = int(input("What rating would you give the book (1–5)? "))
8      return rating
9
10 def display_book_info(book_title, book_author, book_rating):
11     print("Title:", book_title)
12     print("Author:", book_author)
13     print("Rating:", book_rating, "out of 5 stars")
14
15 # main program
16 book_title, book_author = get_book_info()
17 book_rating = get_book_rating()
18 display_book_info(book_title, book_author, book_rating)
```

The solution will be as follows:

Let us first trace the code and predict the output:

- The get_book_info() function is defined. This function prompts the user for the title and author of a book and then returns these two values.
- The get_book_rating() function is defined. This function prompts the user for a rating for the book (on a scale of 1–5) and returns the rating.
- The display_book_info() function is defined. This function takes the book title, author, and rating as input and then prints this information.
- The main function calls the get_book_info() function to get the book title and author, then calls the get_book_rating() function to get the book rating. Finally, it calls the display_book_info() function, passing in the book title, author, and rating.

Now, let us predict the output:

- When the main() function is called, it will call the get_book_info() function.
- The get_book_info() function will prompt the user for the book title and author and then return these values to the main() function.
- The main function will then call the get_book_rating() function.

- The get_book_rating() function will prompt the user for a book rating (on a scale of 1–5) and then return this value to the main() function.
- Finally, the main() function will call the display_book_info() function, passing in the book title, author, and rating.
- The display_book_info() function will then print the book information.

The output of this program will be

> What is the title of the book? The Great Gatsby
> Who is the author of the book? F. Scott Fitzgerald
> What rating would you give the book (1-5)? 4
> Title: The Great Gatsby
> Author: F. Scott Fitzgerald
> Rating: 4 out of 5 stars

The key points to note are as follows: First, the get_book_info() and get_book_rating() functions are called by the main program to obtain the book information and rating. Second, the display_book_info() function is called by the main program to print the book information.

● Exercise 5: Function calls another function – 3

The following code shows how one function calls another function. Trace the code and try to predict what the output of this program will be:

```python
def get_name():
    name = input("What is your name? ")
    return name

def get_age():
    age = int(input("What is your age? "))
    return age

def get_favorite_color():
    color = input("What is your favorite color? ")
    return color

def display_info(person_name, person_age, person_color):
    print("Hello,", person_name)
    print("You are", person_age, "years old.")
    print("Your favorite color is", person_color + ".")

def get_person_info():
    name = get_name()
    age = get_age()
    color = get_favorite_color()
    return name, age, color
```

```
23
24  # main program
25  person_name, person_age, person_color = get_person_info()
26  display_info(person_name, person_age, person_color)
```

The solution will be as follows:

Let us first trace the code and predict the output.

- The get_name() function is defined. This function prompts the user for their name and returns it.
- The get_age() function is defined. This function prompts the user for their age and returns it.
- The get_favorite_color() function is defined. This function prompts the user for their favorite color and returns it.
- The display_info() function is defined. This function takes the person's name, age, and favorite color as input and then prints this information.
- The get_person_info() function is defined. This function calls the get_name(), get_age(), and get_favorite_color() functions and then returns the person's name, age, and favorite color.
- In the main program, the get_person_info() function is called, and its return values are assigned to the variables person_name, person_age, and person_color.
- Finally, the display_info() function is called, with person_name, person_age, and person_color as arguments.

Now, let us predict the output:

- When the main program is executed, the get_person_info() function is called.
- The get_person_info() function calls the get_name(), get_age(), and get_favorite_color() functions in sequence, prompting the user for their name, age, and favorite color and storing the responses in the variables name, age, and color, respectively.
- The get_person_info() function then returns these three values as a tuple.
- The main program assigns the returned values to the variables person_name, person_age, and person_color.
- Finally, the display_info() function is called, with person_name, person_age, and person_color as arguments.
- The display_info() function prints the person's name, age, and favorite color.

● Exercise 6: Recursive Fibonacci

The Fibonacci sequence is a series of numbers where each number is the sum of the previous two, starting with 0 and 1. The sequence goes like this: 0, 1, 1, 2, 3, 5, 8, 13, 21, 34, and so on.

Your task is to write a recursive function that calculates the number n^{th} in the Fibonacci sequence.

Here is an example of the output of the program

> Enter a number: 5
> The Fibonacci of 5 is 3

The solution will be as follows:

```python
def fibonacci(n):
    # Base cases
    if n <= 0:
        return 0
    elif n == 1:
        return 1

    # Recursive case
    return fibonacci(n - 1) + fibonacci(n - 2)
```

● Exercise 7: Find max

Write a program that uses one function to find the maximum of two numbers and another function to find the maximum of three numbers. Compare the length and performance of your functions with the built-in max function.

Here is an example of the output of the program:

> Enter the first number: 20
> Enter the second number: 5
> Enter the third number: 16
> The maximum number is 20

The solution will be as follows:

```python
def max_of_two(a, b):
    return a if a > b else b

def max_of_three(a, b, c):
    return max_of_two(max_of_two(a, b), c)

# main program
num1 = int(input("Enter the first number: "))
num2 = int(input("Enter the second number: "))
```

```
10  num3 = int(input("Enter the third number: "))
11  print(max_of_two(num1,num2)) # using our function
12  print(max_of_two(max_of_two(num1,num2),num3) # using our function
13  print(max(num1,num2)) # using the built–in function
14  print(max(num1,num2,num3)) # using the built–in function
```

From the above code, it is clear that the built-in function is concise and does the job in a single line.

● **Exercise 8: Calculate the factorial of a number**

Write a program that uses a function to calculate the factorial of a number using a loop and another function that calls itself. Compare the length and the performance of your functions with the math.factorial() built-in function.

Here is an example of the output of the program:

Enter a number: 5
The factorial of 5 is 120

The solution will be as follows:

```
1   import math
2
3   def factorial_loop(n):
4     result = 1
5     for i in range(1, n + 1):
6       result *= i
7     return result
8
9   def factorial_recursive(n):
10    if n == 0 or n == 1:
11      return 1
12    else:
13      return n * factorial_recursive(n − 1)
14
15  # main program
16  num = int(input("Enter a number: "))
17  print(factrial_loop(num)) # using the loop function
18  print(factrial_recursive(num)) # using the recursive function
19  print(math.factorial(num)) # using the built–in function
```

We can see in the above code that the built-in function saves many lines of code; hence, it saves efforts and time, and also it works efficiently.

● Exercise 9: Calculate the power of a number

Write a program that uses a function to calculate the power of a number using a loop and another function that calls itself. Compare the length and the performance of your functions with the pow() built-in function.

Here is an example of the output of the program:

Enter the base number: 2
Enter the exponent number: 3
The result of 2 raised to the power of 3 is 8

The solution will be as follows:

```python
import math

def power_loop(base, exponent):
    result = 1
    for _ in range(exponent):
        result *= base
    return result

def power_recursive(base, exponent):
    if exponent == 0:
        return 1
    elif exponent == 1:
        return base
    else:
        return base * power_recursive(base, exponent - 1)

# main program
# Get input from user
base = float(input("Enter the base number: "))
exponent = int(input("Enter the exponent number: "))

print(power_loop(base,exponent)) # using the loop function
print(power_recursive(base,exponent)) # using the recursive function
print(pow(base,exponent)) # using the built—in function
```

We can see in the above code that the built-in function saves many lines of code; hence, it saves efforts and time, and also it works efficiently.

• Exercise 10: Calculate the sum of numbers in a range

Write a program that uses a function to calculate the sum of numbers in a specific range. Compare the length and the performance of your functions with the sum(range(start, end + 1)) built-in function.

Here is an example of the output of the program:

Enter the first number: 2
Enter the end number: 10
The sum of numbers from 2 to 10 is 54

The solution will be as follows:

```
def sum_range_loop(start, end):
    total = 0
    for num in range(start, end + 1):
        total += num
    return total

# main program
# Get input from user
start = int(input("Enter the first number: "))
end = int(input("Enter the end number: "))

print(sum_range_loop(start,end)) # using the loop function
print(sum(range(start, end + 1))) # using the built−in functions
```

We can see in the above code that the built-in function saves many lines of code; hence, it saves efforts and time, and also it works efficiently.

Index

© Alaa Tharwat 2025
A. Tharwat, *Python Adventures for Young Coders*,
https://doi.org/10.1007/979-8-8688-1067-1